Revised

Corporate History

of

Northern Pacific Railway Company

As of June 30, 1917

Prepared in Accordance with

Valuation Order No. 20

of the

Interstate Commerce Commission

Office of Land Assistant, Northern Pacific Railway

St. Paul, Minnesota

August 30, 1921

Centennial Edition

Including a Foreword with Later Corporate Changes

by Rollin R. Davis, Ph.D.

Zea Books
Lincoln, Nebraska
2022

Foreword copyright © 2022 Rollin R. Davis

ISBN 978-1-60962-260-2 paperback
ISBN 978-1-60962-261-9 ebook
doi: 10.32873/unl.dc.zea.1330

Zea Books are published by the
University of Nebraska-Lincoln Libraries.

Electronic (pdf) edition available online at
http://digitalcommons.unl.edu/zeabooks/

Print edition available from
http://www.lulu.com/spotlight/unlib

UNL does not discriminate based upon any protected status.
Please go to http://www.unl.edu/equity/notice-nondiscrimination

Contents

Foreword by Rollin R. Davis, Ph.D. vii

Revised Corporate History of Northern Pacific Railway Company
    As of June 30, 1917 xvii
        Explanation xviii
        Index xx
        The Lake Superior and Mississippi Railroad Company 1
        The Saint Paul and Pacific Railroad Company 8
        Northern Pacific Railroad Company 12
        The Stillwater and St. Paul Railroad Company 41
        Northern Pacific Railway Company 45
        The Minneapolis and Duluth Railroad Company 89
        Minneapolis & St. Louis Railway Company 94
        The Minneapolis and St. Louis Railroad Company 98
        Utah and Northern Railway Company 101
        Montana Union Railway Company 104
        Seattle and Walla Walla Rail Road Company 108
        The Columbia and Puget Sound Railroad Company 111
        Olympia Railroad Union 116
        The Olympia and Chehalis Valley Railroad Company 119
        Port Townsend Southern Railroad Company 123
        Saint Paul and Northern Pacific Railway Company 127
        Taylors Falls and Lake Superior Rail Road Company 133
        Saint Paul and Duluth Railroad Company 138
        Northern Pacific, Fergus, and Black Hills Railroad Company . . 146
        Union Depot, Street Railway and Transfer Company of Stillwater 153
        Stillwater Union Depot & Transfer Company 158
        Union Depot & Transfer Company of Stillwater 162
        Saint Cloud, Grantsburg and Ashland Railway Company 165
        The Grantsburg, Rush City and St. Cloud Railroad Company . . 168
        The Little Falls and Dakota Railroad Company 171
        Mill Creek Flume and Manufacturing Company 175
        The Oregon Railroad and Navigation Company 178
        The Saint Paul, Minneapolis and Manitoba Railway Company . . 181
        Rocky Mountain Railroad Company of Montana 184
        Fargo and Southwestern Railroad Company 187

The Jamestown & Northern Railroad Company 190
Montana Railway Company 194
Sanborn, Coopertown and Turtle Mountain Railroad Company. . 198
The Puget Sound Shore Railroad Company 201
Helena and Jefferson County Railroad Company 204
James River Valley Railroad Company 207
Duluth and Manitoba Railway Company 210
Northern Pacific and Cascade Railroad Company 214
Northern Pacific and Puget Sound Shore Railroad Company. . . 218
The Coeur d'Alene Steam Navigation and Transportation
    Company 222
Seattle, Lake Shore and Eastern Railway Company 225
Spokane and Seattle Railway Company 231
Spokane and Palouse Railway Company 235
The Oregon and Washington Territory Railroad Company . . . 239
Puget Sound and Grays Harbor Railroad and Transportation Co. 243
Helena and Red Mountain Railroad Company 246
Duluth Short Line Railway Company 249
The Coeur d'Alene Railway and Navigation Company 252
Clealum Railroad Company 259
South-Eastern Dakota Railroad Company 262
Spokane Falls and Idaho Railroad Company 266
Helena and Northern Railroad Company 269
Northern Pacific, LaMoure and Missouri River Railroad
    Company 272
Rocky Fork and Cooke City Railway Company 275
The Missoula and Bitter Root Valley Railroad Company . . . 278
The Drummond and Philipsburg Railroad Company 281
Vancouver, Klickitat and Yakima Railroad Company 284
Seattle and West Coast Railway Company 287
Canyon Creek Railroad Company 290
The Central Washington Railroad Company 293
Northern Pacific and Montana Railroad Company 297
Washington Short Line Railway Company 304
The Tacoma, Orting & Southeatern Railroad Company 307
The Duluth, Crookston and Northern Rail Road Company . . . 310
The Snohomish, Skykomish and Spokane Railway and
    Transportation Company 313

Contents

Jamestown and Northern Extension Railroad Company 316
Seattle Terminal Railway and Elevator Company 319
Philadelphia Mortgage and Trust Company 324
Seattle Warehouse and Terminal Company. 328
The Seattle and San Francisco Railway and Navigation Company 332
Northwestern Improvement Company. 337
Wallace and Sunset Railroad Company 340
Yakima and Pacific Coast Railroad Company 343
Tacoma, Olympia and Grays Harbor Railroad Company 346
Duluth Transfer Railway Company 350
Duluth Transfer Railroad Company 353
The United Railroads of Washington 356
Green River and Northern Railroad Company. 362
Little Falls and Southern Railroad Company 365
The Portland and Poget Sound Railroad Company. 368
Washington & Oregon Railway Company 372
Bellingham Bay and Eastern Railroad Company 376
Everett and Monte Cristo Railway Company 380
Monte Cristo Railway Company 385
The Washington and Columbia River Railway Company 388
Montana Southern Railway Company 393
Washburn, Bayfield and Iron River Railway Company 396
Seattle and International Railway Company 399
Gaylord and Ruby Valley Railway Company 404
Portland, Vancouver and Yakima Railway Company 407
Seattle and Montana Railroad Company 411
Western American Company. 414
The Washington Central Railway Company 417
Clearwater Short Line Railway Company 420
Washington Railway & Navigation Company 425
Mill Creek Railroad Company 430
North Yakima and Valley Railway Company 434
Spokane, Portland and Seattle Railway Company 438
Missouri River Railway Company. 442
Western Dakota Railway Company 445
Big Fork and International Falls Railway Company 448
The Shields River Valley Railway Company 451
Toppenish, Simcoe & Western Railway Company 454

Connell Northern Railway Company 457
The Camp Creek Railway Company. 460
Cuyuna Northern Railway Company 463
Cuyuna Dock Company. 466
Missoula and Hamilton Railway Company 469

C.F. Staples to Charles Donnelley, Sept. 30, 1921. 471
Charles Donnelley to C.F. Staples, Oct. 3, 1921 473
Voided and Revised page 102 474
Loan information for microfilming 476

Appendices

Northern Pacific Railway Company, Revised Chart and History Map. . 477

    Northern Pacific Railway Company, Revised Chart — Sheet 2,
        As of June 30, 1917. Propereties owned and Operated. Property
        Operated but not Owned. Properties Owned but not Operated
        by Respondent. Filed under Valuation Order No. 20. 478

    Northern Pacific Railway Company Corporate History Map.
        Revised as of June 30, 1917. Each portion of the present
        Northern Pacific system constructed by a separate corporation
        formed for this purpose is made a corporate history unit. Its
        location is shown by number on the map, together with a
        summary of the chain of title from the oriinal construction
        company to the present owner, the Northern Pacific
        Railway Company. 482

Foreword to the Centennial Edition

Railroads have been important in American history since the mid-nineteenth century for national unification, the settlement of the American West, the industrial revolution, economic growth, models of complex organization for other large corporations, and the transition of America from rural, agrarian society to urban, industrial society. The railroads' transformative influence of technological change and social change has been termed "railroadization" (Schumpeter 1939, 1:325-351). Alfred D. Chandler Jr. (1965, 9-12) characterized the railroad industry as the first big business in America. The transcontinental railroads were especially significant. A transcontinental railroad may be defined as a railroad whose eastern terminal is east of the Continental Divide and whose western terminal is on the Pacific coast. The term transcontinental has traditionally not been applied to railroads that extend between Atlantic coast terminals and mid-continental terminals (e.g., Chicago, St. Louis, and New Orleans).

There were six transcontinental railroads, which were completed between 1869 and 1909. The first transcontinental railroad was the "Overland Route," consisting of the Union Pacific, which was built west from Omaha, Nebraska, and the Central Pacific, which was built east from Sacramento, California (later extended to the Pacific coast at Oakland and San Francisco) to the junction at Promontory, Utah, where the last spike ceremony was held on May 10, 1869 (Athearn 1971, 98; Bain 1999, 658-663; Southern Pacific 1955, 12-14). The junction was later moved to Ogden, Utah (Klein 1987, 255; Southern Pacific 1955, 14). Promontory Point, Utah, which is a peninsula on the north shore of the Great Salt Lake, was reached when the Lucin Cut-off across the Great Salt Lake between Lucin, Utah, and Ogden, Utah, was opened to traffic on March 8, 1904 (Hofsommer 1986, 17; Southern Pacific 1955, 37, 45). The Central Pacific Railroad was leased by the Southern Pacific Company for 99 years on April 1, 1885, and it was reorganized as the Central Pacific Railway on July 29, 1899 (Interstate Commerce Commission 1889, 2:170-171; Interstate Commerce Commission 1900, 13:260-261). The Central Pacific Railway was merged into the Southern Pacific Company on June 30, 1959 (Interstate Commerce Commission 1959, 73:534).

The Union Pacific Railway was sold out of receivership at a foreclosure sale in 1897 and was reorganized as the Union Pacific Railroad by Edward H. Harriman and his associates (Athearn 1971, 372-373; Interstate Commerce Commission 1898, 11:262-263).

The second transcontinental railroad was the "Sunset Route" of the Southern Pacific between New Orleans, Louisiana, and Los Angeles, California, which was completed on January 12, 1883 (Southern Pacific 1955, 25, 33).

The third transcontinental railroad was the Northern Pacific Railroad, which was chartered on July 2, 1864, when President Abraham Lincoln approved *An Act Granting Lands to Aid in the Construction of a Railroad and Telegraph Line From Lake Superior to Puget Sound, on the Pacific Coast, by the Northern Route*. The construction was completed from Duluth, Minnesota, and from St. Paul, Minnesota, to Wallula, Washington, the junction with the Oregon Railway and Navigation Company, which provided the connection along the south bank of the Columbia River to Portland, Oregon (Burlington Northern n.d., 7-8; Burlington Northern Santa Fe Railway 1999, 21-22; Grodinsky 1962, 137; Northern Pacific Railway n.d., 4-7). On page 18 of this book it is stated that the actual completion of the Northern Pacific Railroad occurred at Gold Creek, Montana, on August 22, 1883. On September 8, 1883, rails that had been removed were replaced, and the last spike was driven at Gold Creek, Montana, for the formal ceremony that had been planned by Henry Villard, the president of the Northern Pacific Railroad, to celebrate the official completion of the Northern Pacific Railroad (de Borchgrave 2001, 333-334; Burlington Northern Railroad n.d., 8; Burlington Northern Santa Fe Corporation 1999, 22; Northern Pacific Railway 1953, 1-2; Northern Pacific Railway 1961, 1, 3; Northern Pacific Railway 1964a, 4; Northern Pacific Railway 1964b, 5; Northern Pacific Railway 1965, 2;

Foreword to the Centennial Edition

Northern Pacific Railway n.d., 7-9; Winks 1991, 259; [Winser] 1897, 188; Wood 1968, 42; cf. Schrenk 2002, 23). The 1960 "Northern Pacific Railway Guide to Points of Interest on the Scenic Route across America" identifies Gold Creek, Montana, as the site of both the actual completion on August 22, 1883, and the last spike ceremony on September 8, 1883 (Northern Pacific Railway 1960, 13-14). In addition, the completion site of the Northern Pacific Railroad at Gold Creek, Montana, is listed in the National Register of Historic Places, commemorating both the actual completion on August 22, 1883, and the driving of the last spike ceremony on September 8, 1883 ("Northern Pacific Railroad Completion Site, 1883" 1983, Sections 7-8). In 1903 Amedee Joullin created the oil on canvas mural that depicts the driving of the last spike at Gold Creek, Montana, on September 8, 1883; the mural is above the Grand Stairway in the Montana State Capitol in Helena (Lambert et al. 2002, 50-52). The painting was reproduced on the cover of the Northern Pacific Railway's *Annual Report* for 1962 (Northern Pacific Railway 1962, cover). The names Gold Creek and Independence Creek have been used interchangeably (Nolan 1983, 72; "Northern Pacific Railroad Completion Site, 1883" 1983, Section 8).

In 1884 the construction of the Oregon Short Line (a Union Pacific subsidiary) was completed from Granger, Wyoming (on the main line of the Union Pacific) to Huntington, Oregon, where it connected with the Oregon Railway and Navigation Company, which it leased in 1887 (Athearn 1971, 316, 318, 325; Grodinsky 1962, 156, 250; Hedges 1930, 145; Klein 1987, 438, 560, 564; Lewty 1987, 143; Lewty 1995, 5; Trottman 1966, 182). Thus, it became necessary for the Northern Pacific to build its own line to the Pacific coast (Burlington Northern Santa Fe Railway 1999, 23; Grodinsky 1962, 270, 292, 366-367). On pages 19 and 20 of this book it is stated that the route from Pasco, Washington (fourteen miles north of Wallula) through the Cascade Mountains via temporary switchbacks over Stampede Pass was opened for operation from Pasco, Washington, to Tacoma, Washington, on June 1, 1887. In addition, on page 20 of this book it is stated that the Stampede Tunnel was opened for operation in May 1888. The Northern Pacific Railroad was reorganized as the

Northern Pacific Railway on September 1, 1896 (Interstate Commerce Commission 1897, 10:250-251).

The fourth transcontinental railroad was the Atchison, Topeka and Santa Fe, which was completed between Los Angeles, California, San Francisco, California, and Chicago, Illinois, on December 31, 1887 (Bryant 1982, 138; Marshall 1945, 204; Waters 1950, 88). The Atchison, Topeka and Santa Fe Railroad was reorganized as the Atchison, Topeka and Santa Fe Railway on December 31, 1895 (Interstate Commerce Commission 1896, 9:256-257).

The fifth transcontinental railroad was the Great Northern Railway, which was completed between St. Paul, Minnesota, and Seattle, Washington, on January 6, 1893 (Hidy et al. 2004, 85).

The sixth transcontinental railroad was the Chicago, Milwaukee and St. Paul Railway (the Milwaukee Road), which was completed between Chicago, Illinois, and Seattle, Washington, on May 14, 1909 (Derleth 2002, 187). It was reorganized as the Chicago, Milwaukee, St. Paul and Pacific Railroad on January 13, 1928 (Interstate Commerce Commission 1928, 42:244).

This book, *Revised Corporate History of the Northern Pacific Railway As of June 30, 1917, Prepared in Accordance With Valuation Order No. 20 of the Interstate Commerce Commission,* is the official history of the Northern Pacific Railway, and it documents corporate changes from the Northern Pacific's charter on July 2, 1864, to June 30, 1917. It was prepared in accordance with Valuation Order number 20 of the Interstate Commerce Commission. The official *History of the Northern Pacific Railroad* by Eugene V. Smalley (1883) was finished before the last spike ceremony on September 8, 1883. The history by Renz (1980) does not cite sources.

In order to complete the history of the Northern Pacific Railway it is necessary to add the corporate changes that occurred from 1917 until its merger into the Burlington Northern in 1970. The Interstate Commerce Commission published annual statistical reports that included corporate changes in the railroad industry. The Centralia Eastern Railroad (nine miles of line owned and eleven miles of line operated) was "sold to Northern Pacific Ry. Co., Sept. 1, 1917" (Interstate Commerce Commission 1917, 31:504). The Billings and Central Montana Railway (13 miles owned and 14 miles operated) was "conveyed by deed to Northern Pacific Ry. Co., Oct. 1, 1921" (Interstate Commerce Commission 1921, 35:446). The operations of the Gilmore and Pittsburgh Railroad (120 miles owned), a Northern Pacific subsidiary, were "abandoned, effective July 3, 1940" (Interstate Commerce Commission 1940, 54:548). On July 1, 1901, the Brainerd and Northern Minnesota Railway was reorganized as the Minnesota and International Railway (146 miles owned and 179 miles operated), which was "acquired by Northern Pacific Ry. Co., effective Oct. 23, 1941" (Interstate Commerce Commission 1902, 15:274-275; Interstate Commerce Commission 1941, 55:547). The Big Fork and Northern Railway (32 miles owned) was "acquired by the Northern Pacific Ry. Co., effective Dec. 8, 1942" (Interstate Commerce Commission 1942, 56:547). The Walla Walla Valley Railway (18 miles owned and 19 miles operated), a Northern Pacific subsidiary, was "Reclassified from an electric railway to a Class II line-haul company Jan. 1, 1950" (Interstate Commerce Commission 1950, 64:584).

Burlington Northern was created by the merger of the following four railroads: Northern Pacific Railway (6,360 miles of road owned and 6,769 miles operated), Chicago, Burlington and Quincy Railroad (7,799 miles owned and 8,430 miles operated), Great Northern Railway (7,695 miles owned and 8,274 miles operated), and its subsidiary, the Pacific Coast Railroad (32 miles owned and operated) (Interstate Commerce Commission 1969, 83:340). The Columbia and Puget Sound Railroad Company (56 miles of line owned and operated) was renamed Pacific Coast Railroad Company in 1916 (Armbruster 2018, 33; Best 1964, 135; Interstate Commerce Commission 1916, 29:698). In 1906 the Milwaukee Road leased twenty-three miles of the Columbia and Puget Sound Railroad's line between Seattle and the junction with the Milwaukee Road at Maple Valley, Washington (Armbruster 2018, 29; Best 1964, 135). Operations on Burlington Northern began on March 3, 1970 (Interstate Commerce Commission 1970, 84:340). The Spokane, Portland and Seattle Railway was a subsidiary road that was leased to Burlington Northern on March

2, 1970, for ten years (Interstate Commerce Commission 1970, 84:331). Gaertner (1990, 204) states that the Spokane, Portland and Seattle Railway became part of Burlington Northern on November 1, 1979. Burlington Northern and Santa Fe (Atchison, Topeka and Santa Fe Railway) were merged to form Burlington Northern Santa Fe Railway (BNSF) on September 22, 1995 (Burlington Northern Santa Fe Railway 1999, 3-4).

Montana Rail Link leased the former Northern Pacific main line between Huntley, Montana (thirteen miles east of Billings) and Sandpoint, Idaho, and started operations on October 31, 1987 (*The Historical Guide to North American Railroads* 2014, 197). The route between Billings and Sandpoint was described by Schrenk (2002). On January 10, 2022, it was announced that Montana Rail Link's lease would be terminated and BNSF would resume operations (Stephens 2022, 4-5). Warren Buffett's holding company, Berkshire Hathaway Inc., acquired Burlington Northern Santa Fe Corporation (BNSF) on February 12, 2010 (Securities and Exchange Commission 2010).

A correction is published at the end of this book, including two letters that concern an error on the original page 102, which had stated that the Utah and Northern Railway (a Union Pacific subsidiary) was "still in existence." The first letter was written on September 30, 1921, by C. F. Staples, the Acting Director of the Bureau of Valuation of the Interstate Commerce Commission, to Charles Donnelley, the President of the Northern Pacific Railway. The second letter was written on October 3, 1921, from Donnelley to Staples. Two Union Pacific subsidiaries, the Oregon Short Line Railway and the Utah and Northern Railway, were "Consolidated into the Oregon Short Line and Utah Northern Railway, Aug. 1, 1889" (Interstate Commerce Commission 1890, 3:314-315). Ironically, the correction on page 102 misstates the corporate name as "Oregon Short Line and Utah and Northern Railway Company [sic]." The Oregon Short Line and Utah Northern Railway was reorganized as the Oregon Short Line Railroad (a Union Pacific subsidiary) on February 9, 1897 (Interstate Commerce Commission 1897, 10: 252-253).

I am very grateful to Dr. Paul Royster, the Coordinator of Scholarly Communications at the University of Nebraska-Lincoln Libraries, who

Foreword to the Centennial Edition

made possible this online publication, thereby filling a gap in the knowledge of the history of the transcontinental railroads. I thank Dr. Michael R. Hill for his generous gift of a laptop computer and a rare stereograph showing a Northern Pacific train crossing the Missouri River on the historic bridge between Bismarck and Mandan, North Dakota. Thanks are also due to the Minnesota Historical Society in St. Paul, Molly Kruckenberg, the Director of the Montana Historical Society in Helena, and the library of Montana State University in Bozeman, which loaned the microfilm copy of this book.

Rollin R. Davis, Ph.D.
Linccln, Nebraska
August 30, 2022

References

An Act Granting Lands to Aid in the Construction of a Railroad and Telegraph Line From Lake Superior to Puget Sound, on the Pacific Coast, by the Northern Route. 1864. Washington, DC: Senate and House of Representatives. July 2.

Armbruster, Kurt E. 2018. *Pacific Coast: Seattle's Own Railroad.* Burien, WA: Pacific Northwest Railroad Archive.

Athearn, Robert G. 1971. *Union Pacific Country.* Chicago: Rand McNally.

Bain, David Haward. 1999. *Empire Express: Building the First Transcontinental Railroad.* New York: Viking.

Best, Gerald. 1964. *Ships and Narrow Gauge Rails: The Story of the Pacific Coast Company.* Berkeley: Howell-North.

De Borchgrave, Alexandra Villard and John Cullen. 2001. *Villard: The Life and Times of an American Titan.* New York: Doubleday.

Bryant, Keith L. 1982. *History of the Atchison, Topeka and Santa Fe Railway.* Lincoln: University of Nebraska Press.

Burlington Northern Railroad. n.d. *Historical Background Information: Major Burlington Northern Predecessor Companies.* St. Paul: Burlington Northern Railroad.

Burlington Northern Santa Fe Corporation. 1999. "The History of BNSF: A Legacy for the 21st Century." *Railway: The Employee Magazine of Burlington Northern Santa Fe Corporation.* November/December.

Chandler, Alfred D., Jr., ed. 1965. *The Railroads, the Nation's First Big Business: Sources and Readings.* New York: Harcourt, Brace and World.

Derleth, August. 2002. *The Milwaukee Road: Its First Hundred Years.* Iowa City: University of Iowa Press.

Gaertner, John T. 1990. *North Bank Road: The Spokane, Portland and Seattle Railway.* Pullman: Washington State University Press.

Grodinsky, Julius. 1962. *Transcontinental Railway Strategy, 1869-1893: A Study of Businessmen.* Philadelphia: University of Pennsylvania Press.

Hedges, James Blaine. 1930. *Henry Villard and the Railways of the Northwest.* New Haven: Yale University Press.

Hidy, Ralph W., Muriel E. Hidy, Roy V. Scott, and Don L. Hofsommer. 2004. *The Great Northern Railway: A History.* Minneapolis: University of Minnesota Press.

The Historical Guide to North American Railroads. 2014. Waukesha, WI: Kalmbach Books.

Hofsommer, Don L. 1986. *The Southern Pacific, 1901-1985.* College Station: Texas A & M University Press.

Interstate Commerce Commission. 1888-1953. *Statistics of Railways in the United States.* Washington DC: Government Printing Office.

——. 1954-1994. *Transport Statistics in the United States.* Washington DC: Government Printing Office.

Klein, Maury. 1987. *Union Pacific: The Birth of a Railroad, 1862-1893.* Garden City, NY: Doubleday.

Lambert, Kirby, Patricia M. Burnham, and Susan R. Near. 2002. *Montana's State Capitol: The People's House.* Helena: Montana Historical Society Press.

Lewty, Peter J. 1987. *To the Columbia Gateway: The Oregon Railway and the Northern Pacific, 1879-1884.* Pullman: Washington State University Press.

——. 1995. *Across the Columbia Plain: Railroad Expansion in the Interior Northwest, 1885-1893.* Pullman: Washington State University Press.

Marshall, James. 1945. *Santa Fe: The Railroad That Built an Empire.* New York: Random House.

Nolan, Edward W. 1983. *Northern Pacific Views: The Railroad Photography of F. Jay Haynes, 1876-1905.* Helena: Montana Historical Society Press.

"Northern Pacific Railroad Completion Site, 1883." 1983. *National Register of Historic Places Inventory/Nomination Form.* Washington, DC: Department of the Interior, National Park Service.

Northern Pacific Railway. 1953. "Seventieth Anniversary." *The Tell Tale.* September.

——. 1960. "Northern Pacific Railway Guide to Points of Interest on the Scenic Route across America." St. Paul: Northern Pacific Railway.

——. 1961. "Villards Visit Historic Site." *The Tell Tale.* August.

——. 1962. *Sixty-sixth Annual Report.* St. Paul: Northern Pacific Railway.

——. 1964a. *Construction Era of the Northern Pacific Railway.* St. Paul: Northern Pacific Railway.

——. 1964b. "Villard Pushes NP Line to Completion." *Telltale* [sic]. July.

——. 1965. *The NP Story: Main Street of the Northwest.* St. Paul: Northern Pacific Railway.

———. n.d. *First of the Northern Transcontinental Railroads: Brief History of the Northern Pacific.* St. Paul: Northern Pacific Railway.

Renz, Louis Tuck. 1980. *The History of the Northern Pacific Railroad.* Fairfield, WA: Ye Galleon Press.

Schrenk, Larry. 2002. *Route Guide: Billings, Montana to Sandpoint, Idaho.* N.p.: Northern Pacific Railway Historical Association.

Schumpeter, Joseph A. 1939. *Business Cycles.* Vol. 1. New York: McGraw-Hill.

Securities and Exchange Commission. 2010. *Form 8-K. Berkshire Hathaway.* February 12.

Smalley, Eugene. 1883. *History of the Northern Pacific Railroad.* New York: Putnam.

Southern Pacific Company. 1955. *Southern Pacific's First Century.* San Francisco: Southern Pacific Company.

Stephens, Bill. 2022. "Montana Rail Link to Bow Out." *Trains.* April.

Trottman, Nelson. 1966. *History of the Union Pacific: A Financial and Economic Survey.* New York: Augustus M. Kelley.

Waters, L. L. 1950. *Steel Rails to Santa Fe.* Lawrence: University of Kansas Press.

Winks, Robin W. 1991. *Frederick Billings: A Life.* New York: Oxford University Press.

[Winser, Henry Jacob]. 1897. *The Official Northern Pacific Railway Guide.* St. Paul: W. C. Riley.

Wood, Charles R. 1968. *The Northern Pacific: Main Street of the Northwest.* New York: Bonanza Books.

REVISED

CORPORATE HISTORY

of

NORTHERN PACIFIC RAILWAY COMPANY

As of June 30, 1917

Prepared in accordance with

Valuation Order No.20

of the

Interstate Commerce Commission

Office of Land Assistant

St. Paul, Minnesota

Aug. 30, 1921.

Explanation

Arrangement: The Corporate Details are arranged in accordance with their map numbers, there being a map number for every corporation doing any construction. In cases of corporations doing no construction but which at one time held title to the property, the map number of the constructing company has been given them and they have been placed in their proper sequence following it. Each corporation has also been given a chart and place number, the chart numbers being given in chronological order; the company incorporated first, receiving number one; and the place numbers designate the position of the company on the chart, the numbers being given consecutively from left to right.

Mileage: In all cases where the items herein reported can be identified in the Northern Pacific Railway Company's Annual Report to the Interstate Commerce Commission for the year ending December 31, 1917, adjusted to June 30, 1917, the mileage as given therein has been adopted for the corporate history. There are generally unimportant discrepancies between this mileage and that shown by earlier records caused by line changes, re-measurements and trackage now merged with yards and terminal systems and which cannot be identified.

Abbreviations: It has been found desirable to abbreviate the names of corporations in certain places, but the full name will be found at least once in the chapter in which the abbreviation occurs.

Marginal references to records used are explained as follows:

M.B.128, p.3	Minute Book No.128, page 3
A.S.File 166-15	Assistant Secretary's Correspondence File 166, part 15
A.S.Doc. 86	Assistant Secretary's Document No.86
R.W.Deed 71	Right of Way Deed No.71
L.A.File 140	Land Assistant's File 140

INDEX

Page	
	B.
293	Barney, Charles T. et al (C.W.R.R.Co.)
376	Bellingham Bay and Eastern Railroad Company
448	Big Fork and International Falls Railway Company
69	Butte, Anaconda and Pacific Railway Company
	C.
420	Camas Prairie Railroad Company (C.S.L.Ry.Co.)
460	Camp Creek Railway Company (The)
290	Canyon Creek Railroad Company
380	Cary, E. V. (E.& M.C.Ry.Co.)
259	Clealum Railroad Company
420	Clearwater Short Line Railway Company
293	Central Washington Railroad Company (The)
66	Chicago & North Western Railway Company
66	Chicago, Milwaukee & St. Paul Railway Company
252	Coeur d'Alene Railway and Navigation Company (The)
222	Coeur d'Alene Steam Navigation and Transportation Company (The)
111	Columbia and Puget Sound Railroad Company (The)
457	Connell Northern Railway Company
158	Crosby, Stephen M., Trustee
466	Cuyuna Dock Company
463	Cuyuna Northern Railway Company

Page	
	D.
210	Duluth and Manitoba Railway Company
210	Duluth and Manitoba Railroad Company (The)
310	Duluth, Crookston and Northern Rail Road Company (The)
249	Duluth Short Line Railway Company
353	Duluth Transfer Railroad Company
350	Duluth Transfer Railway Company
62	Duluth Union Depot & Transfer Company
281	Drummond and Philipsburg Railroad Company (The)
284	Durham, R.L., Trustee
	E.
235	Eastern Washington Railway Company (Spok.& Pal.Ry.Co.)
380	Everett and Monte Cristo Railway Company
	F.
187	Fargo and Southwestern Railroad Company
94	Fort Dodge & Fort Ridgeley Railroad Company
	G.
404	Gaylord and Ruby Valley Railway Company
284	Gerlinger, Louis
168	Grantsburg, Rush City and St.Cloud Railroad Company (The)
69	Great Northern Railway Company
362	Green River and Northern Railroad Company

Page	
	H.
75	Hartford Eastern Railway Company
204	Helena and Jefferson County Railroad Company
269	Helena and Northern Railroad Company
246	Helena and Red Mountain Railroad Company
256	Helena, Boulder Valley and Butte Railroad Company
	J.
190	Jamestown & Northern Railroad Company (The)
316	Jamestown and Northern Extension Railroad Company
207	James River Valley Railroad Company
	K.
	L.
1	Lake Superior and Mississippi Railroad Company (The)
171	Little Falls and Dakota Railroad Company (The)
171	Little Falls and Dakota Railroad Company
365	Little Falls and Southern Railroad Company
12	Livingston, Johnston et al (N.P.R.R.)
	M.
89	Minneapolis and Duluth Railroad Company (The)
94	Minneapolis and St. Louis Railway Company (The)

Page	
	M.
94	Minneapolis and St. Louis Railway Company
98	Minneapolis and St. Louis Railroad Company (The)
64	Minneapolis, St. Paul & Sault Ste. Marie Railway Company
8) 127)	Minnesota and Pacific Railroad Company
94	Minnesota & Iowa Southern Railroad Company
146	Minnesota Northern Railroad Company
94) 146)	Minnesota Western Railroad Company
175	Mill Creek Flume and Manufacturing Company
430	Mill Creek Railroad Company
278	Missoula and Bitter Root Valley Railroad Company
469	Missoula and Hamilton Railway Company
442	Missouri River Railway Company
385	Monte Cristo Railway Company
194	Montana Railway Company
393	Montana Southern Railway Company
104	Montana Union Railway Company
	N.
1	Nebraska and Lake Superior Railroad Company (The)
214	Northern Pacific and Cascade Railroad Company
297	Northern Pacific and Montana Railroad Company
218	Northern Pacific and Puget Sound Shore Railroad Company
146	Northern Pacific, Fergus and Black Hills Railroad Company

Page	
	N.
272	Northern Pacific, La Moure and Missouri River Railroad Company
12	Northern Pacific Railroad Company
45	Northern Pacific Railway Company
77	Northern Pacific Terminal Company of Oregon
337	Northwestern Improvement Company
434	North Yakima and Valley Railway Company
	O.
239	Oregon and Washington Territory Railroad Company (The)
368	Oregon Railway Extension Co.
178	Oregon Railroad and Navigation Company (The)
178	Oregon Railway and Navigation Company
76	Oregon-Washington Railroad & Navigation Company
94	Olcott, Frederick P. et al (M.& St.L.Ry.)
119	Olympia & Chehalis Valley Railroad Company (The)
116	Olympia Railroad Union
	P.
225	Paton, Morton S. et al (S.L.S.& E. Ry. Co.)
324	Philadelphia Mortgage and Trust Company
158	Prince, F.M.
368	Portland and Puget Sound Railroad Company (The)
438	Portland and Seattle Railway Company (S.P.& S.Ry.)

Page	
	P.
407	Portland, Vancouver & Yakima Railway Company
123	Port Townsend Southern Railroad Company
243	Puget Sound and Grays Harbor Railroad and Transportation Company
201	Puget Sound Shore Railroad Company (The)
	R.
275	Rocky Fork and Cooke City Railway Company
184	Rocky Mountain Railroad Company of Montana
1) 138)	Rhawn, William H. et al (L.S.& M.R.R.)
	S.
165	Saint Cloud-Grantsburg and Ashland Railway Company
138	Saint Paul and Duluth Railroad Company
127	Saint Paul and Northern Pacific Railway Company
8	Saint Paul and Pacific Railroad Company (The)
181	Saint Paul, Minneapolis and Manitoba Railway Company (The)
62	St. Paul Union Depot Company
198	Sanborn, Cooperstown and Turtle Mountain Railroad Company
399	Seattle and International Railway Company
411	Seattle and Montana Railroad Company
332	Seattle and San Francisco Railway and Navigation Company (The)
108	Seattle and Walla Walla Rail Road and Transportation Company

Page	
	S.
108	Seattle and Walla Walla Rail Road Company
287	Seattle and West Coast Railway Company
225	Seattle, Lake Shore and Eastern Railway Company
319	Seattle Terminal Railway and Elevator Company
328	Seattle Warehouse & Terminal Company
235	Spokane and Palouse Railway Company (East.Wash.Ry.)
231	Spokane and Seattle Railway Company
266	Spokane Falls and Idaho Railroad Company
438	Spokane, Portland and Seattle Railway Company
451	Shields River Valley Railway Company (The)
41	Stillwater and St.Paul Railroad Company (The)
153	Stillwater Street Railway and Transfer Company (The)
158	Stillwater Union Depot & Transfer Company
262	South-Eastern Dakota Railroad Company
313	Snohomish, Skykomish and Spokane Railway and Transportation Company (The)
45	Superior and St.Croix Railroad Company
	T.
346	Tacoma, Olympia and Grays Harbor Railroad Company
307	Tacoma, Orting & Southeastern Railroad Company (The)
133	Taylors Falls and Lake Superior Railroad Company
454	Toppenish, Simcoe & Western Railway Company
119	Thurston County Railroad Construction Company

Page	
	T.
346	Tac. Olympia & Chehalis Valley R.R. Co.(T.O.& C.H.R.R.Co.)
	U.
101	Utah and Northern Railway Company
162	Union Depot & Transfer Company of Stillwater
153	Union Depot Street Railway and Transfer Company of Stillwater
356	United Railroads of Washington (The)
	V.
284	Vancouver, Klickitat and Yakima Railroad Company
	W.
340	Wallace and Sunset Railroad Company
396	Washburn, Bayfield and Iron River Railway Company
388	Washington and Columbia River Railway Company (The)
372	Washington & Oregon Railway Company
417	Washington Central Railway Company (The)
425	Washington Railway & Navigation Company
304	Washington Short Line Railway Company
414	Western American Company
445	Western Dakota Railway Company
127	Western Railroad Company of Minnesota (St.P.& N.P.Ry.)
239	Wright, C.B.

Page	Y.
343	Yakima and Pacific Coast Railroad Company

THE LAKE SUPERIOR AND MISSISSIPPI RAILROAD COMPANY

Chart Nos. 2 & 3 & 16
Place No. 45 & 36 & 25
Map No. 1

1. Incorporation

Chap. XCIII
Session Laws
1857
P. 323 &c.

The Nebraska and Lake Superior Railroad Company was created May 23, 1857, by Act of Legislature of the Territory of Minnesota. The name was changed to Lake Superior and Mississippi Railroad Company by an amendatory act dated March 8, 1861. There was also a second amendatory act, extending the time for construction, dated March 6, 1863.

Chap. I
Spl. Laws
1861
p. 201

Chap. V
Spl. Laws
1863
p. 151

Organization effected November 30, 1861

2. Construction

This company constructed a main line from St. Paul, Minn. to Duluth, Minn., 155.00 miles, between August 12, 1867 and August 1, 1870, as follows:

From	To	Date
# St. Paul	Mile Post 30	Aug. 12, 1867 to Dec. 23, 1868
Mile Post 30	Mile Post 80	Mar. 1869 to Dec. 28, 1869
Mile Post 80	Mile Post 110	Completed June 30, 1870
Mile Post 110	Mile Post 155 (Duluth)	June 1870 to Aug. 1, 1870

Some grading was done on this section in years 1864 and 1865.

3. Operation

L.A. File 140

Operation on the first 10 or 12 miles commenced September 10, 1868, and as further sections were completed they were put in operation. The road was formally opened to Duluth August 22, 1870.

A.S.Doc. R.R.390

June 5, 1871, the line of the Minneapolis and Duluth Railroad Company, extending from M.& D. Junction, Minn. (White Bear) to St.Anthony (now part of Minneapolis), Minn., 13.62 miles, was leased and operated until May 1, 1872, when lease was assigned to the N.P. R.R. Co., who continued the operation; being unable to make rental payments, the lease was reassigned to the L.S.& M.R.R. Co., who surrendered the property to the M.& D. R.R. Co. as of January 1, 1874.

A.S.Doc. 391

A.S.Doc. 775

A.S.Doc. 389

On October 24, 1871, the Minneapolis and St.Louis Railway Co. leased to the L.S.& M.R.R. Co. its line of railroad commencing near First St., Minneapolis, and extending to a point of junction with the St.Paul & Sioux City Railroad Co. in Scott County. Operated by the L.S.& M.R.R.Co. from November 15, 1871 to May 1, 1872, when lease was assigned to the N.P. R.R. Co., who continued the operation. Being unable to make rental payments the line was surrendered to the M.& St.L.Ry. Co. January 1, 1874.

M.B.294 p.85

November 21, 1870, the line of the Stillwater and St.Paul Railroad Company extending from Stillwater, Minn. to White Bear, Minn., 12.74 miles, was leased and operated from December 28, 1870 to May 1, 1872,

A.S.Doc. 365

when lease was assigned to the N.P. R.R. Co. and operation continued by them until terminated by agreement of April 21, 1874, which restored this property to the L.S.& M.R.R. Co. as of Feb. 1, 1874; operated until June 14, 1877.

A.S.Doc. 772

January 1, 1872, an undivided one-half interest in the 22.50 miles of line between Thomson, Minn. and Duluth was deeded to the Northern Pacific Railroad Company and was operated jointly with that company until May 1, 1872.

A.S.Doc. 814

On May 1, 1872, the property of the L.S.& M.R.R.Co. and all of the above lines were leased to the N.P.R.R. Co., who operated them, but being unable to make required payments, the leased lines were reassigned to

A.S.Doc. 365

the L.S.& M.R.R. Co. at various times, until finally the whole arrangement was terminated by an agreement dated April 21, 1874, effective as of February 1, 1874.

A.S.Doc. 853

February 1, 1874, the L.S.& M.R.Co. again took up the operation of its line along with that of the Stillwater & St. P. Co. and continued to operate them until June 14, 1877. The L.S.& M. R.R. Co. having failed, the property was sold at public auction May 1, 1877, and conveyed by deed dated June 14, 1877 from H.E.Mann, Master in Chancery, to a Committee of Bondholders. The committee operated the property from June 14, 1877 to June 30, 1877, and having incorporated the Saint Paul and Duluth Railroad Company, that company operated the property from July 1, 1877, taking title by deed dated July 17, 1877.

A.S.Doc. 1365

Preliminary work on the line from Carlton to Cloquet (Knife Falls R.R.Co.) was done by this company early in 1877.

4. Present Status of Corporation

The deed of conveyance whereby title to this company's property passed to the St.P.& D. R.R. Co. also included the franchise of the L.S.& M. R.R. Co. to be a corporation.

The records are in the custody of Mr. R. H. Relf, Assistant Secretary of the Northern Pacific Railway Company, Saint Paul, Minnesota.

5. Chain of Title

	From	To	Date	Form of Transfer
A.S.Doc. 1364	L.S.& M.R.R.Co. H.E.Mann, Master in Chancery	William H.Rhawn, et al (Committee of Bondholders)	June 14,1877	Deed
A.S.Doc. 1365	William H.Rhawn, et al (Committee of Bondholders)	St.P.& D.R.R.Co.	July 17,1877	Deed

	From	To	Date	Form of Transfer
A.S.Doc. 300	St.P.& D.R.R.Co.	N.P. Ry. Co.	June 15, 1900	Deed

SCHEDULE OF INSTRUMENTS AND RECORDS

File Ref.	Description
A.S.Doc. 390	Lease of June 5, 1871 from Mpls. and Duluth R.R.Co. to The Lake Superior and Mississippi Railroad Co., covering the line from M.& D. Jct. to St.Anthony, 13.62 miles.
M.B.394 p.85	Lease of Nov. 21, 1870 from Stillwater and St.Paul Railroad Company to L.S.& M. R.R. Co.
A.S.Doc. 772	Deed of Jan. 1, 1872, by which L.S.& M. R.R. Co. conveyed to N.P. R.R. Co. a one-half interest in line from Thompson to Duluth.
A.S.Doc. 814	Lease of May 1, 1872, L.S.& M.R.R. Co. to N.P.R.R. Co. covering its entire system.
A.S.Doc. 365	Instrument dated April 21, 1874, terminating the lease of May 1, 1872, by which the properties of Minneapolis and St.Louis, Minneapolis and Duluth Railroad and Stillwater and St.Paul Railroad Companies were operated by the N.P. R.R. Co.
A.S.Doc. 853	Instrument of April 21, 1874, by which L.S.& M.R.R. Company again took up the operation of its property.

A.S.Doc.
1364
Deed of June 14, 1877, by which entire property of L.S.& M. R. R. Co. was conveyed to William H. Rhawn, et al, a Committee of Bond Holders.

A.S.Doc.
1365
Deed of July 17, 1877, by which William H. Rhawn, et al, Committee of Bond Holders, conveyed the property to the St. Paul and Duluth Railroad Co.

A.S.Doc.
300
Deed of June 15, 1900, by which the St.P.& D. R.R. Co. conveyed its entire property to the N.P. Ry. Co. (except land grant)

A.S.Doc.
775
Agreement Nov. 18, 1871 acknowledging possession of the line, covered by lease of Oct. 24, 1871 (A.S.Doc. 391) as of November 15, 1871.

A.S.Doc.
389
Agreement of Nov. 13, 1873 covering possession of line (A.S.Doc.391) by N.P.R.R. Co., reassignment to L.S.& M. R.R. Co. and return of property to M.& St.L. Ry. Co.

A.S.Doc.
391
Lease of Oct. 24, 1871, M.& St.L. Ry. Co. to L.S.& M. R.R. Co., line from Minneapolis to Scott County.

A.S.Doc.
375
Agreement of Nov. 13, 1873, under which the L.S.& M.R.R.Co. restored to the M.& D. R.R. Co. its line from Minneapolis to White Bear.

L.A.File
140
Land Assistant's file "Data used in compiling return to Order No. 20 - Corporate History".

THE SAINT PAUL AND PACIFIC RAILROAD COMPANY

Chart No.1&4
Place No.100 & 91
Map No.2

1. Incorporation

Chap.1
Ex Sess.
Laws
p.3

Minnesota and Pacific Railroad Company was created by an Act of the Legislature of the Territory of Minnesota May 22, 1857. The Act authorized the construction of a main line from Stillwater, Minn. to a point between Big Stone Lake and the Sioux Wood River with a branch line to the Red River via St.Cloud and Crow Wing, Minn. The company issued some First Mortgage Bonds on which it defaulted. The State of Minnesota, having acquired the bonds, foreclosed and became possessed of the property and franchises of the company.

Chap.XX
Spl.Laws
1862
p.247

The Legislature of the State of Minnesota, March 10, 1862, passed an act entitled: "An Act to facilitate the construction of the Minnesota and Pacific Railroad and to amend and continue the Act of Incorporation relating thereto." This Act conferred upon The Saint Paul and Pacific Railroad Company all the rights and privileges which had pertained to the M.& P.R.R.Co. An Act of

Chap.CXLIV
U.S.Stat.
at Large
p.588

Congress of March 3, 1871 authorized, among other things, the construction of a line from Crow Wing, to a connection with the Northern Pacific Railroad at Brainerd, Minn., and this company commenced construction.

2. Construction

L.A.File 140

This company constructed a railroad grade between Watab, Minnesota and Brainerd, Minnesota, about 55 miles, in 1871 and 1872, and laid track on it from Brainerd to a point 5 miles south.

3. Operation

This company operated no lines of interest in this report.

4. Present Status of Corporation

Chap.201
Spl.Laws
1877
p.257

This company having failed to complete the line between Crow Wing and Brainerd, as authorized by Act of Congress, the State Legislature passed an Act declaring forfeited the rights of the St.P.& P.R.R.Co. to this line. The Act provided further that any other Minnesota railroad corporation complying with certain provisions of the Act might acquire the rights forfeited by the St.P.& P.R.R.Co. Under these provisions the line between Brainerd and Watab was appropriated by the Western Railroad Company of Minnesota.

Other property of this company was sold under foreclosure to the St.Paul, Minneapolis and Manitoba Railway Co.

The records are in the custody of Mr.L.E.Katzenbach,

Secretary of the Great Northern Railway Company at St. Paul, Minnesota.

5. Chain of Title

	Line	From	To	Date	Form of Transfer
Chap.201 Spl.Laws 1877 p.257	Brainerd to Watab	St.P.&P.R.R. Co.	W.R.R.Co. of Minn.	Mar.1,1877	Acquisition of forfeited rights under provisions of the Act of the Legislature
A.S.Doc. 1320	Brainerd to Sauk Rapids	W.R.R.Co. of Minn.	St.P.& N.P.Ry. Co.	May 9,1883	Change of name
A.S.Doc. 51	All	St.P.& N.P.Ry. Co.	N.P.Ry. Co.	Nov.2,1896	Deed

SCHEDULE OF INSTRUMENTS AND RECORDS

File Ref.	Description
A.S.Doc. 51	Deed of November 2, 1896, by which the Saint Paul and Northern Pacific Railway Company conveyed its entire property to N.P.Ry.Co.
A.S.Doc. 1320	Amended Articles of Incorporation changing name of W.R.R.Co. of Minn. to St.P.& N.P. Ry. Co.
L.A.File 140	Land Assistant's file "Data used in compiling return to Order No.20 - Corporate History".

NORTHERN PACIFIC RAILROAD COMPANY

Chart No.5 & 35
Place No.11 & 4
Map No.3, 31, 32

1. **Incorporation**

13 Stat. at Large p.365

Incorporated under Act of Congress of July 2, 1864, entitled: "An Act granting lands to aid in the construction of a railroad and telegraph line from Lake Superior to Puget Sound, on the Pacific Coast, by the Northern Route". The Act provided that the construction of the road was to be commenced within two years and completed by July 4, 1876.

M.B.140 p.1

Organization effected December 7, 1864.

By joint resolution of the Senate and House of Representatives on the following dates the Act was amended:

14 Stat. at Large p.355

May 7, 1866; the time for commencing and completing the road was extended two years.

15 Stat. at Large p.255

July 1, 1868; the time for commencing was extended two years more, but it was provided that the road was to be completed by July 4, 1877.

15 Stat. at Large p.346

March 1, 1869, the Company was given the right to issue bonds. "Puget Sound" was defined as meaning all the waters connecting with the Straits of Juan de Fuca.

16 Stat. at Large p.57

April 10, 1869; a line from Portland, Oregon to Puget Sound was provided for; twenty five miles of this was to be constructed by July 2, 1871, and the balance at the rate of 40 miles per year until completed.

16 Stat. at. Large p.378

May 31, 1870; the main line was defined as reaching Puget Sound via the valley of the Columbia River and a branch from the main line to Puget Sound via the Cascade Mountains was authorized.

Spl.Laws 1865 p.228

Pri.&Local Laws 1865 p.290

The State of Minnesota signified its assent to the construction of the line by an Act of Legislature approved March 2, 1865, and the State of Wisconsin by a similar Act approved April 10, 1865.

This company failed and a receiver was appointed April 16, 1875. The property, including all rights and franchises, (except patented and certified lands) was sold at auction August 12, 1875, being purchased by a Bond-holders' committee, consisting of Johnston Livingston et al. The sale was confirmed by the court August 25, 1875 and the property was conveyed to Johnston Livingston et al by Oliver Fiske and Kenneth G. White, Master Commissioners on September 17, 1875. The committee, having been given power of attorney by the bond and stock holders, as soon as it came into possession of the property and franchises became the body politic and corporate known as the Northern Pacific Railroad Company and the first directorate of the reorganized company was elected September 30, 1875. By deed dated March 22, 1882 Johnston Livingston, et al conveyed the property sold under foreclosure on August 12, 1875 to Northern Pacific Railroad Company.

In connection with the foreclosure and reorganization proceedings the following deeds were also executed.

A.S.Doc.
R.R.493
May 1, 1875 Northern Pacific Railroad Company to George W. Cass, Receiver, conveying all real and personal property and land grants.

A.S.Doc.
R.R.2
Sept. 28, 1875, George W. Cass, Receiver to Johnston Livingston et al, conveying all property covered by the deed of May 1, 1875.

A.S.Doc.
R.R.1
Sept. 27, 1875, Jay Cooke and Charlemagne Tower, Trustees to Johnston Livingston et al, conveying all the property sold under foreclosure August 12, 1875.

These deeds were in effect quitclaim deeds, as the deed of September 17, 1875 from Oliver Fiske and Kenneth G. White, Master Commissioner, and the deed from Johnston Livingston, et al, dated March 22, 1882 conveyed proper title.

There were nine deeds dated December 16, 1876 from Geo. W. Cass, Receiver, Jay Cooke and Charlemagne Tower, Trustees to Frederick Billings, Trustee, and nine deeds from Frederick Billings, Trustee to N.P.R.R.Co. conveying land in eight counties in Minnesota and one in North Dakota.

The new company also failed and on August 15, 1893 receivers were appointed by the Federal Courts of the several Circuits traversed by the railroad. The property was sold under foreclosure July 25, 1896, conveyance being made by two deeds dated August 18, 1896 from Alfred L. Cary, Special Master, to the Northern Pacific Railway Company. One deed was known as the "General Railroad Deed" and the other as the "General Land Deed". These deeds conveyed all the main and branch lines, and recite that the court proceedings held in the several Judicial Districts under which the deeds were issued are by reference thereto to be of the same force and effect as though such proceedings and the record thereof were included in and made part of the deeds mentioned.

A.S.Doc. 35

After the sale of July 25, 1896 the following deeds were also executed:

A.S.Doc. 35
October 15, 1896 railroad and land deed from N.P. R.R. Co. to N.P. Ry. Co.

A.S.Doc. 35
October 16, 1896 Trustees' deed from the Farmers Loan and Trust Co. to N.P.Ry. Co. covering same property conveyed in deed of August 18, 1896 from Alfred L. Cary, Special Master.

A.S.Doc. 35
October 30, 1896 Receivers' deed from Edwin H. McHenry, Frank G. Bigelow and Andrew F. Burleigh, Receivers of N.P.R.R. Co. to the N.P. Ry. Co. This deed conveyed the

same property described in the above deeds, dated respectively October 15, 1896 and October 16, 1896.

M.B.141
p.132

Organization of reorganized company effected September 30, 1875.

2. Construction and Purchases

The Northern Pacific Railroad Company constructed lines as follows:

Wisconsin

From	To	Date	Miles
Wis.-Minn.Line	Bluff Creek Superior	July 1881 to Feb.1882	16.20
Bluff Creek Superior	Brule	June to Dec. 1883	24.75
Brule	Ashland	June 1883 to Jan.1885	37.70
So.Superior	Superior	1888	3.98
Superior	Wis.-Minn. Line	1885	2.08
		Total - - -	84.71

Minnesota

From	To	Date	Miles
Carlton (formerly N.P.Jctn.)	Brainerd	Feb.1870 to April 1871	91.40
Brainerd	Minn.-N.Dak. Line	1871	136.70
Carlton	Minn.-Wis. Line	July 1881 to Feb.1882	9.00
Minn.-Wis. Line	Duluth Jctn.	1885	1.65

	From	To	Date	Miles
	Minnesota			
A.S.Doc. 772	One-half interest in line of Lake Superior and Mississippi Railroad Company between Thomson and Duluth was purchased Jan. 1, 1872			22.50
			Total -	261.25
	North Dakota			
	N.Dak-Minn. Line	30 Miles East of Bismarck	Oct.1871 to Oct.1872	165.10
	30 Miles East of Bismarck	Missouri Riv. West of Bismarck	1872 to Spring of 1873	31.30
	Bismarck Bridge Line over Missouri River		Jan.1881 to Nov. 1882	4.58
	Bismarck Missouri Riv.	Little Missouri River	April 1879 to Sept. 1880	150.00
	Little Missouri River	N.Dak.-Mont. Line	Dec.1879 to July 1881	26.90
			Total -	377.88
	Montana			
	Mont.-N.Dak.Line	Glendive	1880 to July 1881	46.30
	Glendive	Ft.Keogh	Oct.1880 to Dec.1881	75.00
	Ft.Keogh	Forsyth	June 1881 to April 1882	50.00
	Forsyth	Billings	Oct.1881 to Sept.1882	100.00

From	To	Date	Miles
Montana			
Billings	Mission	Nov. 1881 to Dec. 1882	100.00
Mission	Lombard	June 1882 to April 1883	75.00
Lombard	East Helena	June 1881 to June 1883	50.00
East Helena	Mullan Tunnel	April 1882 to July 1883	25.00
Mullan - overhead line		June to Aug. 1883	3.36
Mullan Tunnel	Gold Creek	May 1881 to (1) Sept. 1883	36.60
Bozeman - overhead line		Oct. 1882 to Feb. 1883	2.34
Mont.-Ida. Line	Noxon	Aug. 1881 to Sept. 1882	10.98
Noxon	Woodlin	June to Nov. 1882	50.00
Woodlin	Dixon	Sept. 1882 to April 1883	50.00
Dixon	Evaro	Sept. 1882 to June 1883	25.00
Evaro	Bonita	Nov. 1881 to July 1883	50.00
Bonita	Gold Creek	May 1881 to (1) Sept. 1883	38.40
Coal Spur	Cokedale	Completed Aug. 14, 1887	3.59
		Total -	791.57

(1) The tracks of the eastern and western portions of the railroad met at Gold Creek August 22, 1883.

From	To	Date	Miles
Idaho			
Ida.-Wash. Line	Algoma	Sept.1880 to Oct.1881	40.73
Algoma	Ida-Mont. Line	Aug.1881 to Sept.1882	43.90
		Total --	84.63
Washington			
Wallula	Snake River (Ainsworth)	Mar.to Nov. 1880	11.50
Bridge line at Ainsworth		1882 to 1884	0.94
Ainsworth	Ritzville	Oct.1879 to April 1881	84.28
Ritzville	Spokane	June 1880 to Aug. 1881	64.30
Spokane	Wash.-Ida. Line	Sept.1880 to Aug. 1881	18.90
Pasco	Columbia Riv.(Incline track)	1884	2.08
Pasco	Kennewick (Bridge line)	July 1887 to April 1888	3.30
Kennewick	Kiona	July to Dec. 1883	25.20
Kiona	Yakima City	Jan. to Dec. 1884	59.85
Yakima City	Ellensburg	Dec.1884 to May 1886	39.60
Ellensburg	Easton	June to Nov. 1886	40.28

From	To	Date	Miles
Washington			
Easton	# Conn. with line from west on Stampede Switchback	June 1886 to June 1887	11.25
Tacoma	Cascade Jct.	Dec. 1876 to May 1877	26.00
Cascade Jotn.	Eagle Gorge	Sept. 1884 to Nov. 1885	24.10
Eagle Gorge	#Conn. with line from east on Stampede Switchback	June 1886 to June 1887	29.60
Tacoma	Tenino	April 1873 to Mar. 1874	40.10
Tenino	Kalama	1871 to Aug. 1873	65.00
Line through Stampede Tunnel		Feb. 1886 to May 1888	2.92
Cascade Jotn.	Wilkeson	1877	5.23
Cascade Jotn.	Burnett	1881	1.87
Wilkeson	Carbonado	1880	3.60
Meeker	Stuck Jotn.	Nov. 1882 to July 1883	6.93
		Total - -	566.83

\# The connection over the Cascade Mountains via the Switchback was effected June 1, 1887.

From	To	Date	Miles
Oregon			
Portland	Hunters (now Charlton)	May to Sept. 1883	36.25
Hunters (Partly graded in 1883)	Goble	Jan. 1890 to Mar. 1891	2.30
		Total -	38.55

Wisconsin	84.71 Miles
Minnesota	261.25
North Dakota	377.88
Montana	791.57
Idaho	84.63
Washington	566.83
Oregon	38.55

Grand Total - 2205.42 Miles

Owing to line changes, re-measurements, etc. the main and branch line mileage turned over to the Northern Pacific Railway Company by the Northern Pacific Railroad Company August 31, 1896, was:

	Main Line	Branches
Wisconsin	84.29 Miles	
Minnesota	255.19	
North Dakota	376.93	
Montana	783.08	3.59 Miles
Idaho	84.06	
Washington	538.50	13.16
Oregon	39.15	
	2,161.20 Miles	16.75 Miles

Grand Total   2,177.95 Miles

3. **Operation**

L.A. File 140

The Northern Pacific Railroad Company operated the

property from the date each parcel was turned over for operation until August 15, 1893; thereafter the property was operated by the receivers of the N.P.R.R.Co. until August 31, 1896. The details are as follows:

Main Line

From	To	Miles	Date turned over for Operation
Wisconsin			
Minn.-Wis.Line	Superior	16.00	Sept.1,1882
Superior	Ashland	63.30	June 1,1885
South Superior	Wis.-Minn.Line	6.06	Aug. 5,1887 *
	Total	85.36	
Minnesota			
Carlton (formerly N.P.Jctn.)	Brainerd	90.00	Oct. 5,1871
Brainerd	Minn.-N.D.Line	140.00	Oct. 5,1871
Carlton	Minn.-Wis.Line	9.00	Sept.1,1882
Wis.-Minn.Line	Duluth Jctn.	1.65	Aug. 5,1887 *
Thomson	Duluth (owned and operated jointly with Lake Superior and Mississippi Railroad Company)	22.50	Jan. 1,1872
	Total	263.15	

From	To	Miles	Date turned over for Operation
North Dakota			
Minn.-N.D.Line	35 miles E. of Bismarck	160.00	Oct. 7, 1873
35 Miles E. of Bismarck	Bismarck	35.00	Oct. 7, 1873
Bismarck	N.D.-Mont.Line	178.00	Aug. 1, 1881
	Total	373.00	
Montana			
N.D.-Mont.Line	Glendive	40.00	Aug. 1, 1881
Ida.-Mont.Line	Heron	5.94	Mar.31, 1883
Glendive	Billings	225.00	Sept.15, 1882
Billings	Livingston	116.00	Jan. 15, 1883
Heron	Knowles (formerly Olive)	85.00	Mar.31, 1883
Knowles	Dixon (formerly Jocko)	21.00	May 20, 1883
Livingston	Helena	123.00	July 1, 1883
Dixon (formerly Jocko)	Missoula	45.00	July 5, 1883
Missoula	Gold Creek	61.00	Sept.1, 1883
Helena	Gold Creek	58.50	Sept.1, 1883
	Total	780.44	
Idaho			
Mont.-Ida.Line	Ida.-Wash. Line	84.06	May 1, 1882
	Total	84.06	

From	To	Miles	Date turned over for Operation
Washington			
Kalama	Tenine	65.00	Aug. 15, 1873
Tenine	Tacoma	40.00	Mar. 5, 1874
Tacoma	Cascade Jctn.	26.00	1877
Wallula	Wash.-Ida. Line	173.00	May 1, 1882
Pasco	Yakima City	87.50	June 1, 1885
Cascade Jctn.	50 Miles E. of Tacoma	24.00	July 2, 1887
Yakima City	Ellensburg	40.00	May 15, 1886
Ellensburg	Cle Elum	25.00	Dec. 20, 1886
50 Miles E. of Tacoma	Cle Elum	56.10	July 2, 1887

Total - 536.60

Oregon

From	To	Miles	Date turned over for Operation
Portland	Hunters (now Charlton)	36.25	Oct. 9, 1884
Hunters	Goble	2.30	Mar. 1891 approx.

Total - 38.55

```
Wisconsin        85.36 Miles
Minnesota       263.15
North Dakota    373.00
Montana         780.44
Idaho            84.06
Washington      536.60
Oregon           38.55

Grand Total - - 2161.15 Miles
```

BRANCH LINES

From	To	Miles	Date Operation Began	Owning Company	Operating Agreement	File Ref.
Wisconsin		No Branches				
Minnesota						
St.Paul	Duluth	155.00	May 1, 1872	Feb. 1, 1874	L.S.& M.R.R.Co.	Lease of May 1, 1872 with L.S.& M.R.R.Co.	A.S.Doc.8144 A.S.Doc.345 A.S.Doc.R.R. 390
M.& D.Jctn.	St.Anthony	13.62	"	Jan. 1, 1874	M.&D.R.R.Co.		
Stillwater	White Bear	12.74	"	May 1, 1874	S.& St.P.R.R.Co.		A.S.Doc.345
Sauk Rapids	Brainerd	60.50	Nov.1, 1877	Aug.31, 1896	St.P.& N.P.Ry.Co.	Without formal contract and Leases of May 1,1878 and May 1, 1883	A.S.Doc.237& A.S.Doc.R.R. 479
Sauk Rapids	Minneapolis	66.10	July 2, 1884			Lease of May 1, 1883	A.S.Doc.237
Ramsey St.Line in Mpls.		0.76	May 1, 1886			"	"
2nd St.Line in Mpls.		1.01	1886			"	"
Mulberry St.Line in Mpls.		0.68	May 1, 1884			"	"
E.Side Line at St.Paul		1.25	Oct. 1889			"	"
Track to Minn. Tfr.		1.04	1885			"	"
Northtown Jctn.	St.Anthony	5.26	1885			"	"
Northtown Jctn.	Terminal Lot	3.44	July 2, 1884			"	"
20th Ave.Mpls.St.Paul		10.08	Feb. 1886			"	"

From	To	Miles	Date Operated From	Date Operated To	Owning Company	Operating Acct.	File Ref.
Minnesota							
Little Falls	Staples	33.65	Nov. 24, 1889	Aug. 31, 1896	St.P.& N.P.	Lease of May 1, 1883	A.S.Doc.237
L.F.&D.Connec.	Little Falls Canal	1.08	Jan. 1, 1891	"	L.F.&D.R.R. Co.	Without formal contract and contract of Oct.1,1891	A.S.Doc.R.R. 501
Little Falls	Morris	87.85	Nov. 1, 1882	"	L.F.&D.R.R. Co.	Contract of Oct.20,1882 and Nov.7, 1894	A.S.Doc.R.R. 125 and A.S. Doc.Rec.40
Wadena	Breckenridge	75.00	Nov. 10, 1882	"	N.P.F.&B.H. R.R.Co.	Contract of Oct.20,1882 and Nov.12, 1894	A.S.Doc.63 and A.S.Doc. Rec.34
Manitoba Jctn. (formerly Winnipeg Jctn.)	N.Grand Forks	105.00	Apr. 1, 1887	"	D.&M.R.R.Co.	Contract of June 1, 1887 and Nov.8, 1894	A.S.Doc.R.R. 286 and A.S. Doc.433-143-145
Key West	Omera	3.38	"	"	"	"	"
Omera	Sherack	2.95	Oct. 1895	"	"	"	"
Red Lake Falls Jctn.	Red Lake Falls	1.08	Apr. 1, 1887	"	"	"	"
Fertile	Crookston	22.40	Dec. 2, 1889	"	D.C.& N.R.R. Co.	Contract of Aug.1,1890	A.S.Doc. R.R. 354
Crookston	Carthage Jct.	22.10	Sept. 6, 1890	"	"	"	"
	Total	686.20					

From	To	Miles	Date Operated From	Date Operated To	Owning Company	Operating Agent.	File Ref.
North Dakota							
Wahpeton	Wilmor	42.10	Sept. 1, 1883	Aug. 31, 1896	N.P.F.& B.H. R.R.Co.	Contract of Oct. 20, 1882 and Nov. 12, 1894	A.S.Doc.88 and A.S.Doc. Rec.34
Fairview Jct.	Mathews (formerly Fairview and Adams)	3.06	1884	"	"	Contract of Oct. 20, 1882 and Nov. 1, 1889	A.S.Doc.88 and A.S.Doc. 368
Mathews	Great Bend	5.74	Oct. 19, 1887	"	S.E.D.R.R.Co.	Contract of Nov. 1, 1889	A.S.Doc.368
Keystone Jct.	Bayne	6.04	Aug. 1, 1890	"	"	"	"
Grand Forks	Pembina	96.30	Oct. 7, 1887	"	D.& M.R.R.Co.	Contract of June 1, 1887 and Nov. 8, 1894	A.S.Doc.433-143-145
Fargo	Lisbon	60.00	July 1, 1883	"	F.& S.W.R.R. Co.	Contract of July 1, 1882 and Nov. 12, 1894	A.S.Doc.R.R. 96 and A.S. Doc.34
Lisbon	La Moure	27.40	Aug. 25, 1883	"	"	"	"
Jamestown	La Moure	48.55	Dec. 14, 1885	"	J.R.V.R.R.Co.	Contract of Jan. 1, 1886 and Nov. 8, 1894	A.S.Doc.165 A.S.Doc.Rec. 35
Independence Oakes (formerly Valley Jct.)		15.20	Dec. 15, 1886	"	"	"	"
La Moure	Edgeley	21.30	Nov. 1, 1887	"	N.P.LaM.&M.R. R.R.Co.	Contract of June 1, 1887 and Nov. 17, 1894	A.S.Doc.230
Sanborn	Cooperstown	36.78	Dec. 1, 1883	"	S.C.& T.M. R.R.Co.	Contract of Apr. 18, 1883 and Nov. 12, 1894	A.S.Doc.R.R. 120 and A.S. Doc.Rec.34

28

From	To	Miles	Date Operated From	Date Operated To	Opings Company	Operating Agrmt.	File Ref.
North Dakota							
Jamestown	Melville	32.80	July 1, 1883	Aug. 31, 1896	J.&N.R.R.Co.	Contract of July 1, 1882 and Nov.12, 1894	A.S.Doc.97 and A.S.Doc. Rec.34
Melville	New Rockford	25.10	Dec. 1, 1883	"	"	"	"
New Rockford	Kinnewaukan	31.70	Aug. 6, 1885	"	"	"	"
Carrington	Sykeston	12.90	Dec. 1, 1883	"	"	"	"
Kinnewaukan	Leeds	18.03	Dec. 1, 1889	"	J.& N.R.R. Co.	Contract of Sept. 2,1889 and Nov.17, 1894	A.S.Doc.311
	Total	483.00					
Montana							
Laurel	Red Lodge	44.37	Aug. 1, 1890	Aug. 31, 1896	R.P.& C.C. Ry.Co.	No formal contract	
Livingston	Cinnabar	51.70	Sept.16,1883	"	R.M.R.R.Co. of M.	Contract of Aug.1, 1883 and Nov.12, 1894	A.S.Doc.R.R. 215 & A.S. Doc.Hed.34
Logan	Butte	71.00	June 14,1890	"	N.P.& M.R.R. Co.	Contract of Oct.1, 1888 and Nov.12, 1894	A.S.Doc.R.R. 263 and A.S. Doc.Rec.37
Sappington	Norris	20.64	July 10,1890	"	"	"	"
Harrison	Pony	7.08	"	"	"	"	"
Boulder	Elkhorn	20.43	"	"	"	"	"
De Smet	St.Regis	71.40	Jan. 1,1891	"	"	"	"

From	To	Miles	Date Operated From	Date Operated To	Owning Company	Operating Agrmt.	File Ref.
Montana							
St. Regis	Lookout	38.14	Aug. 15, 1891	Aug. 31, 1896	N.P.& M.R.R. Co.	Contract of Oct.1, 1888 and Nov.12, 1894	A.S.Doc.R.R. 283 and A.S. Doc.Rec.57
Whitehall	Parrott	5.75	Sept. 1, 1895	"			
Clough Jctn. (formerly Birdseye)	Marysville	12.58	Nov. 20, 1887	Sept. 7, 1888	H.& M.R.R.Co.	Contract of June 1, 1887	A.S.Doc.R.R. 229
"	"	---	Sept. 7, 1888	Aug. 31, 1896	N.P.& M.R.R.	Contract of Oct. 1, 1888 and Nov. 12, 1894	A.S.Doc.R.R. 283 and A.S. Doc.Rec.57
Jefferson City	Calvin	30.00	Dec. 1, 1887	Sept. 7, 1888	H.B.V.& B.R. R.Co.	Contract of May 1, 1887	A.S.Doc.R.R. 217
"	"	---	Sept. 7, 1888	Aug. 31, 1896	N.P.& M.R.R. Co.	Contract of Oct. 1, 1888 and Nov. 12, 1894	A.S.Doc.R.R. 283 and A.S. Doc.Rec.57
Drummond	Philips- burg	25.80	Nov. 20, 1887	Sept. 7, 1888	D.& P.R.R.Co.	Contract of June 1, 1887	A.S.Doc.R.R. 227
"	"	---	Sept. 7, 1888	Aug. 31, 1896	N.P.& M.R.R.	Contract of Oct. 1, 1888 and Nov. 12, 1894	A.S.Doc.R.R. 283 and A.S. Doc.Rec.57
Philipsburg	Rumsey	6.37	Dec. 15, 1888				
Missoula	Victor	35.85	June 1, 1888	Sept. 7, 1888	M.& B.R.V. R.R.Co.	Contract of June 1, 1887	A.S.Doc.R.R. 239
Victor	Grantsdale	15.00	Aug. 1, 1888	"			
Missoula	"	---	Sept. 7, 1888	Aug. 31, 1896	N.P.& M.R.R. Co.	Contract of Oct. 1, 1888 and Nov.12, 1894	A.S.Doc.R.R. 283 and A.S. Rec.57

From	To	Miles	Date Operated From	Date Operated To	Owning Company	Operating Agmt.	File Ref.
Montana							
East Helena (formerly Prickly Pear Jctn.)	Vicks	20.60	Dec. 18, 1883	Aug. 31, 1896	H.& J.C.R.R. Co.	Contract of Aug.1, 1883	A.S.Doc.R.R. 470
Helena	Rimini	16.37	Dec. 15, 1896	"	H.& R.M.R.R. Co.	Contract of Mar.1, 1887 and Nov.12, 1894	A.S.Doc.216 and A.S.Doc. Rec.35
Coal Spur	Cokedale	3.59	1888	"	N.P.R.R.Co.		
	Total	496.67					
Idaho							
Old Mission	Wallace	24.71	Oct. 1, 1888	Aug. 31, 1896	C.d'A.Ry.& N. Co.	Lease of Sept.14, 1888 and April 25, 1894	A.S.Doc.270 and A.S.Doc. Rec.10
Wallace	Mullan	7.05	June 1889	"	"	"	"
Mullan	Ida.-Mont. Line	11.10	Aug. 15,1891	"	"	"	"
Wallace	Burke	6.83	Oct. 1,1888	"	"	"	"
Coeur d'Alene City (via steamboats)	Old Mission	45.00	"	"	"	"	"
Hauser	Coeur d' Alene City	13.61	Oct. 24,1886	"	S.F.& I.R.R.	Without formal contract and Contract of Oct. 1, 1887	A.S.Doc.250

From	To	Miles	Date Operated From	Date Operated To	Owning Company	Operating Agrmt.	File Ref.
Idaho							
Wash.-Ida.Line	Genesee	7.15	July 1, 1888	Aug. 31, 1896	S.& P.Ry.Co.	Contract of May 1, 1886, June 1,1887 and Nov.17,1894	A.S.Doc.R.R. 177 and A.S. Doc.R.R.604
"	Julaetta	32.99	Sept.15,1891	"	"	"	"
Total(except steamboat line) 103.44							
Washington							
Cascade Jctn.	Wilkeson	5.23	1877	July 1, 1885	N.P.R.R.Co.	Without formal contract and Contract of Oct. 1, 1887	A.S.Doc.R.R. 181
"	"	---	July 1,1885	Aug.31, 1896	N.P.& C.R.R. Co.	"	"
Wilkeson	Carbonado	3.60	Oct. 1881	July 1, 1885	N.P.R.R.Co.	Without formal contract and Contract of Oct. 1, 1887	A.S.Doc.R.R. 181
"	"	---	July 1,1885	Aug.31, 1896	N.P.& C.R.R. Co.	"	"
Cascade Jct.	Burnett	1.87	Oct. 1881	July 1, 1885	N.P.R.R.Co.	"	"
"	"	---	July 1,1885	Aug.31, 1896	N.P.& C.R.R. Co.	"	"
Burnett	Spiketon (formerly Pittsburg)	2.18	Oct. 6, 1890	Aug.31, 1896	"	"	"
Crocker	Wingate(formerly Douty)	5.30	May 6,1889	"	"	"	"

31

From	To	Miles	Date Operated From	Date Operated To	Owning Company	Operating Agmnt.	File Ref.
Washington							
Palmer	Kingley Jctn. (formerly Durham)	2.90	Dec. 1, 1888	Aug. 31, 1896	O.R.& N.R.R. Co.	No formal contract	
Kingley Jct. (formerly Durham)	Mile Post 10½	7.50	June 30,1893	"	"	"	
"	Kingley Mine	1.50	Jan. 1, 1891	"	"	"	
Meeker (formerly Puyallup Jct.)	Stuck Jctn.	7.00	July 6,1884	July 1, 1885	N.P.R.R.Co.	"	
"	"	---	July 1,1885	Aug. 31, 1896	N.P.& P.S.S. R.R.Co.	Contract of Aug.1, 1885, Oct.1,1887 and Nov.1, 1889	A.S.Doc.R.R. 182,R.R.132A and R.R.342
Stuck Jct.	Seattle	23.97	Jan. 17, 1890	"	"	"	
Marshall	Belmont	43.00	Oct. 15, 1886	"	S.& P.Ry.Co.	Contract of May 1, 1886, June 1,1887 and Nov.17, 1894	A.S.Doc.R.R. 177 and A.S. Doc.R.R. 604
Belmont	Wash.-Ida.Line	53.51	July 1, 1888	"	"	"	
Pullman Jct.	"	7.06	Sept.15,1891	"	"	"	
Belmont	Farmington	6.09	Dec. 10, 1890	"	"	"	
Cheney	Davenport	41.40	July 1, 1889	Oct. 31, 1895	C.W.R.R.Co.	Lease of Nov. 1, 1888	A.S.Doc.282
Davenport	Almira	46.10	June 14,1890	"	"	"	
Almira	Coulee City	21.16	Nov. 1,1890	"	"	"	

32

From	In	Miles	Date Operated From	Date Operated To	Owning Company	Operating Arrmt.	File Ref.
Washington							
Orting	Puyallup Riv.	7.64	June 24, 1889	Aug. 31, 1896	T.O.& S.E.R.R.	No formal contract	
Tacoma	Ruston (formerly Barnsea)	3.08	Feb. 8, 1889	"	N.P.R.R.Co.		
Simpson	Montesano	20.80	Feb. 16, 1891	"	T.O.& G.H.R.R. Co. and U.R.R. of W.	No formal contract and Contract of Aug. 5, 1890 and Nov. 24, 1894	A.S.Doc.R.R. 365 and A.S. Doc.Rec.33
Centralia	Elma	32.57	May 1, 1891	"	"	"	"
Lake View	Olympia	23.85	May 1, 1891	"	"	"	"
Olympia	Gate	19.65	Aug. 10, 1891	"	"	"	"
Cosmopolis Jct.	Cosmopolis	1.60	April 11, 1892	"	U.R.R. of W.	Contract of Aug.5, 1890 and Nov.24, 1894	A.S.Doc.R.R. 365 and A.S. Doc.Rec.33
Chehalis Jct.	South Bend	56.68	June 1, 1893	"	"	"	"
Aberdeen Jct.	Aberdeen	2.60	June 1, 1895	"	"	"	"
Montesano	Ocosta	24.70	April 11, 1892	"	"	"	"
Black River Jctn.	Renton	5.60	1893	"	N.P.& P.S.S. Co.	Contract of Aug. 1, 1885, Oct. 1, 1897 and Nov.1, 1889	A.S.Doc.R.R. 182, R.R.1321 and R.R.362
Woodinville (formerly Jacobson)	Kirkland	5.60	"	"	"	"	"
Total		483.57					

33

34

Item	Is	Miles	Date Operation Began	Owning Company	Operating Arrgt.	File Ref.

Spurs
No Branches

4. **Present Status of Corporation**

No action has been taken to dissolve this corporation but having parted with its assets it is not active.

The records are in the custody of Mr. R. H. Relf, Assistant Secretary of the Northern Pacific Railway Company, Saint Paul, Minnesota.

5. **Chain of Title**

From	To	Date	Form of Transfer	File Ref.
Olive Fisks and Kenneth G. White, Master Commissioners	Johnston Livingston, et al	Sept. 17, 1875	Deed	A.S.Doc. R.R.5
N.P.R.R. Co.	Geo. W. Cass, Receiver	May 1, 1875	Deed	A.S.Doc. R.R.493
Jay Cooke and C. Tower, Trustees	Johnston Livingston, et al	Sept. 27, 1875	Deed	A.S.Doc. R.R.1
Geo. W. Cass, Receiver	Johnston Livingston, et al	Sept. 28, 1875	Deed	A.S.Doc. R.R.2
Johnston Livingston, et al	N.P. R.R. Co.	Mar. 22, 1882	Deed	A.S.Doc. R.R.42

The entire property as it existed in August 1896 was conveyed to the Northern Pacific Railway Company by the following deeds:

From	To	Date	Form of Transfer	File Ref.
Alfred L. Cary, Special Master	N.P.Ry.Co.	Aug. 18, 1896	General Railroad Deed	A.S.Doc.35
Alfred L. Cary, Special Master	"	"	General Land Deed	"
Northern Pacific Railroad Co.	"	Oct. 15, 1896	Railroad and Land Deed	"
The Farmers Loan and Trust Company	"	Oct. 16, 1896	Trustees' Deed	"
Edwin H. McHenry, Frank G. Bigelow and Andrew F. Burleigh, Receivers	"	Oct. 30, 1896	Receivers' Deed	"

Prior to the general conveyance of the system the following branch lines had been disposed of:

Line		Transfer				
From	To	From	To	Date	Form	File Ref.
Cascade Jctn., Wash.	Burnett, Wash.	N.P.R.R.Co.	N.P.& C.R.R.Co.	July 1, 1885	Deed	A.S.10230
Cascade Jctn.	Carbonado, Wash.	"	"	"	"	A.S.10230
Meeker, Wash.	Stuck Jctn., Wash.	"	N.P.& P.S.S.R.R. Co.	"	"	R.W.Deed 71

SCHEDULE OF INSTRUMENTS AND RECORDS

File Ref.	Description
A.S.Loc. 35	Five deeds by which the property of the Northern Pacific Railroad Company was conveyed to the Northern Pacific Railway Company.
M.B.140 p.1	Reference to Organization of original N.P.R.R.Co.
M.B.141 p.132	Reference to Reorganization of N.P. R.R. Co.
A.S.Doc. 772	Deed of Jan. 1, 1872 from Lake Superior and Mississippi Railroad Co. to N.P.R.R. Co. conveying one-half interest in line from Thomson to Duluth.
A.S.Docs. 814, 365 and 390	Lease of May 1, 1872, under which N.P.R.R. Co. operated the system of Lake Superior and Mississippi Railroad Co. and reassignment.
A.S.Docs. 237 and R.R.479	Leases of May 1, 1878 and May 1, 1883, under which N.P. R.R. Co. operated the system of the Saint Paul and Northern Pacific Railway Company.
A.S.Doc. R.R.501	Contract of July 31, 1891, under which N.P. R.R. Co. operated the line of the Little Falls and Southern Railroad Co.
A.S.Docs. R.R.125 and Rec.40	Contract of Oct. 20, 1882, under which N.P.R.R.Co. operated the line of The Little Falls and Dakota Railroad

Co. and lease to the Receivers of N.P. R.R. Co. dated Nov. 7, 1894.

A.S.Docs. 88 and Rec.34
Contract of Oct. 20, 1882, under which N.P.R.R.Co. operated the line of the system of the Northern Pacific, Fergus and Black Hills Railroad Co.

A.S.Doc. R.R.286
Contract of June 1, 1887, under which N.P.R.R.Co. operated the system of Duluth and Manitoba Railroad Co.

A.S.Doc. R.R.354
Contract of Aug. 1, 1890, under which N.P.R.R.Co. operated the system of The Duluth, Crookston and Northern Rail Road Co.

A.S.Doc. 368
Contract of Nov. 1, 1889, under which N.P.R.R.Co. operated the system of South-Eastern Dakota Railroad Co.

A.S.Docs. R.R.96 and Rec.34
Contract of July 1, 1882, under which N.P. R.R. Co. operated the system of Fargo and Southwestern Railroad Co. and lease of Nov. 12, 1894 to receivers of the N.P. R.R. Co.

A.S.Docs. 165 and Rec. 36
Contract of Jan. 1, 1886, under which N.P. R.R. Co. operated the system of James River Valley Railroad Co. and lease of Nov. 8, 1894 to Receivers of N.P. R.R. Co.

A.S.Doc. 230
Contract of June 1, 1887, under which N.P.R.R.Co. operated the system of Northern Pacific, LaMoure and Missouri River R.R. Co.

A.S.Doc.　　　　Contract of May 1, 1887, under which the N.P.R.R.
R.R.217　　　　Co. operated the Helena, Boulder Valley & Butte R.R.Co.

A.S.Docs.　　　Contract of April 18, 1883, under which N.P.R.R.Co.
R.R.120
and Rec.34　　 operated the system of Sanborn, Cooperstown and Turtle
　　　　　　　　Mountain Railroad Co. and lease dated Nov. 12, 1894 to
　　　　　　　　Receivers of N.P. R.R. Co.

A.S.Docs.　　　Contract of July 1, 1882, under which N.P. R.R. Co.
97 and
Rec.34　　　　 operated the system of Jamestown and Northern Railroad
　　　　　　　　Co. and lease dated Nov. 12, 1894 to Receivers of N.P.
　　　　　　　　R.R. Co.

A.S.Doc.　　　 Contract of Sept. 2, 1889, under which N.P. R.R. Co.
311　　　　　　 operated the system of Jamestown and Northern Extension
　　　　　　　　Railroad Co.

A.S.Doc.　　　 Contract dated June 1, 1887, under which N.P. R.R.
R.R.229　　　　 Co. operated the Helena & Nor. R. R. Co.

A.S.Docs.　　　Contract of Aug. 1, 1883, under which N.P. R.R. Co.
R.R.213
and Rec.34　　 operated system of Rocky Mountain Railroad Co. of Mon-
　　　　　　　　tana, and lease dated Nov. 12, 1894 to the Receivers of
　　　　　　　　N.P. R.R. Co.

A.S.Docs.　　　Contract of Oct. 1, 1888, under which N.P. R.R. Co.
R.R.383 and
Rec.37　　　　 operated system of Northern Pacific and Montana Railroad
　　　　　　　　Co. and lease dated Nov. 12, 1894 to Receivers of N.P.
　　　　　　　　R.R. Co.

A.S.Doc. 470	Contract of Aug. 1, 1883, under which N.P. R.R. Co. operated system of Helena and Jefferson County Railroad Co.
A.S.Doc. R.R.227	Contract dated June 1, 1887, under which the N.P.R.R. Co. operated the Drummond & Philipsburg R.R. Co.
A.S.Docs. 216 and Rec.35	Lease of Nov. 12, 1894 to Receivers of N.P.R.R. Co. and Contract of Mar. 1, 1887 covering operation of the system of Helena and Red Mountain Railroad Co.
A.S.Doc. R.R.239	Contract dated June 1, 1887, under which the N.P.R.R. Co. operated the Missoula & Bitter Root Valley R.R. Co.
A.S.Docs. 270 and Rec.10	Lease of Oct. 1, 1888, under which N.P.R.R. Co. operated system of The Coeur d'Alene Ry. and Nav. Co. and lease dated April 25, 1894 to Receivers of N.P. R.R. Co.
A.S.Doc. 250	Contract of Oct. 1, 1887, under which N.P. R.R. Co. operated system of Spokane Falls and Idaho Railroad Co.
A.S.Docs. R.R.177 and R.R. 604	Contracts of May 1, 1886 and June 1, 1887, under which N.P. R.R. Co. operated system of Spokane and Palouse Ry. Co. Also lease of Nov. 17, 1894 to Receivers of N.P. R.R. Co.
A.S.Doc. R.R.181	Contract of Oct. 1, 1887, under which N.P. R.R. Co. operated system of Northern Pacific and Cascade Railroad Co.

40

A.S.Doc. R.R.182 and R.R.362
Contracts of Aug. 1, 1885, Oct. 1, 1887 and Nov. 1, 1889, under which N.P.R.R.Co. operated system of Northern Pacific and Puget Sound Shore Railroad Co.

A.S.Doc. 282
Lease of Nov. 1, 1888, under which N.P.R.R.Co. operated system of The Central Washington Railway Co.

A.S.Docs. R.R.855 and Rec. 33
Contract of Aug. 5, 1890, under which N.P.R.R.Co. operated system of The United Railroads of Washington and lease dated Nov. 24, 1894 to Receivers of the N.P.R.R. Co.

A.S.Doc. 10230
Deed of July 1, 1885, by which N.P.R.R. conveyed its lines extending from Cascade Junction to Burnett, Wilkeson and Carbonado to Northern Pacific and Cascade Railroad Co.

R.W.Deed 71
Deed of July 1, 1885, by which N.P.R.R.Co. conveyed its line from Meeker to Stuck Jctn. to Northern Pacific and Puget Sound Shore Railroad Co.

THE STILLWATER AND ST. PAUL RAILROAD COMPANY

Chart No.6
Place No.27
Map No.4

1. Incorporation

A.S.Doc.
10005
    Incorporated under the general laws of the State of Minnesota.

    Articles are not dated but the commencement of the corporation is stated as being January 24, 1867. Articles were filed with the Secretary of State January 27, 1867.

M.B.294
p.5
    Organization effected February 26, 1867.

    Amended Articles filed with the Secretary of State on the following dates:

M.B.294
p.14
    May 29, 1869, increasing amount of indebtedness.

M.B.294
p.55
    November 18, 1870, increasing capital stock.

M.B.294
p.111
    January 8, 1874, re-incorporating the company.

2. Construction

L.A.File
140
    This company constructed the line from Myrtle St., Stillwater, Minnesota to White Bear, Minnesota, 12.74 miles, between September and December 1870.

3. Operation

L.A.File 140 and M.B.294 p.85

The line was operated:

From December 28, 1870 to May 1, 1872, by the Lake Superior and Mississippi Railroad Company under a lease dated November 21, 1870.

A.S.Dec. 365

On May 1, 1872 this lease was assigned to the N.P. R.R. Co. who continued the operation of the property. Being unable to make the payments required under the lease the N.P. R. R. Co. entered into an agreement with the L.S.& M.R. R. Co. April 21, 1874 by which lease of this line was reassigned to the L.S.& M. R. R. Co. as of February 1, 1874.

M.B.294 ps.85 and 111

From February 1, 1874 to June 30, 1877 operated by the L.S.& M. R. R. Co. under the lease of November 21, 1870, and a modification thereof dated February 24, 1874.

From July 1, 1877 to March 2, 1899, by the Saint Paul and Duluth Railroad Company under the lease of November 21, 1870, as modified February 24, 1874.

4. Present Status of Corporation

L.A.File 140

The charter of this company expired by limitation January 24, 1917.

The records are in the custody of Mr. R. H. Relf, Assistant Secretary of the Northern Pacific Railway Company at Saint Paul, Minnesota.

5. <u>Chain of Title</u>

	From	To	Date	Form of Transfer
A.S.Doc. 1030	S.& St.P.R.R.Co.	St.P.& D.R.R.Co.	Mar. 2, 1899	Deed
A.S.Doc. 300	St.P.& D.R.R.Co.	N. P. Ry. Co.	June 15, 1900	Deed

SCHEDULE OF INSTRUMENTS AND RECORDS

File Ref.   **Description**

A.S.Doc.   Articles of Incorporation of The Stillwater and
10005
and   St. Paul Railroad Company and amendments thereto.
M.B.294
ps.1,14,
55,111

M.B.294   Lease of November 21, 1870, from The S.& St.P.R. R.
ps.85
and   Co. to Lake Superior & Mississippi Railroad Company
111
                 and modification of same.

A.S.Doc.   Deed of March 2, 1899, by which The S.& St.P.R.R.
1030
                 Co. conveyed its entire property to the St.Paul and
                 Duluth Railroad Company.

A.S.Doc.   Deed of June 15, 1900, by which the St.P.& D. R.R.
300
                 Co. conveyed its entire property to the N.P. Ry. Co., ex-
                 cepting its land grant.

L.A.File   Land Assistant's file "Data used in compiling re-
140
                 turn to Order NO.20".

NORTHERN PACIFIC RAILWAY COMPANY

Chart No.7,98,126 and 136
Place No.6, 1, 2 and 3
Map No.5

1. Incorporation

A.S.Doc. 1256

The Superior and St.Croix Railroad Company was created by the State of Wisconsin by Special Act approved March 15, 1870 and specially amended January 20, 1871, March 16, 1871 and April 15, 1895. Pursuant to resolution of the Stockholders July 1, 1896 the former title, Superior and St.Croix Railroad Company was changed to the present name, Northern Pacific Railway Company.

M.B.152 p.1

Organization effected February 4, 1871.

2. Construction and Purchases

This company purchased the entire system of the Northern Pacific Railroad Company, title being conveyed by the following deeds:

	Executed by	Date	Description
A.S.Doc. 35	Alfred L.Cary, Special Master	Aug.18,1896	General Railroad Deed
A.S.Doc. 35	Alfred L.Cary, Special Master	Aug.18,1896	General Land Deed
A.S.Doc. 35	Northern Pacific Railroad Co.	Oct.15,1896	Railroad and Land Deed
A.S.Doc. 35	The Farmers Loan & Trust Co.	Oct.16,1896	Trustees' Deed

	Executed by	Date	Description
A.S.Doc. 35	Edwin H.McHenry ⎫ Frank G.Bigelow ⎬ Receivers Andrew F.Burleigh ⎭	Oct.30,1896	Receivers' Deed

The system as purchased extended from Ashland, Wisconsin to Wallula, Washington, and from Pasco, Washington to Portland, Oregon, 2177.95 miles, the mileage in each state being as follows:

Wisconsin	84.29	miles
Minnesota	255.19	"
North Dakota	376.93	"
Montana	786.67	"
Idaho	84.06	"
Washington	551.66	"
Oregon	39.15	"
Total	2177.95	"

The Northern Pacific Railway Company acquired the following lines on dates shown:

Line of Company

Wisconsin

	From	To	Miles	Date deeded to N.P.Ry.Co.	File Ref.
Washburn, Bayfield and Iron River Railway Company	Iron River	Washburn	33.78	June 16, 1902	A.S.Doc.1130
Cayuse Dock Company	Ore Dock on Superior Bay Front		0.18	Aug. 27, 1915	A.S.Doc.8553
Saint Paul and Duluth Railroad Company	St.Croix River	Grantsburg	11.90	June 15, 1900	A.S.Doc. 300
	Minn.-Wis.Line	West Superior	1.54	June 15, 1900	A.S.Doc. 300

Minnesota

	From	To	Miles	Date deeded to N.P.Ry.Co.	File Ref.
Duluth Transfer Railroad Company	Duluth	Spirit Lake	9.06	May 26, 1902	A.S.Doc.1135
Saint Paul and Duluth Railroad Company	St.Paul	Thomson	132.50	June 15, 1900	A.S.Doc. 300
(1)	Thomson	Duluth	22.50	June 15, 1900	A.S.Doc. 300
	Rush City	St.Croix Riv.	5.14	June 15, 1900	A.S.Doc. 300
	White Bear	Stillwater	12.74	June 15, 1900	A.S.Doc. 300
	Wyoming	Taylors Falls	20.59	June 15, 1900	A.S.Doc. 300
	Carlton	Cloquet	6.64	June 15, 1900	A.S.Doc. 300
	Groningen(formerly Miller)	Banning	4.73	June 15, 1900	A.S.Doc. 300
	Thomson	Minn.-Wis.Line	26.21	June 15, 1900	A.S.Doc. 300

(1) One half interest acquired

Minnesota	From	To	Miles	Date deeded to L.P.Ry.Co.	File Ref.
Saint Paul and Northern Pacific Railway Company	All		183.77	Nov. 2, 1896	A.S.Doc.51
The Little Falls and Dakota Railroad Company	Little Falls	Morris	87.85	June 5, 1900	A.S.Doc.490
Northern Pacific, Fergus and Black Hills Railroad Company	Wadena	Breckenridge (Minn.-N.D.Line)	75.00	April 21, 1898	A.S.Doc.130
The Duluth, Crookston and Northern Rail Road Company	Fertile	Carthage Jctn.	44.50	Apr. 21, 1898	A.S.Doc.125
Duluth and Manitoba Railroad Company	Manitoba Jctn.	East Grand Forks	105.00	Apr. 21, 1898	A.S.Doc.123
	Leyvest	Shuruck	6.33	Apr. 21, 1898	A.S.Doc.122
	Red Lake Falls Jctn.	Red Lake Falls	1.04	Apr. 21, 1898	A.S.Doc.122
Union Depot & Transfer Company of Stillwater	Lines in Stillwater	(approx)	10.62	June 21, 1902	A.S.Doc.1240
The Minneapolis & St.Louis Rail-road Company	St. Anthony	M.& D.Jctn.	13.68	Nov. 29, 1901	A.S.Doc.1126
Little Falls and Southern Rail-Road Company	L.F.& D.Gemeo.	Little Falls Canal at Little Falls	1.08	Sept. 4, 1899	A.S.Doc.220
Cuyuna Northern Railway Company	Deerwood	Ironland	3.56	June 18, 1914	A.S.Doc.7033
	Deerwood	Cuyuna-MilleLac Mine	5.16	June 18, 1914	A.S.Doc.7033
Big Fork & International Falls Railway Company	Grand Falls	International Falls	34.01	June 18, 1914	A.S.Doc.7034

48

North Dakota

	From	To	Miles	Date deeded to I.P.R.Co.	File Ref.
Missouri River Railway Company	Mandan	Stanton	52.64	June 20, 1914	A.S.Doc.7935
	Mandan	6 miles south of Cannon Ball	42.41	June 20, 1914	A.S.Doc.7935
Western Dakota Railway Company	Cannon Ball	Mott	91.35	June 20, 1914	A.S.Doc.7936
	Stanton	Golden Valley	35.00	June 20, 1914	A.S.Doc.7936
Fargo and Southwestern Railroad Company	Fargo	LaMoure	87.49	Apr. 21, 1898	A.S.Doc. 124
Northern Pacific, LaMoure and Missouri River Railroad Company	LaMoure	Edgeley	21.30	Apr. 21, 1898	A.S.Doc. 131
Sanborn, Cooperstown and Turtle Mountain Railroad Company	Sanborn	Cooperstown	36.78	Apr. 21, 1898	A.S.Doc. 139
Jamestown and Northern Railroad Company	Jamestown	Minnewaukan	89.60	Apr. 21, 1898	A.S.Doc. 128
	Carrington	Sykeston	12.90	Apr. 21, 1898	A.S.Doc. 128
Jamestown and Northern Extension Railroad Company	Minnewaukan	Leeds	18.03	Apr. 21, 1898	A.S.Doc. 129
South-Eastern Dakota Railroad Company	Mathews (formerly Adams and Fairview)	Great Bend	5.74	Apr. 21, 1898	A.S.Doc. 138
	Keystone Jctn.	Bayne	6.04	Apr. 21, 1898	A.S.Doc. 138
Duluth and Manitoba Railroad Company	Grand Forks	Pembina	96.30	Apr. 21, 1898	A.S.Doc. 122
James River Valley Railroad Company	Jamestown	LaMoure	48.68	Apr. 21, 1898	A.S.Doc. 127
	Independence	Oakes	15.20	Apr. 21, 1898	A.S.Doc. 127

49

North Dakota

	From	To	Miles	Date deeded to N.P.Ry.Co.	File Ref.
Northern Pacific, Fergus and Black Hills Railroad Company	Wahpeton (Minn.-N.D. Line)	Milnor	42.10	Apr. 21, 1898	A.S.Doc. 130
	Fairview Jctn.	Mathews (Formerly Fairview and Adams)	3.06	Apr. 21, 1898	A.S.Doc. 130

Montana

	From	To	Miles	Date deeded to N.P.Ry.Co.	File Ref.
Rocky Mountain Railroad Company of Montana	Livingston	Cinnabar	51.70	Apr. 21, 1898	A.S.Doc. 137
Northern Pacific and Montana Railroad Company	Logan	Butte	71.00	Apr. 21, 1898	A.S.Doc. 133
	Philipsburg	Rumsey	6.37	Apr. 21, 1898	A.S.Doc. 133
	Sappington	Norris	20.64	Apr. 21, 1898	A.S.Doc. 133
	Harrison	Pony	7.08	Apr. 21, 1898	A.S.Doc. 133
	Boulder	Elkhorn	20.43	Apr. 21, 1898	A.S.Doc. 133
	DeSmet	Lookout	109.54	Apr. 21, 1898	A.S.Doc. 133
	Whitehall	Parrott	5.75	Apr. 21, 1898	A.S.Doc. 133
	Clough Jctn.	Marysville	12.58	Apr. 21, 1898	A.S.Doc. 133
	Jefferson City	Calvin	30.00	Apr. 21, 1898	A.S.Doc. 133
	Drummond	Philipsburg	25.80	Apr. 21, 1898	A.S.Doc. 133
	Missoula	Grantsdale	50.85	Apr. 21, 1898	A.S.Doc. 133
Helena and Jefferson County Railroad Company	East Helena (formerly Prickly Pear Jctn.)	Wickes	20.10	Apr. 21, 1898	A.S.Doc. 126

Montana

	From	To	Miles	Date deeded to I.P.R.Co.	File Ref.
Rocky Fork and Cooke City Railway Company.	Laurel	Red Lodge	44.37	Apr. 21, 1898	A.S.Doc. 136
Helena and Red Mountain Railroad Company	Helena	Rimini	16.37	Dec. 15, 1899	A.S.Doc. 238
The Shields River Valley Railway Company	Mission	Wilsall	22.93	June 23, 1914	A.S.Doc.7937
Missouri River Railway Company	Glendive	Sidney	54.81	June 20, 1914	A.S.Doc.7938
The Camp Creek Railway Company	Manhattan	Anceney	15.15	June 22, 1914	A.S.Doc.7938
Gaylord and Ruby Valley Railway Company	Renova	Twin Bridges	21.90	Feb. 28, 1899	A.S.Doc. 197
Montana Railway Company	All		14.83	Oct. 7, 1898	A.S.Doc. 159
Montana Union Railway Company	All		71.98	Oct. 7, 1898	A.S.Doc. 221

Idaho

	From	To	Miles	Date deeded to I.P.R.Co.	File Ref.
The Coeur d'Alene Railway and Navigation Company	Old Mission	Lookout	42.86	Jan. 26, 1897	A.S.Doc. 22
	Wallace	Burke	6.83	Jan. 26, 1897	A.S.Doc. 22
(1) Via steamboats. (1)	Old Mission	Coeur d'Alene City	45.00	Jan. 26, 1897	A.S.Doc. 22
Clearwater Short Line	Arrow	Stites	62.91	June 23, 1914	A.S.Doc.7939
	Joseph	Grangeville	66.78	June 23, 1914	A.S.Doc.7939

52

	From	To	Miles	Date deeded to N.P.Ry.Co.	File Ref.
Idaho					
Wallace and Sunset Railroad Company	Wallace	Sunset	5.56	Nov. 1898	(1)

(1) No record can be found of a deed from this company; all of its stock is owned by N.P.Ry. Co.and its holdings which consisted of a small amount of right of way and some grade were appropriated by N.P.Ry.Co.

	From	To	Miles	Date deeded to N.P.Ry.Co.	File Ref.
Spokane Falls and Idaho Railroad Company	Hauser Jctn.	Coeur d'Alene City	13.61	Apr. 21,1898	A.S.Doc. 140
Spokane and Palouse Railway Company	Wash.-Ida. Line	Julietta	32.99	Feb. 21,1899	A.S.Doc. 203
	Wash.-Ida. Line	Genesee	7.15	Feb. 21,1899	A.S.Doc. 203
Washington					
Clearwater Short Line Railway Company	Snake Riv. Jctn.	Lewiston Jctn.	40.97	June 23,1914	A.S.Doc.7939
Connell Northern Railway Company	Connell	Adco	60.95	June 25,1914	A.S.Doc.7941
	Bassett Jct.	Sohrag	12.54	June 25,1914	A.S.Doc.7941
Spokane and Palouse Railway Company	Marshall	Wash.-Ida.Line	96.51	Feb. 21,1899	A.S.Doc. 203
	Pullman Jctn.	Wash.-Ida.Line	7.06	Feb. 21,1899	A.S.Doc. 203
	Belmont	Farmington	6.09	Feb. 21,1899	A.S.Doc. 203

Washington

	From	To	Miles	Date deeded to N.P.Ry.Co.	File Ref.
The Washington Central Railway Company	Cheney	Coulee City	108.66	June 29, 1914	A.S.Doc.7940
	Coulee Jctn.	Adrian	21.10	June 29, 1914	A.S.Doc.7940
Green River and Northern Pacific Railroad Company	Palmer Jctn.	Mile Post 10¼	11.90	Apr. 21, 1898	A.S.Doc. 125
Northern Pacific and Cascade Railroad Company	Cascade Jctn.	Spiketon (formerly Pittsburgh)	4.05	Apr. 21, 1898	A.S.Doc. 135
	Cascade Jctn.	Carbonado	8.83	Apr. 21, 1898	A.S.Doc. 135
	Crocker	Wingate (formerly Dowty)	5.30	Apr. 21, 1898	A.S.Doc. 135
	Extension beyond Wilkeson		0.93	Apr. 21, 1898	A.S.Doc. 135
Northern Pacific and Puget Sound Shore Rail-Road Company	Meeker (formerly Puyallup Jctn.)	Seattle	30.95	Apr. 21, 1898	A.S.Doc. 134
	Black River Jctn.	Kennydale	6.50	Apr. 21, 1898	A.S.Doc. 134
	Woodinville (formerly Jacobsen)	Kirkland	5.60	Apr. 21, 1898	A.S.Doc. 134
The United Railroads of Washington	Centralia	Ocosta	67.90	Apr. 21, 1898	A.S.Doc. 132
	Chehalis Jctn.	South Bend	56.68	Apr. 21, 1898	A.S.Doc. 132
	Elma	Simpson (formerly Summit)	10.17	Apr. 21, 1898	A.S.Doc. 132
	Lake View	Gate	43.50	Apr. 21, 1898	A.S.Doc. 132
	Aberdeen Jctn.	Aberdeen	2.60	Apr. 21, 1898	A.S.Doc. 132
	Cosmopolis Jctn.	Cosmopolis	1.60	Apr. 21, 1898	A.S.Doc. 132

54

Washington	From	To	Miles	Date deeded to N.P.Ry.Co.	File Ref.
Clealum Railroad Company	Cle Elum	Ronald	5.28	Apr. 21, 1898	A.S.Doc. 121
Tacoma, Orting and South-eastern Railroad Company	Orting	Puyallup River	7.64	Apr. 21, 1898	A.S.Doc. 141
The Washington and Columbia River Railway Company	Ore.-Wash.Line	Dayton	98.08	June 18, 1907	A.S.Doc.3575
	Eureka	Pleasant View	19.73	June 18, 1907	A.S.Doc.3575
	Mill Creek Jctn.	Tracy	6.13	June 18, 1907	A.S.Doc.3575
North Yakima and Valley Railway Company	North Yakima	Naches	13.07	June 24, 1914	A.S.Doc.7942
	North Yakima	Moxee	8.85	June 24, 1914	A.S.Doc.7942
	Granger	Parker	17.06	June 24, 1914	A.S.Doc.7942
	Cowiche Jctn.	Weibel	5.07	June 24, 1914	A.S.Doc.7942
	Wesley Jctn.	Parren	8.57	June 24, 1914	A.S.Doc.7942
Western American Company	Carbonado	Fairfax	7.10	Aug. 3, 1901	A.S.Doc. 665
Spokane and Seattle Railway Company	Spokane	Davenport	50.05	Mar. 17, 1899 and Oct. 3, 1900	A.S.Doc. 198 and A.S.Doc. 402
Seattle and International Railway Company	Seattle	Sallal Prairie	63.32	Mar. 21, 1901	A.S.Doc. 310
	Woodinville	Sumas	102.90	Mar. 21, 1901	A.S.Doc. 310
	Snohomish	Everett	11.41	Mar. 21, 1901	A.S.Doc. 310
	Arlington	Darrington	28.08	Mar. 21, 1901	A.S.Doc. 310
Monte Cristo Railway Company	Hartford	Monte Cristo	42.12	July 31, 1903	A.S.Doc.1467

Washington

	From	To	Miles	Date deeded to N.P.Ry.Co.	File Ref.
Bellingham Bay and Eastern Rail-Road Company	Wickersham	Bellingham	23.37	July 1, 1902	A.S.Doc. 1362
Northwestern Improvement Company	Seattle	West Seattle	3.20	Oct. 21, 1903	A.S.Doc. 1516
Washington Short Line Railway Company	Tacoma	Ruston (formerly Smasen)	3.08	Aug. 22, 1900	A.S.Doc. 426
Port Townsend Southern Railroad Company	Tenino	West Olympia	15.00	June 25, 1914	A.S.Doc. 7943
Washington Railway & Navigation Company	Kalama	Vancouver	28.90	Oct. 19, 1903	A.S.Doc. 1517
	Vancouver Jctn.	Yacolt	30.12	Oct. 19, 1903	A.S.Doc. 1517
Seattle and Montana Railroad Company	(1) Passenger Terminal at Seattle		0.84	Nov. 16, 1907	R/W Deed 398
(1) one-half interest acquired.	(1) Tunnel approach to Passenger Terminal at Seattle		2.24	Nov. 25, 1907	R/W Deed 400

Oregon

	From	To	Miles	Date deeded to N.P.Ry.Co.	File Ref.
The Washington and Columbia River Railway Company	Pendleton	Ore.-Wash. Line	30.42	June 18, 1907	A.S.Doc. 3575
	Eureka (formerly Killian Jctn.)	Athena (formerly Centerville)	14.39	June 18, 1907	A.S.Doc. 3575
Spokane, Portland and Seattle Railway Company	(1) Vancouver	Willbridge	5.41	April 28, 1908	A.S.Doc. 4102

(1) one-third interest acquired.

The Northern Pacific Railway Company constructed the following lines:

Main Line

State	From	To	Miles	Date
Wisconsin	Walbridge	Wis.-Minn.Line	3.15	July 1896
Minnesota	Wis.-Minn. Line	State Line Station	0.10	July 1896
Minnesota	West Side Line at Little Falls		2.12	1900
Montana	St.Regis	Paradise	21.80	Dec.1906 to Feb.1909
Washington	Palmer Jct.	Auburn	21.70	July 1899 to Aug. 1900
Washington	Tacoma (via Plumb)	Tenino	43.44	Feb.1912 to Dec.15,1914

Branch Lines

From	To	Miles	Date
Wisconsin			
Newton Ave. to Cuyuna Dock at Superior		1.50	1913
Minnesota			
Cedar Lake	Soo Connection	0.80	Aug.1,1914 to Oct. 1914
(1) D.B.Junction	Duluth-Brainerd Mine	2.69	Aug.1914
(1) Loerch	Woodrow	1.65	April 1915
North Dakota			
Milnor	Oakes	32.50	May 1900 to Nov.1900

(1) Partly constructed when acquired

From	To	Miles	Date
North Dakota			
Casselton	Marion	60.13	April 1900 to Nov. 1906
Cooperstown	McHenry	26.10	May 1899 to Sept. 1899
Edgeley	Streeter	39.90	June 24, 1903 to Nov. 1903 & April 1905 to Nov. 1905
Pingree	Wilton	92.40	April 1910 to July 1912
Sykeston	Bowdon	15.02	May 1899 to August 1899
Bowdon	Denhoff	26.49	July 1901 to Nov. 1902
Denhoff	Turtle Lake	30.42	April 1905 to Dec. 1905
Oberon	Esmond	28.08	May 1901 to Oct. 1901
McKenzie	Linton	45.31	June 1902 to Oct. 1903

(Includes 1.11 miles at Linton owned jointly with C.M.& St.P.Ry.Co.)

From	To	Miles	Date
Golden Valley	Killdeer	33.73	Nov. 23, 1914
Beach	Nor.Dak.-Mont.Line	17.90	Aug. 1914 to Sept. 1, 1915
Montana			
Nor.Dak-Mont. Line	Ollie	8.50	Aug. 1914 to Sept. 1, 1915
Silesia	Bridger	19.74	June 1898 to Nov. 1898

(1) Partly constructed when acquired

	From	To	Miles	Date
		Montana		
(1)	Cinnabar	Gardiner	2.90	May to Nov. 1902
	Twin Bridges	Alder	19.40	July 1901 to Dec. 1901
	Grantsdale	Charles	6.53	Dec.1899 to April 1900
	Charles	Darby	7.44	June 1904 to Dec.1904
	Extension beyond Darby		1.65	May 1910 to Oct.30,1910
	Further Extension beyond Darby		.73	1913
	Idaho			
(1)	Wallace	Sunset	5.56	1898 to Nov. 1899
	Juliaetta	Lewiston	21.16	Feb. to Oct. 1898
	Washington			
	Sunnyside Jctn.	Grand View	20.09	June 1905 to Nov.1906
	Ronald	Lakedale	1.80	Dec.1907 to May 1910
	Kanaskat	Green Riv.Br. Connection	0.80	1902
	Puyallup River	Lake Kapowsin	2.68	April 1909 to Sept.1910
(1)	Black River Jctn.	Woodinville	24.11	April 1903 to Oct.1904
	Mile Post 10	Kerriston	4.70	Sept.1901 to June 1902
	Kruse	Edgecomb	4.39	Aug.1913 to Nov.1914
	Bromart	Great Northern Connection		

(1) Partly constructed when acquired

From	To	Miles	Date
Washington			
Aberdeen	Hoquiam	4.23	Oct.1897 to Nov.1898
Hoquiam	Moclips	27.75	July 1901 to Dec.1904
Ocosta	Bay City	2.80	June 1911 to Aug.14,1911
New West Seattle Line		2.20	1905
(1) Parron	Harrah	1.33	April 1915 to Aug.1915
(1) Harrah	White Swan	9.25	May to Dec. 1916
(1) Arlington	Darrington	28.06	Mar.to June 1901

The Northern Pacific Railway Company has also purchased portions of the right of way for but has not yet constructed the following branch lines:

From	To	Miles	Date
Edgeley, N.D.	Cannonball, N.D.	110.00	1910-13
Streeter, N.D.	Dawson, N.D.	20.60	1903-4
Turtle Lake, N.D.	Coal Harbor, N.D.	23.60	1903-4
Cannon Ball, N.D.	Nesedak, N.D.	29.60	June 20,1914
Almont, N.D.	State Line	65.00	1903-4
Mott, N.D.	Marmarth, N.D.	79.00	June 20,1914
Hesper, Mont.	Lake Basin, Mont.	51.40	1913
Lo Lo, Mont.	Summit, Mont.	18.00	June 23,1914
Grandview, Wash.	Gibbon, Wash.	12.05	1910-11
Pullman, Wash.	Penawawa, Wash.	36.00	June 23,1914
Clarkston(Lewiston)Wash.	Riparia, Wash.	70.00	June 23,1914

(1) Partly constructed when acquired

From	To	Miles	Date
Riverside, Wash.	Covelle, Wash.	32.00	June 18, 1907
Schrag, Wash.	Ritzville, Wash.	24.60	June 25, 1914
Bassett Jct. Wash.	Ellensburg, Wash.	82.50	June 25, 1914

The Northern Pacific Railway Company has ceased to operate the following lines:

From	To	Miles	Date
Fond du Lac, Minn.	Thomson, Minn.	7.19	1897
Winnipeg Jctn.	Manitoba Jctn. Minn.	0.99	1910
Coal Spur	Cokedale, Mont.	3.62	1906
Jefferson	Boulder Jctn.	10.99	1898
E. Helena	Wickes	33.43	1905
Boulder Jctn.	Boulder		
Boomerang	Calvin		
Queen Siding	Elkhorn	4.07	1914
Renova, Mont.	Parrot, Mont.	.53 / .92	1905 / 1906
Philipsburg, Mont.	Rumsey, Mont.	6.23	1904
Butte Mill Line, Montana		6.25	1900
Wallace, Ida.	Old Mission, Ida.	22.00	1902
Spokane, Wash.	Ditmar, Wash.	29.20	1900
Palmer Jctn., Wash.	Green Riv. Br. Connection	0.99	1900
Nisqually, Wash.	St. Clair, Wash.	3.55	1914
Vancouver, Wash.	Connec. Yacolt	4.70	1903
Tenino, Wash.	Plumb, Wash.	5.00	1914
Plumb, Wash.	Tumwater, Wash.	6.10	1916

3. **Operation**

L.A.File 140

The Northern Pacific Railway Company operated Main Line and Branch Lines as follows:

Wisconsin	Miles Main Line	Br.Line	Date
Ashland to Minn.-Wis. State Line	77.88		Sept.1,1896 to June 30,1917
Central Ave.Superior to Center St.Louis Bay Bridge	6.06		Sept.1,1896 to June 30,1917
Bay Front Line, Superior	1.08		1908 to June 30, 1917
Walbridge to Minn.-Wis. State Line	3.15		Sept.1,1896 to June 30, 1917
Joint Tracks in Ashland	0.54		Sept.1,1896 to June 30, 1917
Iron River to Washburn (Washburn Br.)		33.78	June 16,1902 to June 30,1917
West Superior Branch		1.41	July 1,1900 to June 30,1917
St.Croix River to Grantsburg (Grantsburg Br.)		12.00	July 1,1900 to June 30,1917
Total -	88.71	47.19	

Minnesota

Wis.-Minn.State Line to Minn.-N.Dak.State Line	239.07		Sept.1,1896 to June 30,1917
Center St.Louis Bay Bridge to Duluth	1.63		Sept.1,1896 to June 30,1917

	Miles		
Minnesota	**Main Line**	**Br. Line**	**Date**
Walbridge Line	.10		Sept. 1, 1896 to June 30, 1917
St. Paul to Staples (The single track lines of G.N.Ry.Co., N.P.Ry.Co. Northtown Jct. to St. Cloud are operated by both Co's. as a double track Railway)	139.31		Sept. 1, 1896 to June 30, 1917
Little Falls to Brainerd	32.91		Sept. 1, 1896 to June 30, 1917
St. Paul to Duluth	152.06		July 1, 1900 to June 30, 1917
St. Paul Union Depot Co. (Joint)	0.56		Sept. 1, 1896 to June 30, 1917
M. & St. L. R. R. Co. in Minneapolis (Joint)	1.63		Sept. 1, 1896 to June 30, 1917
G.N.Ry.Co. St. Paul to Minneapolis (joint)	10.26		Sept. 1, 1896 to June 30, 1917
Line "A" Broadway to Mississippi St. St. Paul	1.53		Sept. 1, 1896 to June 30, 1917
Line "A" St. Anthony Pk. to 20th Ave. So. Minneapolis	2.57		Sept. 1, 1896 to June 30, 1917
Line from Terminal Yard Minneapolis to Northtown Jctn.	3.42		Sept. 1, 1896 to June 30, 1917
Duluth Union Depot Co. Duluth (owned)	0.25		Sept. 1, 1896 to June 30, 1917
Minneapolis to White Bear		13.75	July 1, 1900 to June 30, 1917

	Miles		
Minnesota	Main Line	Br.Line	Date
West Duluth to Fond du Lac (½ interest owned prior to June 15,1900)		8.97	Sept.1,1896 to June 30,1917
Fond du Lac to 3.23 miles beyond Fond du Lac to G.N.Power Co.		3.23	1905 to June 30,1917
West Superior Branch		2.33	July 1,1900 to June 30,1917
Carlton to Cloquet, Cloquet Branch		6.95	July 1,1900 to June 30,1917
Deerwood to Cuyuna-Mille Lacs Mine) Cuyuna Nor. Br.North		5.16	Dec.29,1912 to June 30,1917
D.B.Jctn.to Duluth Brainerd Mine)		2.69	Oct. 1,1914 to June 30,1917
Deerwood to Oreland Cuyuna Nor.Br.So.		3.56	Dec.29,1912 to June 30,1917
Loerch to Woodrow Cuyuna Northern Ry.		1.65	Oct.1,1914 to June 30,1917
Cedar Lake to "Soo" Connection-Cuyuna Northern Ry.		0.80	Oct.15,1914 to June 30,1917
St.Croix River to Rush City,Grantsburg Br.		5.04	July 1,1900 to June 30,1917
Groningen (formerly Miller) to Banning		4.42	July 1,1900 to June 30,1917
Wyoming to Taylors Falls		20.59	July 1,1900 to June 30,1917
White Bear to Stillwater		12.76	July 1,1900 to June 30,1917
Little Falls to Morris L.F.& D.Br.		87.90	Sept.1,1896 to June 30,1917

64

Minnesota	Miles Main Line	Br. Line	Date
Wadena to Breckenridge (Minn.-N.D.State Line) Fergus Falls Br.		74.87	Sept.1,1896 to June 30,1917
Winnipeg Jctn. to Manitoba Jctn., Red River Br.	(1)	.99	Sept.1,1896 to May 1907
Manitoba Jctn. to East Grand Forks (N.D.-Minn. State Line) Red River Br.		94.16	Sept.1,1896 to June 30,1917
Fertile to Carthage Jctn., Red Lake Falls Br.		53.30	Sept.1,1896 to June 30,1917
Red Lake Falls Jctn. to Red Lake Falls, Red Lake Falls Br.		1.16	Sept.1,1896 to June 30,1917
Keywest to Sherack Keystone Br.		6.13	Sept.1,1896 to June 30,1917
M.St.P.& S.Ste.M.Ry.Co. Kennedy Mine & Ironton & Crosby (Joint)		4.69	July 26,1915 to June 30,1917
Total	585.30	414.21	

North Dakota	Miles Main Line	Br. Line	Date
N.D.-Minn.State Line to N.D.-Mont.State Line	376.94		Sept.1, 1896 to June 30,1917
Grand Forks(N.D.-Minn. State Line) to Pembina, Red River Br.		96.24	Sept.1,1896 to June 30,1917
Wahpeton N.D.-Minn. State Line to Milnor Fergus Falls Br.		42.03	Sept.1,1896 to June 30,1917
Milnor to Oakes, Fergus Falls Br.		32.50	Nov.1,1900 to June 30,1917

| | Miles | | |
North Dakota	Main Line	Br. Line	Date
Fairview Jct. to Bayne & Great Bend, Fairview Br.		14.83	Sept.1,1896 to June 30,1917
Fargo to Edgeley Fargo & Southwestern Br.		108.70	Sept.1,1896 to June 30,1917
Edgeley Jct. to Gackle Fargo & Southwestern Br.		28.62	Sept.10,1905 to June 30,1917
Gackle to Streeter Fargo to Southwestern Br.		11.29	Nov.22,1905 to June 30,1917
Casselton to Marion N.P.Ry. Casselton Br.		60.13	Jan.1,1901 to June 30,1917
Sanborn to Cooperstown Cooperstown Br.		36.98	Sept.1,1896 to June 30,1917
Cooperstown to McHenry Cooperstown Br.		25.90	Oct.25,1899 to June 30,1917
Jamestown to LaMoure James Riv. Br.		48.51	Sept.1,1896 to June 30,1917
Independence to Oakes, Oakes Br.		15.26	Sept.1,1896 to June 30,1917
Jamestown to Leeds Devils Lake Br.		107.48	Sept.1,1896 to June 30,1917
Carrington to Sykeston, Sykeston Br.		13.10	Sept.1,1896 to June 30,1917
Sykeston to Bowdon Sykeston Br.		15.02	Sept.1,1899 to June 30,1917
Bowdon to Denhoff Sykeston Br.		26.49	Aug.1,1902 to June 30,1917
Denhoff to Turtle Lake Sykeston Br.		30.42	Jan.4,1906 to June 30,1917
Oberon to Esmond Oberon Branch		28.08	Nov.1,1901 to June 30,1917

	Miles		
North Dakota	Main Line	Br.Line	Date
McKenzie to Linton Linton Br.		44.20	Nov.5,1903 to June 30,1917
Joint Tracks in Linton (with C.M.& St.P. Ry.Co.)		1.11	Nov.5,1903 to June 30,1917
Pingree to Wilton Wilton Br.		92.40	Aug.1,1912 to June 30,1917
Mandan to Stanton Mo.River Br.North		52.64	Aug.1,1912 to June 30,1917
Mandan to Cannon Ball (6.30 miles beyond Cannon Ball not operated) M.R.Br.South		36.11 (1) 6.30	Nov.1,1910 to June 30,1917
Stanton to Golden Valley Spring Creek Br.		35.00	Mar.1,1914 to June 30,1917
Golden Valley to Killdeer,Spring Creek Br.		33.73	Nov.23,1914 to June 30,1917
Cannon Ball Jct.to Mott West Dak.Br.		91.35	Nov.1,1910 to June 30,1917
Beach to N.D.-Mont.State Line,Golden Valley Br.		17.39	Oct.1,1915 to June 30,1917
Joint tracks in Oakes (with C.& N.W.Ry.Co.)		0.12	1908 to June 30,1917
Total - -	376.94	1145.63	
Montana			
Mont.-N.D.State Line Mont.-Ida.State Line	776.83		Sept.1,1896 to June 30,1917
Butte Line-Logan to Butte		(1) 72.03	Sept.1,1896 to 1899-1900
Butte Line-Logan to Butte	72.03		1899-1900 to June 30,1917

	Miles		
Montana	**Main Line**	**Br. Line**	**Date**
Butte Line-Butte to Garrison		(1) 52.30	Oct.7,1898 to 1899-1900
Butte Line-Butte to Garrison (999 year lease)	52.30		1899-1900 to June 30,1917
De Smet to St. Regis		(1) 71.25	Sept.1,1896 to Mar. 31, 1909
De Smet to St. Regis	71.25		Mar.31,1909 to June 30,1917
St. Regis to Paradise	21.85		Mar.31,1909 to June 30,1917
N.D.-Mont. State Line to Ollie, Golden Valley Branch		8.51	Oct.1,1915 to June 30,1917
Glendive to Sidney Glendive East Br.		54.81	Aug.1,1912 to June 30,1917
Laurel to Red Lodge Rocky Fork Br.		44.14	Sept.1,1896 to June 30,1917
Silesia to Bridger Clarks Fork Br.		19.74	Dec.15,1898 to June 30,1917
Mission to Wilsall Shields Riv.Br.		22.93	Dec.21,1909 to June 30,1917
Livingston to Cinnabar, Park Br.		51.40	Sept.1,1896 to June 30,1917
Cinnabar to Gardiner, Park Br.		2.87	Dec. 15,1902 to June 30,1917
Coal Spur to Cokedale		(1) 3.62	Sept.1,1896 to 1906
Manhattan to Anceny, Camp Creek Br.		15.15	Jan.23,1912 to June 30,1917
Whitehall to Renova Gaylord & Ruby Valley Br.		4.30	Sept.1,1896 to June 30,1917

	Miles		
Montana	Main Line	Br.Line	Date
Renova to Twin Bridges Gaylerd & Ruby Valley Br.		21.90	Aug.1,1898 to June 30,1917
Renova to Parrott Gaylerd & Ruby Valley Br.		(1) 1.45	Sept.1,1896 to 1906
Twin Bridges to Alder,Gaylerd & Ruby Valley Br.		19.53	Dec.1,1901 to June 30,1917
Sappington to Norris Red Bluff Br.		20.99	Sept.1,1896 to June 30,1917
Harrison to Pony, Pony Br.		6.65	Sept.1,1896 to June 30,1917
Calvin to Boomerang (G.N.Tfr.) Boulder Jct.to Boulder & E.Helena (P.P.Jctn.) to Wickes		(1) 33.39	Sept.1,1896 to 1905
Jefferson to Boulder Jctn.		(1) 10.99	Sept.1,1896 to 1898
G.N.Transfer to Boulder,Boulder Br.		6.02	Sept.1,1896 to June 30,1917
Boulder to Queen Siding, Elkhorn Br.		16.06	Sept.1,1896 to June 30,1917
Queen Siding to Elkhorn		(1) 4.07	Sept.1,1896 to 1914
Helena to Rimini Red Mountain Br.		16.37	Sept.1,1896 to June 30,1917
Clough Jct.to Marysville Marysville Br.		12.58	Sept.1,1896 to June 30,1917
Drummond to Philipsburg Philipsburg Br.		25.94	Sept.1,1896 to June 30,1917
Philipsburg to Rumsey		(1) 6.23	Sept.1,1896 to 1904

	Miles		
Montana	Main Line	By.Line	Date
Missoula to Grantsdale Bitter Root Br.		50.85	Sept.1,1896 to June 30,1917
Grantsdale to Charles Bitter Root Br.		6.53	May 15,1900 to June 30,1917
Charles to Darby Bitter Root Br.		8.99	June 15,1905 to June 30,1917
St.Regis to Lookout (Mont.-Ida.State Line) Coeur d'Alene Line		38.33	Sept.1,1896 to June 30,1917
Stuart to Anaconda (leased to B.A.& P.Ry.Co.) Anaconda Br.	(1)	8.52	Not operated by N.P.Ry.Co.
Great Northern Ry.Co. Helena to Hyndman (joint)		38.33	April 20,1905 to June 30,1917
Total	994.26	512.92	

Idaho

Ida.-Mont.State Line to Ida.-Wash.State Line	83.64		Sept.1,1896 to June 30,1917
Ida.-Mont.State Line (Lookout) to Wallace Coeur d'Alene Line		20.41	Sept.1,1896 to June 30,1917
Wallace to Old Mission	(1)	22.40	Sept.1,1896 to 1898
Wallace to Burke, Burke Br.		6.66	Sept.1,1896 to June 30,1917
Wallace to Sunset, Sunset Br.		5.56	Nov.1,1900 to June 30,1917
Hauser Jctn.to Coeur d'Alene, Fort Sherman Br.		13.61	Sept.1,1896 to June 30,1917

	Miles		
Idaho	**Main Line**	**Br. Line**	**Date**
Coeur d'Alene to Old Mission & Harrison (via steamboat)	(1) 45.00		Sept.1,1896 to 1906
Wash.-Ida. State Line to Juliaetta, Pal. & Lewiston Br.		32.99	Sept.1,1896 to June 30,1917
Juliaetta to Lewiston Pal.& Lewiston Br.		21.64	Oct.1,1898 to June 30,1917
Wash.-Ida. State Line to Genesee, Genesee Br.		7.26	Sept.1,1896 to June 30,1917
Arrow to Oro Fino, Clearwater Short Line		29.00	Nov.15,1899 to June 30,1917
Oro Fino to Stites Clearwater Short Line		33.91	May 15,1900 to June 30,1917
(2) Joseph to Culdesac Lapwai Br.		12.00	Nov.15,1899 to Dec.3,1909
(2) Culdesac to Craigmont (formerly Vollmer) Lapwai Br.		23.00	Mar.1,1908 to Dec.3,1909
(2) Craigmont to Grangeville Lapwai Br.		31.78	Dec.31,1908 to Dec.3,1909
O.W.R.R.& N.Co. Lewiston to State Line (joint)		0.96	Operated by Camas P.R.R. Co.
Connection at Lewiston with O.W.R.R.& N.Co.		0.81	1914 to June 30,1917
Joint tracks in Burke with O.W.R.R.& N.Co.(joint)		0.34	Feb.1,1908 to June 30,1917

(2) Lapwai Branch operated by Camas Prairie Railroad Co. subsequent to Dec.3,1909 in interest of O.W.R.& N.Co. and N.P.Ry.Co.

Total - - -   83.64   239.93

	Miles		
Washington	**Main Line**	**Br. Line**	**Date**
Wash.-Ida. State Line to Palmer	371.88		Sept.1,1896 to June 30,1917
Drawbridge Line in Tacoma	1.38		Sept.1,1896 to June 30,1917
Palmer to Meeker via Buckley	(1)33.54		Sept.1,1896 to Sept.1,1900
Palmer to Meeker via Buckley		33.54	Sept.1,1900 to June 30,1917
Meeker to Tacoma	9.56		Sept.1,1896 to June 30,1917
Tenino to Tacoma via Plumb	43.44		Dec.15,1914 to June 30,1917
Tacoma to Tenino via Lakeview	39.49		Sept.1,1896 to June 30,1917
Tenino to Kalama	63.99		Sept.1,1896 to June 30,1917
Kalama to Vancouver		(1)29.00	Sept.1,1902 to 1908
Kalama to Vancouver	29.00		1908 to June 30, 1917
Auburn to Seattle		(1)22.49	Sept.1,1896 to Sept.1,1900
Auburn to Seattle	22.49		Sept.1,1900 to June 30,1917
Palmer to Auburn	21.66		Sept.1,1900 to June 30,1917
Auburn to Meeker	8.67		Sept.1,1900 to June 30,1917
Auburn to Meeker		(1) 8.67	Sept.1,1896 to Sept.1,1900
Seattle to Sumas	126.66		Mar.31,1901 to June 30,1917

	Mi	les	
Washington	Main Line	Br. Line	Date
Line through tunnel in Seattle (joint)	2.24		May 10, 1906 to June 30, 1917
Colorado Street Line in Seattle	3.28		1907 to June 30, 1917
S.P.& S.Ry.Co. in Vancouver (joint)	0.09		1909 to June 30, 1917
Marshall to Wash.-Ida. State Line, Pal. & Lewiston Br.		84.04	Sept. 1, 1896 to June 30, 1917
Pullman Jctn. to Wash. Ida.-State Line, Genesee Br.		20.34	Sept. 1, 1896 to June 30, 1917
Belmont to Farmington, Farmington Br.		5.89	Sept. 1, 1896 to June 30, 1917
Davenport to Ditmar, Spok.Seattle Ry. (Not operated)		(1) 18.13	
Cheney to Coulee City, Wash.Cent.Br.		108.66	June 1, 1898 to June 30, 1917
Coulee Jct. to Adrian Wash.Cent.Br.		21.10	Dec. 1, 1903 to June 30, 1917
Pasco to Wallula Line	(1) 13.89		Sept. 1, 1896 to June 30, 1907
Pasco to Wallula Line		13.89	June 30, 1907 to June 30, 1917
Attalia to Dayton, Dayton Br.		86.20	July 1, 1907 to June 30, 1917
Eureka to Pleasant View, Pleasant View Br.		19.73	July 1, 1907 to June 30, 1917
Mill Creek Jctn. to Tracy, Tracy Br.		6.12	July 1, 1907 to June 30, 1917
Attalia to Wash.-Ore. State Line, Pendleton Br.		10.68	July 1, 1907 to June 30, 1917

	Miles		
Washington	Main Line	Br. Line	Date
Snake River Jctn. to Riparia, Snake Riv. Br.		40.97	May 3, 1909 to June 30, 1917
Sunnyside Jctn. to Grandview, Sunnyside Br.		20.09	April 21, 1906 to June 30, 1917
Grandview to Gibbon, Sunnyside Br.		11.76	June 20, 1917 to June 30, 1917
Connell to Adco, Connell Nor. Br.		60.95	Nov. 1, 1910 to June 30, 1917
Bassett Jct. to Schrag Ritsville Br.		12.54	Nov. 1, 1910 to June 30, 1917
North Yakima to Naches		13.07	July 1, 1914 to June 30, 1917
North Yakima to Moxee Moxee Br.		8.85	July 1, 1914 to June 30, 1917
Parker to Granger Parker-Zillah Br.		17.09	July 1, 1914 to June 30, 1917
Wesley Jctn. to Farren, Simcoe Br.		8.57	July 1, 1914 to June 30, 1917
Farron to Harrah Simcoe Br.		1.34	July 1915 to June 30, 1917
Cowiche Jctn. to Spitzenberg, Cowiche Br.		2.50	July 1, 1914 to June 30, 1917
Harrah to White Swan Simcoe Br.		9.25	Nov. 4, 1916 to June 30, 1917
Spitzenberg to Weikel Cowiche Br.		2.57	Aug. 23, 1914 to June 30, 1917
Cle Elum to Ronald Roslyn Br.		5.40	Oct. 1896 to June 30, 1917

Washington	Main Line	Br. Line	Date
Ronald to Beekman Roslyn Br.		1.00	May 1908 to June 30, 1917
Beekman to Lakedale Roslyn Br.		0.80	May 1910 to June 30, 1917
Palmer Jctn. to Kanaskat	(1) 0.99		Sept. 1, 1896 to 1900
Kanaskat to Mile Post 10½, Green River Br.		10.51	Sept. 1, 1896 to June 30, 1917
Mile Post 10½ to Kerriston, Green River Br.		4.10	June 15, 1902 to June 30, 1917
Kangley Jct. to Kangley, Green River Branch		1.50	Sept. 1, 1896 to June 30, 1917
Cascade Jctn. to Spiketon, Burnett Br.		3.63	Sept. 1, 1896 to June 30, 1917
Cascade Jctn. to Wilkeson to Carbonado Wilkesen Br.		8.70	Sept. 1, 1896 to June 30, 1917
Carbonado to Fairfax Wilkeson Br.		8.24	Aug. 3, 1901 to June 30, 1917
Crocker to Wingate Crocker Br.		5.44	Sept. 1, 1896 to June 30, 1917
Orting to Puyallup River, Orting Br.		7.64	Sept. 1, 1896 to June 30, 1917
Puyallup River to Lake Kapowsin (Electron) Orting Br.		2.39	Oct. 30, 1910 to June 30, 1917
Black River Jctn. to Woodinville, Seattle Belt Line		24.14	Oct. 24, 1904 to June 30, 1917

	Miles		
Washington	Main Line	Br. Line	Date
Snohomish to Everett Everett Br.		11.37	Mar. 31, 1901 to June 30, 1917
Woodinville to Sallal (formerly Sallal Prairie) Snoqualmie Br.		38.32	Mar. 31, 1901 to June 30, 1917
Arlington to Darrington, Darrington Br.		28.08	July 1, 1901 to June 30, 1917
Hartford to Monte Cristo Monte Cristo Br. (Lease Hartford East Ry. Co. from July 11, 1915)	(1) 42.12		Aug. 1, 1903 to July 11, 1915
Edgecomb to Kruse and Connection at Snohomish		3.83	Dec. 12, 1914 to June 30, 1917
Wickersham to South Bellingham, Bellingham Br.		22.75	Oct. 11, 1902 to June 30, 1917
Tenino to Plumb	(1) 5.00		July 1, 1914 to Dec. 15, 1914
Plumb to Tumwater	(1) 6.10		July 1, 1914 to March 1916
Tumwater to Olympia, Tumwater Br.		3.90	July 1, 1914 to June 30, 1917
Tacoma to Dempsey Mill		1.05	1906 to June 30, 1917
Lakeview to Nisqually, Olympia Br.		11.60	Sept. 1, 1896 to June 30, 1917
Nisqually to St. Clair, Olympia Br.	(1) 3.80		Sept. 1, 1896 to Dec. 15, 1914

	Washington	Miles Main Line	Br. Line	Date
	St. Clair to Gate, Olympia Br.		28.43	Sept. 1, 1896 to June 30, 1917
	Centralia to Ocosta, Grays' Harbor Br.		65.85	Sept. 1, 1896 to June 30, 1917
	Ocosta to Bay City Gray's Harbor Br.		2.74	Nov. 30, 1911 to June 30, 1917
	Cosmopolis Jctn. to Cosmopolis, Cosmopolis Br.		1.89	Sept. 1, 1896 to June 30, 1917
	Aberdeen Jctn. to Aberdeen, Peninsular Br.		2.30	Sept. 1, 1896 to June 30, 1917
	Aberdeen to Hoquiam, Peninsular Br.		4.23	Nov. 5, 1898 to June 30, 1917
	Hoquiam to Moclips Peninsular Br.		27.75	July 1, 1905 to June 30, 1917
	Chehalis Jctn. to South Bend, Willapa Harbor Br.		56.67	Sept. 1, 1896 to June 30, 1917
	Vancouver Jctn. to Yacolt Yacolt Br.		27.25	July 1, 1903 to June 30, 1917
	Elma to Stimson (formerly Simpson & Summit) Elma Br.		10.29	Sept. 1, 1896 to June 30, 1917
(2)	O.W.R.R.& N.Co. State Line to Riparia (Joint)	70.50		
	O.W.R.R.& N.Co. in Centralia (Joint)		1.37	Mar. 1, 1914 to June 30, 1917
	O.W.R.R.& N.Co. in Grays Harbor (Joint)		2.90	Mar. 1, 1914 to June 30, 1917
	O.W.R.R.& N.Co. Yakima River Crossing (Joint)		0.13	July 1, 1914 to June 30, 1917

	Miles		
Washington	Main Line	Br. Line	Date
Seattle Southwestern Ry.Co. in Selleck (Joint)		0.27	Dec.1,1914 to June 30,1917
McCleary Timber Ry.Co. in McCleary (Joint)		0.42	1915 to June 30, 1917
S.P.& S.Ry.Co.-Pasco to Snake River Jctn. (Joint)		24.83	Jan.31,1910 to June 30,1917
G.N.Ry.Co.Connections at Snohomish & Everett		0.82	Dec.12,1914 to June 30,1917
G.N.Ry.Co.Snohomish to Kruse (Joint)		11.73	Sept.1,1915 to June 30,1917
Total	743.83	1164.50	

(2) Operated by Camas Prairie R.R.Co. in interest of O.W.R.& N. Co. and N.P.Ry. Co.

Oregon

Willbridge to Portland	3.56	Sept.1,1896 to June 30,1917
Willbridge to Goble (1)	35.29	Sept.1,1896 to June 30,1910
Willbridge to Goble (1) Leased to S.P.& S.Ry.Co.	35.29	Leased to A.& C R.R.Co.(new S.P.& S.Ry. Co.)Jan. 12, 1911
S.P.& S.Ry.Co. State Line to Willbridge (Joint)	5.28	Jan.1,1909 to June 30,1917
Northern Pacific Terminal Co. of Ore.Portland (Joint)	0.92	Sept.1,1896 to June 30,1917

	Miles		
Oregon	Main Line	Br. Line	Date
Pendleton to Ore.-Wash. State Line, Pendleton Br.		30.42	July 1, 1907 to June 30, 1917
Smeltz (formerly Killian Jctn.) to Athena, Athena Br.		14.54	July 1, 1907 to June 30, 1917
Total	9.76	44.96	
Wisconsin	88.71	47.19	
Minnesota	585.30	414.21	
North Dakota	376.94	1145.63	
Montana	994.26	512.92	
Idaho	83.64	239.93	
Washington	743.83	1164.50	
Oregon	9.76	44.96	
Total	2882.44	3569.34	

Total Main Line   2882.44
Total Branch Line 3569.34

Grand Total - 6451.78 Miles

As operated June 30, 1917.

(1) Not being operated as of June 30, 1917 and not included in total mileage.

4. **Present Status of Corporation**

   This corporation is in existence and is active.

   The records are in the custody of Mr. R. H. Relf, Assistant Secretary of the Northern Pacific Railway Co. at Saint Paul, Minnesota.

5. **Chain of Title**

   See Pages 45 to 55 inclusive.

SCHEDULE OF INSTRUMENTS AND RECORDS

File Ref.   **Description**

A.S.Doc.   Charter of Northern Pacific Railway Company (for-
1256   merly Superior and St.Croix Railroad Company) and laws
                    relating thereto.

M.B.152   Reference to organization of N.P. Ry. Co.
p.1

A.S.Doc.   Five deeds by which the property of the Northern
35   Pacific Railroad Company was conveyed to the N.P. Ry.Co.

A.S.Doc.   Deed of Nov. 2, 1896, by which the Saint Paul and
51   Northern Pacific Railway Company conveyed its entire
                    property to the N.P. Ry. Co.

A.S.Doc.   Deed of June 5, 1900, by which The Little Falls
490   and Dakota Railroad Company conveyed its entire proper-
                    ty to the N.P. Ry. Co.

A.S.Doc.   Deed of April 21, 1898, by which the Northern Pa-
130   cific, Fergus and Black Hills Railroad Company conveyed
                    its entire property to the N.P. Ry. Co.

A.S.Doc.   Deed of April 21, 1898, by which The Duluth, Crook-
123   ston and Northern Rail Road Company conveyed its entire
                    property to the N.P. Ry. Co.

A.S.Doc. 122 — Deed of April 21, 1898, by which the Duluth and Manitoba Railroad Company conveyed its entire property to the N.P. Ry. Co.

A.S.Doc. 124 — Deed of April 21, 1898, by which the Fargo and Southwestern Railroad Company conveyed its entire property to the N.P. Ry. Co.

A.S.Doc. 131 — Deed of April 21, 1898, by which the Northern Pacific, LaMoure and Missouri River Railroad Company conveyed its entire property to the N.P. Ry. Co.

A.S.Doc. 130 — Deed of April 21, 1898, by which the Sanborn, Cooperstown and Turtle Mountain Railroad Company conveyed its entire property to the N.P. Ry. Co.

A.S.Doc. 128 — Deed of April 21, 1898, by which the Jamestown and Northern Railroad Company conveyed its entire property to the N.P. Ry. Co.

A.S.Doc. 129 — Deed of April 21, 1898, by which the Jamestown and Northern Extension Railroad Company conveyed its entire property to the N.P. Ry. Co.

A.S.Doc. 138 — Deed of April 21, 1898, by which the South-Eastern Dakota Railroad Company conveyed its entire property to the N.P. Ry. Co.

82

A.S.Doc. 137 — Deed of April 21, 1898, by which the Rocky Mountain Railroad Company of Montana conveyed its entire property to the N.P. Ry. Co.

A.S.Doc. 133 — Deed of April 21, 1898, by which the Northern Pacific and Montana Railroad Company conveyed its entire property to the N.P. Ry. Co.

A.S.Doc. 136 — Deed of April 21, 1898, by which the Helena and Jefferson County Railroad Company conveyed its entire property to the N.P. Ry. Co.

A.S.Doc. 136 — Deed of April 21, 1898, by which the Rocky Fork and Cooke City Railroad Company conveyed its entire property to the N.P. Ry. Co.

A.S.Doc. 238 — Deed of Dec. 15, 1899, by which the Helena and Red Mountain Railroad Company conveyed its entire property to the N.P. Ry. Co.

A.S.Doc. 140 — Deed of April 21, 1898, by which the Spokane Falls and Idaho Railroad Company conveyed its entire property to the N.P. Ry. Co.

A.S.Doc. 203 — Deed of Feb. 21, 1899, by which the Spokane and Palouse Railway Company conveyed its entire property to the N.P. Ry. Co.

83

A.S.Doc. 496
Deed of June 1, 1898, by which The Central Washington Railroad Company by a Committee of Bondholders conveyed its entire property to The Washington Central Railway Company.

A.S.Doc. 7940
Deed of June 29, 1914, by which The Washington Central Railway Company conveyed its entire property to the N.P. Ry. Co.

A.S.Doc. 125
Deed of April 21, 1898, by which the Green River and Northern Railroad Company conveyed its entire property to the N.P. Ry. Co.

A.S.Doc. 135
Deed of April 21, 1898, by which the Northern Pacific and Cascade Railroad Company conveyed its lines from Cascade Jctn. to Spiketon and Carbonado, and Crocker to Wingate to the N.P. Ry. Co.

A.S.Doc. 134
Deed of April 21, 1898, by which the Northern Pacific and Puget Sound Shore Rail-Road Company conveyed its entire property to the N.P. Ry. Co.

A.S.Doc. 132
Deed of April 21, 1898, by which The United Railroads of Washington conveyed its entire property to the N.P.Ry.Co.

A.S.Doc. 121
Deed of April 21, 1898, by which the Clealum Railroad Company conveyed its entire property to the N.P. Ry.Co.

A.S.Dec. 141 — Deed of April 21, 1898, by which the Tacoma, Orting and Southeastern Railroad Company conveyed its entire property to the N.P. Ry. Co.

A.S.Doc. 1130 — Deed of June 16, 1902, by which the Washburn, Bayfield and Iron River Railway Company conveyed its entire property to the N.P. Ry. Co.

A.S.Dec. 8553 — Deed of Aug. 27, 1915, by which the Cuyuna Dock Company conveyed its entire property to the N.P. Ry.Co.

A.S.Dec. 300 — Deed of June 15, 1900, by which the Saint Paul and Duluth Railroad Company conveyed its entire railroad system to the N.P. Ry.Co.

A.S.Doc. 1125 — Deed of May 26, 1902, by which the Duluth Transfer Railroad Company conveyed its entire property to the N.P. Ry. Co.

A.S.Dec. 1240 — Deed of June 21, 1902, by which the Union Depot & Transfer Company of Stillwater conveyed its entire property to the N.P.Ry.Co.

A.S.Dec. 1128 — Deed of Nov. 29, 1901, from The Minneapolis & St.Louis Railroad Company to N.P. Ry. Co. conveying line from M. & D. Junction to St.Anthony, 13.62 miles.

85

A.S.Doc. 220 — Deed of Sept. 4, 1899, by which the Little Falls and Southern Rail-Road Company conveyed its entire property to the N.P. Ry. Co.

A.S.Doc. 7933 — Deed of June 18, 1914, by which the Cuyuna Northern Railway Company conveyed its entire property to the N.P. Ry. Co.

A.S.Doc. 7934 — Deed of June 18, 1914, by which the Big Fork & International Falls Railway Company conveyed its entire property to the N.P. Ry. Co.

A.S.Doc. 7935 — Deed of June 20, 1914, by which the Missouri River Railway Company conveyed its entire property to the N.P. Ry. Co.

A.S.Doc. 7936 — Deed of June 20, 1914, by which the Western Dakota Railway Company conveyed its entire property to the N.P. Ry.Co.

A.S.Doc. 7937 — Deed of June 23, 1914, by which The Shields River Valley Railway Company conveyed its entire property to the N.P. Ry. Co.

A.S.Doc. 7938 — Deed of June 22, 1914, by which The Camp Creek Railway Company conveyed its entire property to the N.P.Ry. Co.

86

A.S.Doc. 197 — Deed of Feb. 28, 1899, by which the Gaylord and Ruby Valley Railway Company conveyed its entire property to the N.P. Ry. Co.

A.S.Doc. 159 — Deed of Oct. 7, 1898, by which the Montana Railway Company conveyed its entire property to the N.P. Ry. Co.

A.S.Doc. 221 — Deed of Oct. 7, 1898, by which the Montana Union Railway Company conveyed its entire property to the N.P. Ry.Co.

A.S.Doc. 7939 — Deed of June 23, 1914, by which the Clearwater Short Line Railway Company conveyed its entire property to the N.P. Ry. Co.

A.S.Doc. 22 — Deed of Jan. 26, 1897, by which The Coeur d'Alene Railway and Navigation Company conveyed its entire property to the N.P. Ry. Co.

A.S.Doc. 7941 — Deed of June 25, 1914, by which the Connell Northern Railway Company conveyed its entire property to the N.P. Ry.Co.

A.S.Doc. 3575 — Deed of June 18, 1907, by which The Washington and Columbia River Railway Company conveyed its entire property to the N.P. Ry. Co.

A.S.Doc. 7942 — Deed of June 24, 1914, by which the North Yakima and Valley Railway Company conveyed its entire property to the N.P. Ry. Co.

A.S.Doc.
665

Deed of Aug. 3, 1901, ny which the Western American Company conveyed its line from Carbenado to Fairfax to the N.P. Ry. Co.

A.S.Docs.
402
and
198

Deeds of Oct. 3, 1900 and March 17, 1899, by which the Spokane and Seattle Railway Company conveyed its entire property to the N.P. Ry. Co.

A.S.Doc.
310

Deed of Mar. 21, 1901, by which the Seattle and International Railway Company conveyed its entire property to the N.P. Ry. Co.

A.S.Doc.
1467

Deed of July 31, 1903, by which the Monte Cristo Railway Company conveyed its entire property to the N.P. Ry. Co.

A.S.Doc.
1362

Deed of July 1, 1902, by which the Bellingham Bay and Eastern Rail-road Company conveyed its entire property to the N.P. Ry. Co.

A.S.Doc.
1516

Deed of Oct. 21, 1903, by which the Northwestern Improvement Company conveyed to the N.P. Ry. Co. the railroad property of The Seattle and San Francisco Railway & Navigation Company.

A.S.Doc.
426

Deed of Aug. 22, 1900, by which the Washington Short Line Railway Company conveyed its entire property to the N.P. Ry. Co.

88

A.S.Doc. 7943 — Deed of June 25, 1914, by which the Port Townsend Southern Railroad Company conveyed its line from Tenino to West Olympia to the N.P. Ry. Co.

A.S.Doc. 1517 — Deed of Oct. 19, 1903, by which the Washington Railway & Navigation Company conveyed its entire property to the N.P. Ry. Co.

R.W.Deed 398 — Deed of Nov. 16, 1907, by which the Seattle and Montana Railroad Company conveys to the N.P. Ry. Co. a one-half interest in passenger terminal at Seattle.

R.W.Deed 400 — Deed of Nov. 25, 1907, by which the S.& M. R.R. Co. conveys to the N.P. Ry. Co. a one-half interest in tunnel at Seattle.

A.S.Doc. 4102 — Deed of April 28, 1908, by which Spokane, Portland and Seattle Railway Company conveyed to N.P. Ry.Co. one-third interest in its line from Vancouver to Willbridge.

A.S.Doc. 127 — Deed of April 21, 1898, by which the James River Valley Railroad Co. conveyed its entire property to the N.P. Ry. Co.

A.S.Doc. 130 — Deed of April 21, 1898, by which the Northern Pacific, Fergus and Black Hills Railroad Co. conveyed its entire property to the N.P. Ry. Co.

THE MINNEAPOLIS AND DULUTH RAILROAD COMPANY

Chart No.8
Place No.119
Map No.6

1. <u>Incorporation</u>

M.B.486
p.1

Incorporated under the general laws of the State of Minnesota.

Articles are dated April 24, 1871, and were filed with the Secretary of State May 16, 1871.

M.B.486
p.6

Organization effected May 12, 1871. (According to ruling of the Interstate Commerce Commission meetings for organization purposes must be held after articles of incorporation are filed to be legal.)

Chap.66
Spl.Laws
1853
and
L.A.File
140

Minnesota Western Railroad Company was created by special act of the Legislature of the Territory of Minnesota March 3, 1853. The name was changed to Minneapolis & St. Louis Railway Company May 26, 1870 by authority of a special Act of the Legislature of that year.

Chap.57
Spl.Laws
1870

Under this Act certain holders of special stock of the M.& St. L. Ry. Co. incorporated The Minneapolis and Duluth Railroad Company for the purpose of constructing a railroad from Minneapolis to White Bear. The M.& St.L. Ry. Co. issued a public notice that all its interests in this particular line were transferred to the M.& D. R.R.Co., which notice was filed with the Secretary of

State May 25, 1871.

M.B.486
ps.159-
174

By Articles of Consolidation dated April 20, 1881, effective June 1, 1881, the Minneapolis & St.Louis Railway Company, The Minneapolis & Duluth Railroad Company, the Minnesota & Iowa Southern Railroad Company and the Fort Dodge & Fort Ridgley Railroad Company formed The Minneapolis and St.Louis Railway Company, a railroad corporation of Minnesota and Iowa. June 25, 1888, The Minneapolis and St.Louis Railway Company went into the hands of a receiver. Its property was sold under decree of foreclosure on October 11, 1894 and conveyed to F.P. Olcott, et al, by James H.Ege, Sheriff of Hennepin County,

L.A.File
140

by deed dated November 28, 1894. F.P.Olcott et al conveyed the property to the M. and St.L.R.R.Co., a reorganization of the old company, by deed dated November 2, 1894.

L.A.File
140

2. Construction

The Minneapolis and Duluth Railroad Company constructed the line from St.Anthony (now part of Minneapolis), Minn. to M. & D. Junction, Minn., 13.62 miles, between April 1871 and August 15, 1871.

3. Operation

The line was operated as follows:

	From	To	Miles	Date
L.A.File 140	(1) St.Anthony	M.& D.Jctn.	13.62	Aug.15,1871 to Jan. 1, 1874
	(2) St.Anthony	M.& D.Jctn.	13.62	Jan. 1,1874 to Aug. 1, 1882
	(3) St.Anthony	M.& D.Jctn.	13.62	Aug. 1, 1882 to July 1, 1900
	(4) St.Anthony	M.& D.Jctn.	13.62	July 1, 1900 to Nov. 29, 1901

A.S.Doc. R.R.390

(1) By Lake Superior and Mississippi Railroad Company under lease dated June 5, 1871 until May 1, 1872, when lease was assigned to the N.P. R.R. Co. who operated the property, but being unable to make necessary payments reassigned the lease to the L.S.& M. R.R. Co., who surrendered the property to the M.& D. R.R. Co. as of Jan. 1, 1874.

M.B.486 ps.80 & 100 to 109

(2) By the Minneapolis & St. Louis Railway Company under agreement dated November 13, 1873 from January 1, 1874 to December 30,1876, on which date a new agreement was made and operation continued under the terms thereof until June 1, 1881, when the new organization, The M.& St.L. Ry. Co. took over the property and operated it until August 1, 1882. Line was then leased to the St.P.& D. R.R.Co. by lease dated July 5,1883, effective Aug.1,1882.

(3) Operated by Saint Paul and Duluth Railroad Company under lease dated July 5, 1883. Term 99 years from August 1, 1882. The rights of the St.P.& D.R.R.Co.under this lease were transferred to the N.P.Ry.Co. when road was sold June 15, 1900.

A.S.Doc. 1128

(4) Operated by Northern Pacific Railway Company under the lease of July 5, 1883 until September 4, 1901, on which date notice of cancellation went into effect. Operated by the N.P.Ry.Co. thereafter without a formal contract until line was purchased from the M.& St.L. R.R.Co. November 29, 1901.

4. Present Status of Corporation

M.B.486 ps.159-174

This Company consolidated with others, by Articles of Consolidation dated April 20, 1881, effective June 1, 1881, to form The Minneapolis and St.Louis Railway Co.

The records are in the custody of Mr. R. H. Relf, the Assistant Secretary of the Northern Pacific Ry.Co. at Saint Paul, Minnesota.

5. Chain of Title

	From	To	Date	Form of Transfer
M.B.486 ps.159-174	M.& D.R.R.Co.	The M.& St.L.Ry. Co.	April 20,1881	Articles of Consolidation
L.A.File 40	James H.Ege, Sheriff of Hennepin Co.	F.P.Olcott,et al	Nov. 28,1894	Deed
L.A.File 40	F.P.Olcott, et al	The M.& St.L. R.R.Co.	Nov. 2,1894	Deed
A.S.Doc. 1128	The M.& St.L. R.R.Co.	N.P.Ry.Co.	Nov. 29,1901	Deed

SCHEDULE OF INSTRUMENTS AND RECORDS

File Ref.	Description
M.B.486 p.1	Articles of Incorporation of The Minneapolis and Duluth Railroad Company.
A.S.Doc. R.R.390	Lease of June 5, 1871 from M.& D. R. R. Co. to Lake Superior and Mississippi Railroad Company.
M.B.486 ps.80 & 100to109	Agreements dated November 13, 1873 and December 30, 1876 between Mpls. & St. Louis Ry. Co. and M. & D. R.R. Co.
M.B.486 ps.159-174	Articles of Consolidation dated April 20, 1881, effective June 1, 1881, M.& D. R.R. Co. et al forming The M.& St. L. Ry. Co.
A.S.Doc. R.R.392	Lease of July 5, 1883 from The M. and St.Louis Ry.Co. to Saint Paul and Duluth Railroad Company.
A.S.Doc. 1128	Deed of November 29, 1901 by which M. and St.L. R.R.Co. conveyed to the N.P.Ry.Co. the line from M.& D. Jct. to St.Anthony, 13.62 miles.
L.A.File 40	Land Assistant's File "Corporate History".
L.A.File 140	Land Assistant's file "Data used in compiling return to Order No.20 - Corporate History".

MINNEAPOLIS & ST. LOUIS RAILWAY COMPANY

Chart No. 27 & 92
Place No. 110 & 104
Map No. 6

1. Incorporation

Chap. 66
Spl. Laws
1853

Chap. 57
Spl. Laws
1870

M.B. 486
P. 159-174

Minnesota Western Railroad Company was created by special Act of the Legislature of the Territory of Minnesota March 3, 1853, and on May 26, 1870 the name was changed to Minneapolis & St. Louis Railway Company by authority of a special Act of the Legislature of the State of Minnesota.

Under date of April 20, 1881, the Minneapolis & St. Louis Railway Company, The Minneapolis & Duluth Railroad Company, Minnesota & Iowa Southern Railroad Company and Fort Dodge & Fort Ridgley Railroad Company were consolidated under the name The Minneapolis & St. Louis Railway Company, a corporation of Minnesota and Iowa, consolidation effective June 1, 1881.

2. Construction

This company constructed no lines of interest in this report.

3. Operation

This company operated the following lines of interest in this report:

	From	To	Miles	Date
(1)	St. Anthony, Minn.	M.& D. Jctn., Minn.	13.62	Jan. 1, 1874 to Aug. 1, 1882
(2)	Wyoming, Minn.	Centre City, Minn.	10.50	Aug. 23, 1880 to Aug. 1, 1883
(2)	Centre City	Taylors Falls, Minn.	9.70	Nov. 8, 1880 to Aug. 1, 1883

M.B.486 ps.80 & 100to109

A.S.Doc. 370

(1) Property of The Minneapolis and Duluth Railroad Company operated under agreements of November 13, 1873 and December 30, 1876, until the consolidation of the companies June 1, 1881, after which time the property was operated by The Minneapolis and St. Louis Railway Company until August 1, 1882, on which date The M.& St.L. Ry.Co. leased it to the St.P.& D. R.R.Co.

A.S.Doc. 370

(2) Property of Taylors Falls and Lake Superior Railroad Company operated under lease of October 12, 1880 until August 1, 1883, on which date St. Paul and Duluth Railroad Company took up operation.

A.S.Doc. R.R.368

In addition to the above the M.& St.L.Ry.Co. had trackage rights over the St.Paul & Duluth Railroad between M.& D. Jct., Minn. and Wyoming, Minn. and between M.& D. Jct., Minn. and Duluth, Minn. by agreements dated May 1, 1880, which were canceled July 5, 1883 as of July 28, 1882.

L.A.File 140

4. **Present Status of Corporation**

June 25, 1888, this company went into the hands of

a receiver and its property was sold under foreclosure October 11, 1894 by James H. Ege, Sheriff of Hennepin County to F.P. Olcott, et al and conveyed by deed dated November 28, 1894; F. P. Olcott et al conveyed the property to the M.& St.L.R.R.Co., a reorganization of the old company, by deed dated November 2, 1894.

The records are in the custody of Mr. A.E. Smith, Auditor of The Minneapolis & St. Louis Railroad Company, Minneapolis, Minnesota.

5. **Chain of Title**

	From	To	Miles	Date
M.B.486 ps.159-174	M.& D.R.R.Co.	The M.& St.L. Ry.Co.	April 20,1881	Articles of Consolidation
L.A.File 40	James H. Ege, Sheriff Hennepin Co.	F.P.Olcott, et al	Nov. 28,1894	Deed
L.A.File 40	F.P.Olcott, et al	The M.& St.L. R.R.Co.	Nov. 2,1894	Deed
A.S.Doc. 1128	The M.& St.L. R.R.Co.	N.P.Ry.Co.	Nov. 29,1901	Deed

SCHEDULE OF INSTRUMENTS AND RECORDS

File Ref.   **Description**

M.B.486   Agreements dated November 13, 1873 and December
ps.80,100 30, 1875 between Mpls. & St. Louis Ry.Co. and Mpls.
-109   and Duluth Railroad Co.

A.S.Doc.   Lease of October 12, 1880 from Taylors Falls and
370   Lake Superior Railroad Company to M. & St. L. Ry. Co.,
           entire property.

M.B.486   Articles of Consolidation forming The Minneapolis
ps.159-   and St.Louis Railway Company.
174

A.S.Doc.   Deed of Nov. 29, 1901 from Minneapolis & St.Louis
1128   Railroad Co. to N.P.Ry.Co. conveying line from M. & D.
           Junction to St.Anthony, 13.62 miles.

A.S.Doc.   Surrender of leases of May 1, 1880 between M.& St.L.
368   Ry. Company and St.Paul and Duluth Railroad Company.

A.S.Doc.   Lease of July 5, 1883 from The M.& St.L.Ry.Co. to
392   the St.P.& D. R. R. Co. covering its line from St.An-
           thony to M.& D. Jct., 13.62 miles.

L.A.File   Land Assistant's file "Corporate History".
40

L.A.File   Land Assistant's file "Data used in compiling re-
140   turn to Order No.20 - Corporate History".

THE MINNEAPOLIS AND ST. LOUIS RAILROAD COMPANY

Chart No.93
Place No.98
Map No.6

1. Incorporation

L.A.File 140

This company is a re-organization of the Minneapolis & St. Louis Railway Company, a corporation of Minnesota and Iowa, which was sold under foreclosure October 11, 1894. Articles of Incorporation are dated November 2, 1894 and were filed with the Secretary of State of Minnesota November 12, 1894. The present corporation is under the general laws of Minnesota and Iowa.

2. Construction and Acquisitions

L.A.File 40

This company constructed no lines of interest in this report but acquired, with other lines, from its predecessor the line formerly owned by The Minneapolis and Duluth Railroad Company from St.Anthony (now part of Minneapolis), Minnesota to M.& D. Junction, Minnesota, 13.62 miles.

3. Operation

A.S.Dec.
R.R.392

This company operated no lines of interest in this report. At time of re-organization its line from

St. Anthony, Minn. to M.& D. Jct. was under lease to the St. Paul and Duluth Railroad Company, who operated the line until July 1, 1900, when that property was purchased by the N.P.Ry. Company who assumed the lease and operated the line until November 29, 1901, when The M. & St. L. R. R. Co. conveyed the property to the N.P.Ry.Co.

4. **Present Status of Corporation**

L.A.File 140

This company is still in existence and its records are in the custody of Mr. A. E. Smith, Auditor, The Minneapolis & St. Louis Railroad Company, Minneapolis, Minnesota.

5. **Chain of Title**

	From	To	Date	Form of Transfer
M.B.484 p.159-174	M.& D.R.R.Co.	The M.& St.L.Ry. Co.	April 20, 1881	Article of Consolidation
L.A.File 40	James H. Ege Sheriff of Hennepin Co.	F.P.Olcott, et al	Nov. 28, 1894	Deed
L.A.File 40	F.L.Olcott, et al	The M.& St.L.R.R. Co.	Nov. 2, 1894	Deed
A.S.Doc. 1128	The M.& St.L. R.R.Co.	N. P. Ry.Co.	Nov. 29, 1901	Deed

SCHEDULE OF INSTRUMENTS AND RECORDS

File Ref.	Description
M.B.486 p.159-174	Articles of Consolidation forming The Minneapolis and St. Louis Railway Company.
A.S.Doc. R.R.392	Lease of July 5, 1883 from The M.& St.L.Ry.Co. to the St.P.& D.R.R.Co. covering line from St.Anthony, Minn. to M. & D. Jct., 13.62 miles.
L.A.File 40	Land Assistant's file " Corporate History".
L.A.File 140	Land Assistant's File "Data used in compiling return to Order No.20 - Corporate History".
A.S.Doc. 1128	Deed of November 29, 1901, by which The Minneapolis and St. Louis Railroad Co. conveyed to the N.P.Ry.Co. its line from M.& D. Jct. to St.Anthony, 13.62 miles.

UTAH AND NORTHERN RAILWAY COMPANY

Chart No. 20
Place No. 19
Map No. 7

1. **Incorporation**

Chap. 362
45th Cong.
Sess. II

Incorporated in the Territories of Utah, Idaho and Montana by Act of Congress of June 20, 1878.

Articles were filed with the Secretary of Territory of Utah May 29, 1883, and with the Auditor of Public Accounts of Territory of Utah February 24, 1879.

L.A. File 140

Organization effected April 1, 1878.

2. **Construction**

L.A. File 140

This report covers only that portion of this company's lines listed below. They were originally narrow-gauge and constructed on dates shown:

From	To	Miles	Date
Silver Bow, Mont.	Butte, Mont.	9.20	1881
Butte	Anaconda Mine	3.40	1884
Silver Bow	Garrison, Mont.	44.50	1881 and 1882

Above lines changed to standard gauge in 1886 and 1887.

3. **Operation**

L.A. File 140

The lines were operated as follows:

From	To	Miles	Date
Silver Bow	Butte	9.20	Dec. 23, 1881 to Aug. 1, 1886
Butte	Anaconda Mine	3.40	1884 to Aug. 1, 1886
Silver Bow	Garrison	44.50	Sept. 29, 1883 to Aug. 1, 1886

4. **Present Status of Corporation**

The property of the Utah and Northern Railway Company was consolidated on July 27, 1889, with seven other companies to form the Oregon Short Line and Utah and Northern Railroad Company, which consolidation dissolved said Utah and Northern Railway Company and terminated its corporate existence.

The records are in the custody of Mr. Alex Millar, Secretary of the Union Pacific System, 165 Broadway, New York City.

5. **Chain of Title**

	From	To	Date	Form of Transfer
A.S.Doc. 221	U. & N. Ry.Co.	M.U. Ry.Co.	Aug. 1, 1886	Lease for 999 years
A.S.Doc. 221	M.U. Ry.Co.	N.P. Ry.Co.	Oct. 7, 1898	Deed and Assignment of Lease

SCHEDULE OF INSTRUMENTS AND RECORDS

File Ref.   Description

A.S.Doc.   Lease of Aug. 1, 1886 for 999 years from Utah and
221   Northern Railway Company to Montana Union Railway Company line from Butte to Garrison and spur to Anaconda Mine.

A.S.Doc.   Instrument dated Oct. 7, 1898, by which M.U. Ry.Co.
221   conveyed its entire property to the N.P. Ry. Co. and also assigned all interest in the above lease.

L.A.File   Land Assistant's file "Data used in compiling re-
140   turn to Order No.20 - Corporate History".

MONTANA UNION RAILWAY COMPANY

Chart No.53
Place No.8
Map No.7

1. Incorporation

A.S.Doc. 1145

Incorporated under the general laws of the Territory of Montana.

Articles are dated June 14, 1886, and were filed with the Secretary of Territory June 28, 1886.

Organization effected June 30, 1886.

2. Construction and Leases

L.A.File 140

This company did no construction with the exception of spur tracks, but it leased railroad properties as follows:

A.S.Doc. 221

From the Utah and Northern Railway Company under lease dated August 1, 1886 for a term of 999 years:

	From	To	Miles
Main Line	Garrison, Mont.	Butte, Mont.	53.70
Br. Line	Butte, Mont.	Anaconda Mine	3.40

A.S.Doc. 222

From the Montana Railway Company under lease dated August 1, 1886 for a term of 999 years:

From	To	Miles
Stuart, Mont.	Anaconda, Mont.	9.00
Walkerville, Mont.	High Ore	1.36

	From	To	Miles
	Anaconda Mine	Walkerville	2.81
	Haggins Mine Spur		1.66

A.S.Doc. 97

The above lease was modified and the line from Stuart to Anaconda leased to the Butte, Anaconda and Pacific Ry.Co. from May 18, 1898.

A.S.Doc. 160

By agreement of October 6, 1898 lease of August 1, 1886 was canceled.

3. Operation

L.A.File 140

This company operated lines as follows:

	From	To	Miles	Date
Main Line	Garrison	Butte	53.70	Aug.1,1886 to Oct.31,1898
Br. Line	Butte	Anaconda Mine	3.40	Aug.1,1886 to Oct.31,1898
Br. Line	Stuart	Anaconda	9.00	Aug.1,1886 to May 17,1898
Br. Line	Walkerville	High Ore	1.36	1887 to Oct.31, 1898
Br. Line	Anaconda Mine	Walkerville	2.81	1887 to Oct.31, 1898
	Haggins Mine Spur		1.66	1887 to Oct.31, 1898

4. Present Status of Corporation

A.S.Doc. 1145

No action has been taken to dissolve this corporation, but having parted with its assets it is not active.

The records are in the custody of Mr. R. H. Relf, the Assistant Secretary of the Northern Pacific Railway

Co. at Saint Paul, Minnesota.

5. <u>Chain of Title</u>

	Portion of Line	From	To	Date	Form of Transfer
A.S.Doc. 221	Garrison to Butte and to Anaconda Mine	M.U.Ry.Co.	N.P.Ry.Co.	Oct.7,1898	Assignment of leasehold interest and general conveyance

SCHEDULE OF INSTRUMENTS AND RECORDS

File Ref.	Description
A.S.Doc. 1145	Articles of Incorporation of Montana Union Railway Company.
A.S.Doc. 221	Lease of Aug. 1, 1886 for 999 years from Utah and Northern Ry. Co. to M.U. Ry. Co. Line from Garrison to Butte and spurs to mines in vicinity of Butte. Also assignment of interests to N.P. Ry. Co. Oct. 6, 1898.
A.S.Doc. 222	Lease of Aug. 1, 1886 for 999 years from Montana Railway Company to M.U.Ry.Co.
A.S.Doc. 97	Modifying lease of Aug. 1, 1886. Agreement of May 5, 1898.
A.S.Doc. 160	Agreement of Oct. 6, 1898, cancelling lease of Aug. 1, 1886 (A.S.Doc.222).
L.A.File 140	Land Assistant's file "Data used in compiling return to Corporate History".

SEATTLE AND WALLA WALLA RAIL ROAD COMPANY

Chart No.13 & 9
Place No.78 & 87
Map No.8

1. Incorporation

A.S.Doc. 9965

Seattle and Walla Walla Rail Road and Transportation Company was incorporated under the general laws of the Territory of Washington.

Articles are dated July 19, 1873, and were filed with the Secretary of Territory July 23, 1873.

Date of organization is unknown.

By an amendment and certificate of re-incorporation dated October 28, 1876, and filed with the Secretary of Territory November 2, 1876, the name was changed to Seattle and Walla Walla Rail Road Company and by deed

R.W.Deed 283H

dated November 8, 1876 the property was conveyed to the latter company.

2. Construction

L.A.File 140

This property consisted of a narrow-gauge road extending from Newcastle, Wash. Territory to Seattle, Washington Territory, 22.50 miles, which was constructed prior to February 8, 1877. No details of this construction are available, but the deed from the original company to the new organization conveyed all property, including rolling stock, and as road was opened three months later, the indications are that construction was practically completed when road was conveyed.

3. Operation

This line was opened for operation February 8, 1877 but records covering this operation are not in the possession of the reporting carrier. By deed dated Nov. 30, 1880 the property was conveyed to the Columbia and Puget Sound Railroad Co.

4. Present Status of Corporation

L.A.File 140

The name of this company was stricken from the records of the Secretary of State of Washington August 23, 1909, for failure to pay annual license fees.

The records are in the custody of Mr. J. W. Smith, Auditor of the C.& P.S. R. R. Co., 77 Washington Street, Seattle, Washington.

5. Chain of Title

	From	To	Date	Form of Transfer
R.W.Deed 283H	S.&W.W.R.R.&T.Co.	S.&W.W.R.R.Co.	Nov. 8, 1876	Deed
R.W.Deed 283	S.&W.W.R.R.Co.	C.&P.S.R.R.Co.	Nov. 30, 1880	Deed
R.W.Deed 283	C.&P.S.R.R.Co.	N.P.Ry.Co.	Oct. 15, 1902	Deed

SCHEDULE OF INSTRUMENTS AND RECORDS

File Ref.	Description
A.S.Doc. 9965	Articles of Incorporation of the S.& W.W.R.R. and T. Co.
R.W.Deed 283	Deed of Nov. 30, 1880, by which the S.& W.W.R.R.Co. conveyed its entire property to the C.& P.S. R.R. Co.
R.W.Deed 283	Deed of October 15, 1902 of C.& P. S. R. R. Co. to N. P. Ry. Co.
R.W.Deed 283H	Deed of Nov. 8, 1876, by which the S.&W.R.R.& T. Co. conveyed its entire property to the S.& W.W. R.R. Co.
L.A.File 140	Land Assistant's file "Data used in compiling return to Order No.20 - Corporate History".

THE COLUMBIA AND PUGET SOUND RAILROAD COMPANY

Chart No. 26
Place No. 69
Map No. 8

1. Incorporation

A.S.Doc. 9966

Incorporated under the general laws of the Territory of Washington.

Articles are dated November 26, 1880, and were filed with the Secretary of Territory November 27, 1880.

Date of organization is unknown.

2. Construction and Purchases

R.W.Deed 283H

This company constructed no lines of interest in connection with this report but purchased November 30, 1880 from the Seattle and Walla Walla Railroad Company a narrow-gauge line extending from Newcastle, Washington to Seattle, Washington, 22.50 miles. Only that portion of this company's road from Seattle to Black River Jct., 10.10 miles, is covered by the information reported herein.

3. Operation

L.A.File 140

This line was operated as follows:

From	To	Operated by
Nov. 30, 1880	July 6, 1884	C.& P.S.R.R.Co.
July 6, 1884	Jan. 17, 1890	C.& P.S.R.R.Co. and P.S.S. R.R.Co. jointly

From	To	Operated by
Jan. 17, 1890	Apr. 21, 1898	C.& P.S.R.R.Co. and N.P. and P.S.S.R.R.Co. Jointly (N.P.R.R.Co. operating for N.P.& P.S.S.R.R.Co.)
April 21, 1898	Sept. 13, 1902	C.& P.S.R.R.Co. and N.P.Ry.Co. jointly

4. Present Status of Corporation

L.A.File 140

This corporation is still in existence.

The records are in the custody of Mr. J. W. Smith, Secretary and Auditor of Columbia & Puget Sound Railroad Company, 77 Washington Street, Seattle, Washington.

5. Chain of Title

L.A.File 140

A.S.Doc. 583

A.S.Doc. 357

A.S.Doc. 134

September 2, 1882, an agreement was entered into permitting the Puget Sound Shore Railroad Company to reconstruct the roadbed of this company and lay a standard gauge track thereon; placing one of the old narrow-gauge rails between the rails of the standard gauge to accommodate the narrow-gauge equipment. The P.S.S.R.R.Co. conveyed its interest to Northern Pacific and Puget Sound Shore Rail-Road Company October 31, 1889 and that company conveyed to Northern Pacific Railway Company April 21, 1898.

A.S.Doc. 914

By agreement dated November 18, 1901 a partition of interests was made and deeds were exchanged between the C.& P.S.R.R.Co. and N.P.Ry.Co. dated October 15, 1902

R.W.Deed 283
R.W.Deed 284

and November 4, 1902, respectively, under which the line between Black River Jct. and N.P. Jct. (Argo) was divided, each company acquiring one-half of the right of way and each company being provided with its own standard gauge main track. The work of widening the grade and installing double track system was done by the N.P. Ry..Co. between December 29, 1901 and September 1902, being turned over for operation September 14, 1902. The N.P.Ry.Co. under the deed of October 15, 1902 acquired certain other property in the City of Seattle and all interest in City of Seattle Franchises Nos.3915 and 6350.

A further partition of interests was agreed upon February 3, 1903, under which the C.& P.S. R.R. Co., among other considerations, acquired the line of the N.P.Ry.Co. from Argo to Atlantic St., Seattle, via Colorado St., giving in return its so-called "Shore Line" from Argo to Seattle and other interests. These properties were exchanged as of August 1, 1904.

	From	To	Date	Form of Transfer
R.W.Deed 283H	S.& W.W.R.R. & T.Co.	S.& W.W.R.R. Co.	Nov. 8, 1876	Deed
R.W.Deed 283	S.& W.W.R.R. Co.	C.& P.S.R.R. Co.	Nov. 30, 1880	Deed

SCHEDULE OF INSTRUMENTS AND RECORDS

File Ref.	Description
A.S.Doc. 9966	Articles of Incorporation Columbia & Puget Sound Railroad Co.
A.S.Doc. 357	Deed of Oct. 31, 1889, by which Puget Sound Shore Railroad Company conveyed its interest to Northern Pacific and Puget Sound Shore Rail-Road Company.
A.S.Doc. 134	Deed of April 21, 1898, by which the N.P.& P.S.S. R.R.Co. conveyed its property to N.P. Ry. Co.
A.S.Doc. 583	Agreement dated September 2, 1882, under which P.S.S.R.R.Co. built a standard gauge track on line of C.& P.S. R.R. Co. from Black River Junction to Seattle, 10.10 miles, and operated over same.
A.S.Doc. 914	Agreement of Nov. 18, 1901 between C.&P.S.R.R.Co. and N.P.Ry.Co. covering partition of interests.
R.W.Deed 283	Deed of Oct. 15, 1902 from C.& P.S.R.R. Co. to the N.P.Ry.Co. to carry out agreement of Nov. 11, 1901.
R.W.Deed 284	Deed of Nov. 4, 1902 from N.P.Ry.Co. to the C.& P.S. R.R.Co. to carry out agreement of Nov. 18, 1901.
L.A.File 140	Land Assistant's file "Data used in compiling return to Order No.20 - Corporate History".

R.W.Deed 283H   Deed of November 8, 1876, by which the S.& W.W. R.R. & T.Co. conveyed its property to S.& W.W.R.R.Co.

R.W.Deed 283   Deed of November 30, 1880, by which the S.& W.W. R.R.Co. conveyed its property to C.& P.S.R.R.Co.

OLYMPIA RAILROAD UNION

Chart No.10
Place No.103
Map No.9

1. Incorporation

A.S.Doc. 9956

Incorporated under the general laws of the Territory of Washington.

Articles are dated January 2, 1874, and were filed with the Secretary of Territory January 5, 1874.

Date of organization is unknown.

2. Construction

R.W.Deed 108

This company carried on no construction but acquired a small part of the right of way for a line between Tenino, Washington and Olympia, Washington. The right of way was deeded to Thurston County Railroad Construction Company July 28, 1877.

3. Operation

This company operated no lines.

4. Present Status of Corporation

A.S.Doc. 9956

The N.P.Ry.Co. has no knowledge as to the location of the records of this corporation and does not know who is their custodian.

The name of this corporation was stricken from the records of the State of Washington for failure to pay annual license fees, August 23, 1909.

5. <u>Chain of Title</u>

	From	To	Date	Form of Transfer
R.W.Deed 108	O.R.R.U.	T.C.R.R.Const.Co.	July 28,1877	Deed
R.W.Deed 108	T.C.R.R.Const.Co.	O.& C.V.R.R.Co.	Aug. 1,1881	Change of name
R.W.Deed 252	O.& C.V.R.R.Co.	P.T.S.R.R.Co.	June 2,1891	Deed
A.S.Doc. 7943	P.T.S.R.R.Co.	N.P.Ry.Co.	June 25,1914	Deed

SCHEDULE OF INSTRUMENTS AND RECORDS

File Ref.	Description
R.W.Deed 108	Deed of July 28, 1877, by which Olympia Railroad Union conveyed some right of way to The Thurston County Railroad Construction Company.
R.W.Deed 108	Copy of Amended Articles of Incorporation under which the T. C. R. R. Const. Co. changed its name to Olympia & Chehalis Valley Railroad Co.
R.W.Deed 252	Deed of June 2, 1891, by which O. and C. V. R.R. Co. conveyed its entire property to the Port Townsend Southern Railroad Company.
A.S.Doc. 7943	Deed of June 25, 1914, by which the P. T. S. R. R. Co. conveyed its property between Tenino and West Olympia to N. P. Ry. Co.
A.S.Doc. 9956	Articles of Incorporation, Olympia Railroad Union.

THE OLYMPIA & CHEHALIS VALLEY RAILROAD COMPANY

Chart No.30 & 14
Place No.86 & 94
Map No.9

1. Incorporation

A.S.Doc.
9967

Thurston County Railroad Construction Company.

Incorporated under the general laws of the Territory of Washington.

Date of organization is unknown.

Articles are dated June 2, 1877, and were filed with the Secretary of Territory June 4, 1877

Amended Articles filed August 6, 1877.

R.W.Deed
108

Amended Articles changing the name to The Olympia & Chehalis Valley Railroad Company were filed with the Secretary of Territory August 1, 1881.

Organization effected August 6, 1881.

L.A.File
140

Amended Articles providing for the construction of some additional lines were filed with the Secretary of Territory July 5, 1886.

Amended Articles filed September 6, 1886; and amended and supplemental articles filed March 1, 1890.

2. Construction and Purchases

R.W.Deed
108

The Thurston County R.R. Const. Co. July 28, 1877 purchased from the Olympia Railroad Union a portion of the right of way for a line between Tenino, Washington

L.A.File 140

and Olympia, Washington, 14.50 miles, and thereafter constructed a narrow-gauge main line, completing the same August 1, 1878.

The line was afterward changed to standard gauge, being completed September 10, 1890.

The work of changing gauge to standard was done by the Port Townsend Southern Railroad Co. prior to acquisition of road by them.

3. Operation

L.A.File 140

The T.C.R.R.Co. operated this line from August 2, 1878 to August 1, 1881, when name was changed to O.& C.V. R.R.Co. Operation continued under the latter company until September 10, 1890, when the line was standardized and turned over to the Port Townsend Southern Railroad Co.

4. Present Status of Corporation

The N. P. Ry. Co. has no knowledge as to the location of the records of this corporation and does not know who is their custodian.

The name of this corporation was stricken from the records of the State of Washington August 23, 1909, for failure to pay annual license fees.

5. Chain of Title

	From	To	Date	Form of Transfer
R.W.Deed 108	O.R.R.U.	T.C.R.R.Const.Co.	July 28, 1877	Deed

	From	To	Date	Form of Transfer
R.W.Deed 108	T.C.R.R.Const.Co.	O.&C.V.R.R.Co.	Aug. 1,1881	Change of name
R.W.Deed 252	O.&C.V.R.R.Co.	P.T.S.R.R.Co.	June 2,1891	Deed
A.S.Doc. 7943	P.T.S.R.R.Co.	N.P.Ry.Co.	June 25,1914	Deed

SCHEDULE OF INSTRUMENTS AND RECORDS

File Ref.	Description
A.S.Doc. 9967	Articles of Incorporation, Thurston County Railroad Const. Co.
R.W.Deed 108	Deed of July 28, 1877, by which the Olympia Railroad Union conveyed some right of way to The Thurston County Railroad Construction Company.
R.W.Deed 108	Copy of Amended Articles of Incorporation under which The T.C.R.R. Const. Co. changed its name to Olympia & Chehalis Valley Railroad Company.
R.W.Deed 252	Deed of June 2, 1891, by which O.& C.V. R.R. Co. conveyed its entire property to the Port Townsend Southern Railroad Company.
A.S.Doc. 7943	Deed of June 25, 1914, by which the P.T.S.R.R.Co. conveyed its property between Tenino and West Olympia to the N.P.Ry.Co.
L.A.File 140	Land Assistant's file "Data used in compiling return to Order No.20 - Corporate History".

PORT TOWNSEND SOUTHERN RAILROAD COMPANY

Chart No.68
Place No.77
Map No.9

1. Incorporation

A.S.Doc. 1266

Incorporated under the general laws of the Territory of Washington.

Articles are dated August 19, 1887, and were filed with the Secretary of Territory September 28, 1887.

L.A.File 140

Organization effected August 19, 1887. (According to ruling of the Interstate Commerce Commission a meeting for organization purposes to be legal must be held after filing Articles of Incorporation.)

2. Construction and Purchases

R.W.Deed 252

By deed dated June 2, 1891 this company acquired the entire property of the Olympia & Chehalis Valley Railroad Co. including a narrow-gauge main line from Tenino to Olympia, Wash., 14.50 miles. In 1890, prior to acquisition of above property, the P.T.S.R.R.Co. changed the gauge to standard, the work being completed September 10,

L.A.File 140

1890. It also extended this line 3.00 miles to West Olympia (Butler's Cove) between August 1890 and January 1891.

R.W.Deed 160

In 1906 and 1907 this company purchased a considerable portion of the right of way for a line from Tenino to

Tacoma, Wash., title being taken in the name of the
P.T.S.R.R.Co. only as a matter of convenience to the
N.P.Ry.Co., who reimbursed them for their expenditures,
and by deed dated September 28, 1907 acquired title to
the right of way and every interest of the P.T.S.R.R.Co.
in this line.

This company's line from Port Townsend to Quilcene
was not conveyed to the N.P.Ry.Co. and is not included
in this report.

3. Operation

This company operated its line, Tenino to Olympia,
17.50 miles, from September 11, 1890 to July 1, 1914.

Owing to track changes the line as conveyed to the
N.P.Ry.Co. June 25, 1914 was only 15.00 miles in length.

4. Present Status of Corporation

A.S.Doc.
1266

This corporation is still in existence.

The records of this company of which the N.P.Ry.Co.
has any knowledge were forwarded in May 1917 to Mr. C.H.J.
Stoltenberg, Secretary, address, Colman Dock, Seattle,
Washington.

5. Chain of Title

	From	To	Date	Form of Transfer
R.W.Deed 108	Olympia Railroad Union	Thurston County R.R.Const.Co.	July 28, 1877	Deed

	From	To	Date	Form of Transfer
R.W.Deed 108	T.C.R.R.Const. Co.	O.&C.V.R.R.Co.	Aug.1, 1881	Change of name
R.W.Deed 252	O.&C.V.R.R.Co.	P.T.S.R.R.Co.	June 2, 1891	Deed
A.S.Doc. 7943	P.T.S.R.R.Co.	N.P.Ry.Co.	June 25, 1914	Deed

SCHEDULE OF INSTRUMENTS AND RECORDS

File Ref. **Description**

A.S.Doc. 1266 — Articles of Incorporation of Port Townsend Southern Railroad Company.

R.W.Deed 252 — Deed of June 2, 1891, by which Olympia and Chehalis Valley Railroad Company conveyed its entire property to the P.T.S.R.R. Co.

A.S.Doc. 7943 — Deed of June 25, 1914, by which the P.T.S.R.R.Co. conveyed its property between Tenino and West Olympia to N.P.Ry.Co.

R.W.Deed 108 — Deed of July 28, 1877, by which Olympia Railroad Union conveyed some right of way to the Thurston County Railroad Const. Co. Amended Articles of Incorporation of T.C.R.R.C.Co. changing name to O.& C.V.R.R.Co. are also in the file.

L.A.File 140 — Land Assistant's file "Data used in compiling return to Order No.20 - Corporate History".

SAINT PAUL AND NORTHERN PACIFIC RAILWAY COMPANY

Chart No.38 & 11
Place No.73 & 82
Map No.2 & 10

1. **Incorporation**

Chap.1
Ex.Sess.
Laws
1857
p.3

Minnesota and Pacific Railroad Company was created by an Act of the Legislature of the Territory of Minnesota May 22, 1857. The Act authorized the construction of a main line from Stillwater, Minnesota to a point between Big Stone Lake and the Sioux Wood River with a branch line to the Red River via St.Cloud and Crow Wing, Minnesota. The company issued some First Mortgage Bonds on which it defaulted. The State of Minnesota, having acquired the bonds, foreclosed and became possessed of the property and franchises of the company.

Chap.XX
Spl.Laws
1862
p.247

The Legislature of the State of Minnesota, March 10, 1862, passed an Act entitled: "An Act to facilitate the construction of the Minnesota and Pacific Railroad and to amend and continue the act of incorporation relating thereto". This act conferred upon The St.Paul and Pacific Railroad Company all the rights and privileges which had pertained to the M.& P.R.R.Co. An Act of Congress March 3, 1871, authorized, among other things, the construction of a line from Crow Wing to a connection with the Northern Pacific Railroad at Brainerd, Minnesota. The St.P.&P.R.R. Co. graded this line from Brainerd to Watab and laid track

Chap.CXLIV
U.S.Stat.
p.588

Chap.201
Spl.Laws
1877
p.257

from Brainered to a point 5 miles south, but having failed to complete the line the Legislature passed an Act March 1, 1877, declaring forfeited the rights of that company to this line and providing that any railroad company incorporated in Minnesota might acquire the right to complete and operate it.

A.S.Doc.
1320

Western Railroad Company of Minnesota was incorporated under the general laws of the State of Minnesota and succeeded to the rights forfeited by the St.P.& P. R.R. Co.

Articles are dated January 29, 1874, and were filed with the Secretary of State January 31, 1874.

Organization effected February 7, 1874.

A.S.Doc.
1320

By amended articles filed with the Secretary of State May 9, 1883, the name was changed to Saint Paul and Northern Pacific Railway Company. The W.R.R.Co. of Minn. finished the grading between Brainerd and Sauk Rapids commenced by the St.P. and P.R.R.Co. and laid the steel to connect with the old track south of Brainerd, work being done in August and September 1877.

A.S.Doc.
1320

Amended articles were filed with the Secretary of State December 29, 1884, which authorized construction of the line between Little Falls and Staples.

L.A.File
140

2. <u>Construction</u>

Details of construction by above companies:

From	To	Miles	Date
Sauk Rapids, Minn.	Brainerd, Minn.	60.50	1871 to Sept. 1877
Sauk Rapids	Minneapolis, Minn. (Northtown Jct.)	66.10	1883 to 1884
Northtown	Terminal Lot (Mpls.)	3.44	July 1883 to Sept. 1884
Line A 20th Ave. at Minneapolis	St. Paul, Minn. (7th St.)	10.08	April 30, 1885 to 1886
East Side Line at St. Paul		1.25	Nov. 1888 to Oct. 1889

Main Line Total - - - 141.37

From	To	Miles	Date
Little Falls	Staples, Minn.	33.40	April to Sept. 1889
Line B Northtown Jct. Minn.	St. Anthony Park, Minn.	5.26	May to Sept. 1885
Line C Ramsey St. Line, Mpls.		0.76	Sept. 1885 to Mar. 1886
Line D Second St. Line, Mpls.		1.01	May to Aug. 1885
Line E Mulberry St. Line, Mpls.		0.88	Aug. to Dec. 1885
Connection with Minnesota Transfer Ry. Co.		1.09	June to Oct. 1885

Branch Line Total - 42.40

The tracks leading to the State Fair Grounds were constructed by the St.P.M.&M.Ry. (Great Nor.Ry.Co.) from June to October 1885, the St.P. and N.P.Ry.Co. acquiring an one-half interest by paying one-half of the cost.

A.S.Doc. 189

Under an agreement made January 1, 1886, the St.P.& N.P.Ry.Co. purchased the terminal property of the N.P.R.R.Co. at St.Paul, consisting of about 10 acres of land extending from Pine St. to 7th St; conveyance being made by deed dated February 28, 1893.

3. <u>Operation</u>

L.A.File 140

The lines were operated as follows:

	From	To	Miles	Date
(1)	Sauk Rapids	Brainerd	60.50	Nov. 1,1877 to May 1, 1883
(2)	Sauk Rapids	Brainerd	60.50	May 1, 1883 to Nov.2, 1896
(2)	Sauk Rapids	Minneapolis	66.10	July 2,1884 to Nov.2,1896
(2)	20th Ave. Minneapolis	St.Paul	10.08	Feb.1886 to Nov.2,1896
(2)	Northtown Jct.	St.Anthony Park	5.26	Part in 1885 and part May 1,1886 to Nov.2,1896
(2)	East Side Line at St.Paul		1.25	Oct.1889 to Nov.2,1896
(2)	Little Falls	Staples	33.65	Nov.24,1889 to Nov.2,1896
(2)	Ramsey St.Line,Mpls.		0.76	May 1, 1886 to Nov. 2, 1896
(2)	Second St.Line,Mpls.		1.01	1885 to Nov.2, 1896
(2)	Mulberry St.Line,Mpls.		0.88	May 1, 1886 to Nov. 2, 1896
(2)	Tracks to Minn.Transfer		1.09	1885 to Nov.2, 1896
(2)	Northtown Jct.Terminal Lot		3.44	July 2, 1884 to November 2, 1896

A.S.Doc.
R.R.479

(1) Operated by Northern Pacific Railroad Company without formal authority until execution of lease dated May 1, 1878. On May 1, 1883 this was canceled and a new lease was entered into.

A.S.Doc.
237

(2) Operated under lease dated June 1, 1883, effective May 1, 1883 by Northern Pacific Railroad Company until August 15, 1893; by the receivers of the N.P.R.R. Co. from August 15, 1893 to August 31, 1896 and from September 1, 1896 to November 2, 1896 by the N.P.Ry.Co.

4. Present Status of Corporation

No action has been taken to dissolve the corporation but having parted with its assets it is not active.

The records are in the custody of Mr. R. H. Relf, the Assistant Secretary of the Northern Pacific Railway Company at Saint Paul, Minnesota.

5. Chain of Title

	Line	From	To	Date	Form of Transfer
Chap.201 Spl.Laws p. 257	Brainerd to Watab	St.P.&P.R.R. Co.	W.R.R.Co. of M.	Mar.1,1877	Acquisition of forfeited rights under provisions of the Act of the Legislature
A.S.Doc. 1320	Brainerd to Sauk Rapids	W.R.R.Co.of M.	St.P.& N.P.Ry.	May 9,1883	Change of name
A.S.Doc. 51	All	St.P.& N.P. Ry.Co.	N.P.Ry.	Nov.2,1896	Deed

SCHEDULE OF INSTRUMENTS AND RECORDS

File Ref.	Description
A.S.Doc. 1320	Articles of Incorporation of Western Railroad Company of Minnesota. Amended Articles dated May 9, 1883, changing name to Saint Paul and Northern Pacific Railway Company. Amended Articles dated December 29, 1884, providing for cut off Little Falls to Staples.
A.S.Doc. 237	Lease of May 1, 1883, by which the N.P.R.R.Co. et al operated the property.
A.S.Doc. 51	Deed of November 2, 1896, by which the St.P.& N.P. Ry.Co. conveyed its entire property to the N.P.Ry.Co.
A.S.Doc. R.R.479	Lease dated May 1, 1878, under which the N.P.R.R.Co. operated the property of the W.R.R.of Minn.
L.A.File 140	Land Assistant's file "Data used in compiling return to Order No.20 - Corporate History".
A.S.Doc. 189	Agreement of Jan. 1, 1886, under which the N.P.R.R. Co. sold its terminal yard in St.Paul to the St.P.& N.P. Ry.Co.

TAYLORS FALLS AND LAKE SUPERIOR RAIL ROAD COMPANY

Chart No.12
Place No.26
Map No.11

1. **Incorporation**

A.S.Doc. 10011

Incorporated under the general laws of the State of Minnesota.

Articles are dated February 8, 1875 and were filed with the Secretary of State February 9, 1875.

Organization effected February 20, 1875.

L.A.File 140

The articles of this company authorize the construction of a line from Taylors Falls, Minnesota to a connection with the Lake Superior and Mississippi Railroad Co. at Wyoming. The control became vested in the Minneapolis and St. Louis Railway Company May 1, 1880, which at that time contemplated a line from White Bear, Minnesota to Taylors Falls, Minnesota, with an ultimate extension to Lake Superior. The Saint Paul and Duluth Railroad Company was constructing a line from Wyoming, Minnesota to Taylors Falls and to avoid the construction of competitive lines to the same point an agreement was entered into May 1, 1880, under which the line from White Bear was abandoned.

2. **Construction and Purchases**

L.A.File 140

This company constructed the line from Centre City,

Minnesota to Taylors Falls, Minnesota, a distance of 10.09 miles, between May and November 1880.

M.B.128
p.135

The line from Wyoming, Minnesota to Centre City, 10.50 miles, was purchased from the Saint Paul and Duluth Railroad Company May 1, 1880. It was constructed between August 1879 and August 1880.

3. Operation

	From	To	Miles	Date
(1)	Wyoming	Centre City	10.50	Aug.23,1880 to Oct.12,1880
(2)	Wyoming	Centre City	10.50	Oct.12,1880 to Aug. 1,1883
(2)	Centre City	Taylors Falls	10.09	Nov. 8,1880 to Aug. 1,1883
(3)	Wyoming	Taylors Falls	20.59	Aug. 1,1883 to Nov.12,1898

L.A.File 140

(1) Operated by the M. and St.L.Ry.Co. under agreement dated May 1, 1880.

A.S.Docs.
370
and
368

(2) Operated jointly by the M. & St.L. Ry.Co. and the St.P.& D. R.R. Co. under lease of October 12,1880, in which the St.P.& D. R.R. Co. had a half interest.

(3) August 1, 1883 the St.P.& D. R.R. Co. acquired the other half interest in the lease and from that time on conducted sole operation.

4. Present Status of Corporation

No action has been taken to dissolve the corporation

but having parted with its assets it is not active.

The records are in the custody of Mr. R. H. Relf, the Assistant Secretary of the Northern Pacific Railway Co. at Saint Paul, Minnesota.

5. <u>Chain of Title</u>

	Portion of Line	From	To	Date	Form of Transfer
M.B.128 p.135	Wyoming to Centre City	St.P.& D. R.R.Co.	T.F.& L.S. R.R.Co.	May 1,1880	Deed
A.S.Doc. 1036	All	T.F.& L. S.R.R.Co.	St.P.& D. R.R.Co.	Nov.12,1898	Deed
A.S.Doc. 300	All	St.P.& D. R.R.Co.	N.P.Ry.Co.	June 15,1900	Deed

SCHEDULE OF INSTRUMENTS AND RECORDS

File Ref.	Description
A.S.Doc. 10011	Articles of Incorperation of Taylor Falls and Lake Superior Railroad Company.
M.B.128 p.135	Deed of May 1, 1880, by which the St.P. and D.R.R. Co. conveyed its line from Wyoming to Centre City to T. F. and L.S.R.R.Co.
A.S.Doc. 370	Lease of Oct. 12, 1880 from T.F.& L.S.R.R.Co. to Minneapolis and Saint Louis Railway Company.
A.S.Doc. 368	Lease of Oct. 12, 1880 covering the System of T.F.& L.S.R.R.Co. which lease was held jointly by St.P.& D.R.R.Co. and M.& St.L.R.R.Co. until August 1, 1883 when St.P.& D.R.R.Co. acquired the full interest in the lease.
A.S.Doc. 1036	Deed of Nov. 12, 1898 by which T.F. and L.S.R.R.Co. conveyed its property to St.P.& D.R.R.Co., excepting its land grant, proceeds from sale of these lands, etc.
A.S.Doc. 300	Deed of June 15, 1900, by which St.P.& D.R.R.Co. conveyed its entire property (except land grant) to N.P.Ry.Co.

L.A.File 140 — Land Assistant's file "Data used in compiling return to Order No.20 - Corporate History".

SAINT PAUL AND DULUTH RAILROAD COMPANY

Chart No.15
Place No.18
Map No.12 & 12¹

1. Incorporation

A.S.Doc. 1191

Incorporated under the general laws of the State of Minnesota.

Articles are dated June 27, 1877 and were filed with the Secretary of State June 28, 1877, and filed a second time November 28, 1898.

Organization effected June 27, 1877.

L.A.File 140

2. Construction and Purchases

The following lines were constructed:

	From	To	Miles	Date
Br.Line	Carlton (formerly N.P.Jct.) Minn.	Cloquet, Minn.	5.48 / 1.16	July 1,1877 to Dec.1879 / Late in 1880
Br.Line	Groningen (formerly Miller) Minn.	Banning, Minn.	4.73	July 1891 to June 1892
# Br.Line	Wyoming, Minn.	Centre City, Minn.	10.50	Aug.1879 to Aug.1880

M.B.128 p.135

\# Deeded May 1, 1880 to Taylors Falls and Lake Superior Railroad Company.

The following lines were purchased:

A.S.Doc. 1365

Main line of Lake Superior and Mississippi Railroad

A.S.Doc. 772

Company from St.Paul, Minn. to Duluth, Minn., 155.00 miles July 17, 1877. The N.P. R.R. Co. owned an one-half interest in this line between Duluth and Thomson.

A.S.Doc. 8857

Main line of The Grantsburg, Rush City and St.Cloud Railroad Company from Rush City, Minn. to the St.Croix River, 5.14 miles March 2, 1899.

A.S.Doc. 1029

Main line of the St.Cloud, Grantsburg and Ashland Railway Company from the St.Croix River to Grantsburg, Wis., 11.90 miles, March 2, 1899.

A.S.Doc. 1030

Main line of The Stillwater and St.Paul Railroad Company from White Bear, Minn. to Stillwater, Minn., 12.74 miles, March 2, 1899.

A.S.Doc. 1036

Main line of the Taylors Falls and Lake Superior Railroad Company from Wyoming, Minn. to Taylors Falls, 20.59 miles, November 12, 1898.

A.S.Doc. 712

Main line of the Duluth Shortline Railway Company from Thomson, Minn. to West Superior, Wis., 17.75 miles, November 11, 1898.

3. Operation

The following lines were operated for the periods stated; the lines of the Lake Superior and Mississippi Railroad and Duluth Shortline Railway being operated as main line and the others as branch lines:

	From	To	Miles	From	To
(1)	St. Paul	Thomson	132.50	July 1, 1877	June 30, 1900
(1)	Thomson	Fond du Lac	7.19	July 1, 1877	1892
(1)	Fond du Lac	Duluth	15.31	July 1, 1877	June 30, 1900
(2)	Thomson	Minn-Wis. Line	16.21	Jan. 16, 1888	June 30, 1900
(2)	Minn.-Wis. Line	W. Superior, Wis.	1.54	"	"
	Carlton	Cloquet	5.48)	Dec. 1, 1879	June 30, 1900
			1.16)	Late in 1880	"
	Groningen	Banning	4.73	June 1, 1892	June 30, 1900
(3)	Rush City	St. Croix, River	5.14	Jan. 24, 1884	June 30, 1900
(4)	St. Croix River	Grantsburg	11.90	Jan. 24, 1884	June 30, 1900
(5)	White Bear	Stillwater	12.74	July 1, 1877	June 30, 1900
(6)	Wyoming	Taylors Falls	20.59	Oct. 12, 1880	June 30, 1900
(7)	M.&D. Jct.	St. Anthony	13.62	Aug. 1, 1882	June 30, 1900

A.S. Doc. 1365

(1) This line was purchased at public auction by Wm. H. Rhawn et al, who incorporated the Saint Paul and Duluth Railroad Company on June 27, 1877, which company began operating the property July 1, 1877, although deed was not made until July 17, 1877. Operation of the portion of the line between Thomson and Fond du Lac was

discontinued after 1892 and the track gradually removed between 1892 and 1898.

A.S.Doc. 363
(2) Operated under a lease dated September 1, 1886 until conveyed to St.P.& D.R.R.Co.

A.S.Doc. 362
(3) Operated from January 24, 1884 under a lease dated June 14, 1881 until conveyed to St.P.& D. R.R. Co.

A.S.Doc. 358
(4) Operated from January 24, 1884 under a contract dated June 1, 1897, retroactive to January 1, 1884 until conveyed to St.P.& D. R. R. Co.

M.B.294 p.85
(5) Operated under the lease made with the Lake Superior and Mississippi Railroad Company November 21, 1870, and modified February 24, 1874, until conveyed to St.P.& D. R. R. Co.

A.S.Doc. 368
(6) The St.P.& D. R. R. Co. held a half interest in a lease dated October 12, 1880, the other half interest being held by the Minneapolis and St.Louis Railroad Company, the property being operated jointly. On August 1, 1883, the St.P.& D. R. R. Co. acquired the other half interest in this lease and conducted sole operation under its terms, until it received a conveyance of the property.

A.S.Doc. 392
(7) Operated under a lease made with M.& St.L.Ry. Co. July 5, 1883. Term 99 years from August 1, 1882.

4. <u>Present Status of Corporation</u>

No action has been taken to dissolve the corporation

but having parted with its assets it is not active.

The records are in the custody of Mr. R. H. Relf, the Assistant Secretary of the Northern Pacific Railway Company at Saint Paul, Minnesota.

5. Chain of Title

	From	To	Date	Form of Transfer
A.S.Doc. 1365	L.S.& M.R.R.Co.	St.P.& D.R.R. Co.	July 17, 1877	Deed
A.S.Doc. 712	D.S.L.Ry.Co.	St.P.& D.R.R. Co.	Nov. 11, 1898	Deed
A.S.Doc. 1036	T.F.& L.S.R.R. Co.	St.P.& D.R.R. Co.	Nov. 12, 1898	Deed
A.S.Doc. 1029	St.C.G.& A.Ry. Co.	St.P.& D.R.R. Co.	Mar. 2, 1899	Deed
A.S.Doc. 8857	G.R.C.& St.C. R.R.Co.	St.P.& D.R.R. Co.	Mar. 2, 1899	Deed
A.S.Doc. 1030	S.& St.P.R.R. Co.	St.P.& D.R.R. Co.	Mar. 2, 1899	Deed
A.S.Doc. 300	St.P.& D.R.R. Co.	N.P.Ry.Co.	June 15, 1900	Deed

SCHEDULE OF INSTRUMENTS AND RECORDS

File Ref.	Description
A.S.Doc. 1191	Articles of Incorporation of Saint Paul and Duluth Railroad Company.
M.B.128 p.135	Reference to deed of May 1, 1880, from St.P.& D. R. R. Co. to Taylors Falls and Lake Superior Railroad Company conveying line extending from Wyoming, Minnesota, to Centre City, Minnesota, 10.50 miles.
A.S.Doc. 1365	Deed of July 17, 1877, by which Lake Superior and Mississippi Railroad Company conveyed its entire property to St.P.& D. R. R. Co.
A.S.Doc. 772	Deed Jan. 1, 1872, L.S.&M. R. R. to N.P.R.R.Co. one-half interest in line Thomson to Duluth.
A.S.Doc. 8857	Deed of March 2, 1899, by which The Grantsburg, Rush City and St.Cloud Railroad Company conveyed its entire property to St.P.& D. R. R. Co.
A.S.Doc. 1029	Deed of March 2, 1899, by which St.Cloud, Grantsburg and Ashland Railway Company conveyed its entire property to St.P.& D. R. R. Co.
A.S.Doc. 1030	Deed of March 2, 1899, by which The Stillwater and

St. Paul Railroad Company conveyed its entire property to St.P.& D. R. R. Co.

A.S.Doc. 1036
Deed of November 12, 1898, by which Taylors Falls and Lake Superior Railroad Company conveyed its entire property to St.P.& D. R. R. Co.

A.S.Doc. 712
Deed of November 11, 1898, by which Duluth Short Line Railway Company conveyed its entire property to St.P.& D. R. R. Co.

A.S.Doc. 363
Lease of September 1, 1886, under which St.P.& D. R. R. Co. operated the entire system of Duluth Shortline Railway Company.

A.S.Doc. 362
Lease of June 14, 1881, under which St.P.& D. R.R. Co. operated the entire system of The Grantsburg, Rush City and St. Cloud Railroad Company.

A.S.Doc. 358
Contract of June 1, 1897, under which St.P.& D.R.R. Co. operated the entire system of St.Cloud, Grantsburg and Ashland Railway Company.

M.B.294 p.85
Reference to lease of November 21, 1870, modified February 24, 1874, under which St.P.& D. R. R. Co. operated the entire system of The Stillwater and St.Paul Railroad Company.

A.S.Doc. 368   Lease of October 12, 1880, covering the system of Taylors Falls and Lake Superior Railroad Company, which lease was held jointly by St.P.& D.R.R. Co. and Minneapolis and St.Louis Railroad Company until August 1, 1883, when St.P.& D.R.R.Co. acquired the full interest in the lease.

A.S.Doc. 392   Lease of July 5, 1883, from Minneapolis & St.Louis Railway Company to St.P.& D.R.R.Co. covering the line of the Minneapolis and Duluth Railroad Company extending from M.& D. Jctn., Minn. to St.Anthony, Minn., 13.62 miles.

A.S.Doc. 300   Deed of June 15, 1900, by which St.P.& D.R.R.Co. conveyed its entire property (except Land Grant) to Northern Pacific Railway Company.

L.A.File 140   Land Assistant's file "Data used in compiling return to Order No.20 - Corporate History".

NORTHERN PACIFIC, FERGUS AND BLACK HILLS RAILROAD COMPANY

Chart No.28 & 17
Place No.35 & 44
Map No.13

1. Incorporation

Chap.66
Spl.Laws
1853

Chap.57
Spl.Laws
1870

M.B.362
p.2 to
7 and
L.A.File
140

A.S.599-16

A.S.599-16

Minnesota Western Railroad Company was created by Act of the Legislature of the Territory of Minnesota March 3, 1853, and by authority of a Special Act of 1870 the name was changed to Minneapolis and St.Louis Railway Company.

The two acts referred to authorized, among other things, a railroad running from Fergus Falls, Minn. to connections with the Northern Pacific Railroad and St.Paul and Pacific Railroad. The M.& St.L.Ry.Co. issued special stock covering the line, which stock was held by George B.Wright, James Compton and Walter C.Bacon, whom the M.& St.L.Ry.Co. authorized February 10, 1875, to form the Minnesota Northern Railroad Co. The company was incorporated under the general laws of the State of Minnesota; its articles are dated January 21, 1878, and were filed with the Secretary of State February 5, 1878.

Organization effected February 5, 1878.

Amended articles providing for the construction of additional lines were filed with the Secretary of State January 4, 1881, and further amended articles providing

for other additional lines and changing the name to
Northern Pacific, Fergus and Black Hills Railroad Company were filed with the Secretary of State April 18, 1881.

2. Construction

L.A.File 140

The N.P.R.R.Co. constructed for account of the N.P.F. and B.H. R.R. Co. the following lines:

	From	To	Miles	Date
Main Line	Wadena, Minn.	Breckenridge, Minn.	75.00	June 1881 to Nov. 1882
# Main Line	Breckenridge, Minn.	Milnor, N.D.	42.10	Oct. 1882 approx. to Aug. 22, 1883

Main Line Total - 117.10

Br. Line	Fergus Falls, Minn.	Pelican Rapids, Minn.	32.20	June 1881 to Oct. 1882
Br. Line	Fairview Jct.	Adams (formerly Fairview) now Mathews	3.06	Aug. to Sept. 1884

Branch Line Total - 25.26

A.S.Doc. R.R.67

#October 1, 1882, an agreement was made between the St. Paul, Minneapolis and Manitoba Railway Company and the N.P.R.R.Co., under which the St.P.M.& M. Ry.Co. conveyed to the N.P.F.& B.H.R.R.Co. the right of way and grade of the line between Wahpeton (near Breckenridge) and Milnor, the construction being completed by the N.P.R.R.Co. for account of the N.P.F. and B.H.R.R.Co.

This agreement was a general settlement between the companies concerned and provided for the sale and use of various lines.

3. Operation

A.S.Doc. 88

This company's property operated by N.P.R.R.Co. under a contract dated October 20, 1882 until August 15, 1893; by the receivers of the N.P.R.R.Co. from August 15, 1893 to August 31, 1896 without a contract until lease was made November 12, 1894; and by the N.P.Ry.Co. from September 1, 1896 to April 21, 1898 with no formal agreement.

A.S.Doc. Rec.34

Receivers were appointed for this company's line in Minnesota, October 18, 1893 and in North Dakota October 13, 1893.

L.A.File 140

Details of operation as follows:

		From	To	Miles	Date
	Main Line	Wadena	Breckenridge	75.00	Nov.10,1882 to April 21,1898
	Main Line	Wahpeton	Milnor	42.10	Sept.1.1883 to April 21,1898
(1)	Br. Line	Fergus Falls	Pelican Rapids	22.20	
(2)	Br. Line	Fairview Jct.	Adams(formerly Fairview)	3.06	1884 to Oct. 19, 1887

(1) Sold to St.P.M.& M.Ry.Co. Not operated.

(2) Operated as part of the South-Eastern Dakota R.R.Co. after October 19, 1887.

4. **Present Status of Corporation**

L.A.File 140

No action has been taken to dissolve this corporation but having parted with its assets it is not active.

The records are in the custody of Mr. R. H. Relf, the Assistant Secretary of the Northern Pacific Railway Co. at Saint Paul, Minnesota.

5. **Chain of Title**

	Portion of Line	From	To	Date	Form of Transfer
A.S.Doc. 1202	Wahpeton to Milnor	St.P.M.&M. Ry.Co.	N.P.F.& B. H.R.R.Co.	April 12,1883	Deed
A.S.Doc. 54	Fergus Falls to Pelican Rapids	N.P.F.& B.H.R.R. Co.	St.P.M.&M. Ry.Co.	Nov. 28,1882	Deed
A.S.Doc. 130	Wadena to Milnor and Fairview Jct. to Adams	N.P.F.& B.H.R.R. Co.	N.P.Ry. Co.	April 21,1898 # Jan. 6,1900	Deed Deed

\# Deed of January 6, 1900 given to replace deed of April 21, 1898, which was destroyed by fire.

The portion of the line from Fairview Jct. to Adams is specifically covered by the deed of the South-Eastern Dakota Railroad Co. to the N.P.Ry.Co. April 21, 1898. The title to the property, however, stood in the name of the N.P.F.and B.H. Co., and there being no conveyance to the S.E.D.R.R.Co., title is considered as having passed to the N.P.Ry.Co. by deed A.S.Doc.130 as referenced above.

SCHEDULE OF INSTRUMENTS AND RECORDS

File Ref.	Description
A.S. File 599-16	Articles of Incorporation of Minnesota Northern Railroad Company.
A.S. File 599-16	Amended Articles providing for Construction of additional lines and change of name to Northern Pacific, Fergus and Black Hills Railroad Company.
A.S. Doc. R.R. 67	Agreement of Oct. 1, 1882 between St. Paul, Minneapolis and Manitoba Railway Company and N.P.R.R.Co. covering sale and use of various properties.
A.S. Doc. 88	Contract of Oct. 20, 1882, by which the N.P.R.R.Co. operated the property of the N.P.F.& B.H.R.R.Co.
A.S. Doc. 54	Deed of Nov. 28, 1882, by which the N.P.F.& B.H.R.R. conveyed its line from Fergus Falls to Pelican Rapids to the St.P.M.& M.Ry.Co.
A.S. Doc. 130	Deed of April 21, 1898, by which the N.P.F.& B.H.R.R.Co. conveyed its entire system to the N.P.Ry.Co.
A.S. Doc. 1202	Deed of April 12, 1883, by which the St.P.M.& M.Ry.Co. conveyed its line from Wahpeton to Milnor to N.P.F.& B.H.R.R.Co.

L.A.File   Land Assistant's file "Data used in compiling re-
   140   turn to Order No.20 - Corporate History".

UNION DEPOT, STREET RAILWAY AND TRANSFER COMPANY
OF STILLWATER

Chart No.33 & 18
Place No.47 & 56
Map No.14

1. Incorporation

A.S.Doc. 10012

The Stillwater Street Railway and Transfer Company was incorporated under the general laws of the State of Minnesota.

Articles are dated March 14, 1878, and were filed with the Secretary of State March 15, 1878.

Date of organization is unknown.

Amended articles were filed with the Secretary of State November 25, 1881, changing the name to Union Depot, Street Railway and Transfer Company of Stillwater.

2. Construction

L.A.File 140

This company constructed and maintained a terminal system in Stillwater, Minnesota for the transfer of freight and passengers between the railroads entering the city from the north and those entering it from the south, with the necessary switches, sidings, depots, station grounds, warehouses and connecting tracks. First track was laid in Stimpson's Alley (now Water St.) in 1878, and in 1882 this was extended on Water and Lake Streets as far north as Laurel St. This company owned or controlled practically all the property between the north line of Myrtle St. and Pine St., and lying east of their tracks in Stimpson's Alley, with scattered pieces of land, and franchise rights, as far north as E.Sycamore St. In 1887 the receivers of this company constructed a union station which was opened to the public in January 1888.

L.A.File 140

3. **Operation**

This property was operated as the S.St.Ry.& Tfr. Co. from 1878 until November 25, 1881, when name was changed to U.D.St.Ry.& Tfr. Co. of Stillwater and operation under this company continued until early in 1885, when Geo. M. Brush was appointed receiver. He resigned and E.D.Buffington was appointed in his stead June 28, 1887; the U.D.St.Ry. & Tfr. Co. conveying all its property and rights to him by deed dated August 6, 1887. J.C.O'Gorman was appointed co-receiver with Buffington Sept. 20, 1887. Operation under the receivership continued until April 23, 1888, when property was sold to F. M. Prince, conveyance to him being executed by E. D. Buffington and J.C.O'Gorman as receivers on May 28, 1888. On the same date F.M.Prince conveyed the property to the Stillwater Union Depot & Transfer Co., excepting certain real estate as described in the deed.

R.W.Deed 46

A.S.Doc. 10058

A.S.Doc. 10058

4. Present Status of Corporation

No action has been taken to dissolve the corporation but having parted with its assets it is not active.

The Northern Pacific Ry. Co. is not in possession of the records of this company and does not know who is their custodian.

5. Chain of Title

	From	To	Date	Form of Transfer
A.S.Doc. 10012	S.St.Ry.& T.Co.	U.D.,St.Ry.& T. Co. of S.	Nov. 25, 1881	Change of name
R.W.Deed 46	U.D.,St.R.& T. Co. of S.	E.D.Buffington, Receiver	Aug. 6, 1887	Deed
A.S.Doc. 10058	E.D.Buffington & J.C.O'Gorman Receivers	F.M.Prince	May 28, 1888	Deed
A.S.Doc. 10058	F.M.Prince	S.U.D.&T.Co.	May 28, 1888	Deed
A.S.Doc. 10058	S.U.D.&T.Co. by Edward Simonton, Master in Chancery	Stephen M.Crosby, Trustee	May 25, 1896	Master's Deed
A.S.Doc. 10058	Stephen M.Crosby, Trustee	U.D.&T.Co. of S.	Dec. 1, 1896	Deed
A.S.Doc. 1240	U.D.& T.Co. of S.	N.P.Ry.Co.	June 21, 1902	Deed

SCHEDULE OF INSTRUMENTS AND RECORDS

File Ref.	Description
A.S.Doc. 10012	Articles of Incorporation of the S.St.Ry.& Tfr. Co.
A.S.Doc. 10012	Amended Articles changing name to U.D.St.Ry.& Tfr. Co. of Stillwater.
R.W.Deed 46	Deed dated Aug. 6, 1887 by which U.D.St.Ry.& Tfr. Co. of Stillwater conveyed all its property and rights to E. D. Buffington, as receiver.
A.S.Doc. 10058	Deed dated May 28, 1888 by which E.D.Buffington and J.C.O'Gorman, receivers, conveyed to F.M.Prince all the property of the U.D.St.Ry.& Tfr.Co. of Stillwater.
A.S.Doc. 10058	Deed dated May 28, 1888 by which F.M.Prince conveyed to the S.U.D.& Tfr. Co. the property of the U.D.St.Ry.& Tfr. Co. of Stillwater, excepting certain real estate.
A.S.Doc. 10058	Deed dated May 25, 1896 by which Edward Simonton, Master in Chancery, conveyed to Stephen M.Crosby, Trustee, the property of the S.U.D.& Tfr. Co.
A.S.Doc. 10058	Deed dated Dec. 1, 1896 by which Stephen M.Crosby, Trustee, conveyed the above property to the U.D.& Tfr.Co.

of Stillwater.

A.S.Doc. 1240 — Deed of June 21, 1902, by which the Union Depot & Transfer Company of Stillwater conveyed its entire property to the N.P.Ry.Co.

L.A.File 140 — Land Assistant's File "Data used in compiling return to Order 20, Corporate History."

STILLWATER UNION DEPOT & TRANSFER COMPANY

Chart No.70, 73 and 101
Place No.29, 38 and 20
Map No.14

1. Incorporation

A.S.Doc. 10013

Incorporated under the general laws of the State of Minnesota.

Articles are dated March 28, 1888, and were filed with the Secretary of State April 17, 1888.

M.B.659 p.10

Date of organization May 25, 1888.

2. Construction and Purchases

A.S.Doc. 10058
and
L.A.File 140

R.W.Deed 73

The property of the Union Depot Street Railway and Transfer Co., except certain real estate, was conveyed to this Company by F.M.Prince, May 28, 1888. This property consisted of an extensive terminal system with appurtenant spurs, sidings, engine facilities and a union depot. By deed dated April 18, 1891 land was acquired which included office building known as the Lumberman's Exchange Building.

3. Operation

L.A.File 140

The property was operated by this company from May 28, 1888 to Sept. 13, 1893, on which date E.D.Buffington was appointed receiver, and the receiver operated the property until discharged by the court July 8, 1896. On May 8, 1896 the property was sold by order

A.S.Doc. 10058 — of the court, and Edward Simonton, Master in Chancery, executed conveyance to Stephen M. Crosby, Trustee, May 25, 1896. Operation under Crosby continued until Dec. 1, 1896, on which date he conveyed the property to the Union Depot & Transfer Co. of Stillwater.

4. Present Status of Corporation

No action has been taken to dissolve this corporation, but having parted with its assets it is not active. The records are in the custody of Mr. R.H.Relf, the Assistant Secretary of the Northern Pacific Ry.Co. at Saint Paul, Minnesota.

5. Chain of Title

	From	To	Date	Form of Transfer
A.S.Doc. 10058	U.D.St.Ry.&Tfr.Co.	F.M.Prince	May 28,1888	Deed
A.S.Doc. 10058	F.M.Prince, et ux	S.U.D.&Tfr. Co.	May 28,1888	Deed
A.S.Doc. 10058	S.U.D.& T.Co. by Edward Simonton, Master in Chancery	Stephen M. Crosby, Trustee	May 25,1896	Master's Deed
A.S.Doc. 10058	Stephen M.Crosby, Trustee	U.D.& T.Co. of S.	Dec. 1,1896	Deed
A.S.Doc. 1240	U.D.& T.Co.of S.	N.P.Ry.Co.	June 21,1902	Deed

160

SCHEDULE OF INSTRUMENTS AND RECORDS

File Ref.	Description
A.S.Doc. 10013	Articles of Incorporation, Stillwater Union Depot & Transfer Co.
A.S.Doc. 1240	Deed of June 21, 1902, by which the Union Depot & Transfer Company of Stillwater conveyed its entire property to N.P. Ry. Co.
M.B.659 p.10	Location of date of organization in Minute Book.
A.S.Doc. 10058	Deed dated May 28, 1888, by which the U.D.St.Ry. & Tfr. Co. property and rights were conveyed to F.M. Prince.
A.S.Doc. 10058	Deed dated May 28, 1888, by which F.M. Prince conveyed above property to S.U.D.& Tfr. Co., excepting certain real estate.
A.S.Doc. 10058	Deed dated May 25, 1896, by which Edward Simonton, Master in Chancery, conveyed the property of the S.U.D. & Tfr. Co. to Stephen M. Crosby, Trustee.
A.S.Doc. 10058	Deed dated Dec. 1, 1896, by which Stephen M.Crosby, Crosby, Trustee, conveyed all the property and rights of the S.U.D.& Tfr. Co. to the U.D.& Tfr. Co. of Stillwater.

L.A.File   Land Assistant's file "Data used in compiling
   140   return to Order No.20 - Corporate History".

UNION DEPOT & TRANSFER COMPANY OF STILLWATER

Chart No.102
Place No.13
Map No.14

1. Incorporation

A.S.Doc. 10014

Incorporated under the general laws of the State of Minnesota.

Articles are dated October 24, 1896, and were filed with the Secretary of State October 24, 1896.

Date of organization November 9, 1896.

2. Construction and Purchases

A.S.Doc. 10058

and

L.A.File 140

This company constructed no lines but purchased December 1, 1896 from Stephen M. Crosby, Trustee, the property of the Stillwater Union Depot & Transfer Company, which was a terminal system, with appurtenant spurs, sidings, engine facilities, a union depot and an office building known as the Lumberman's Exchange Building.

3. Operation

L.A.File 140

The property was operated by this company from December 1, 1896 to June 21, 1902.

4. Present Status of Corporation

No action has been taken to dissolve the corporation, but having parted with its assets it is not active.

The records are in the custody of Mr. R. H. Relf, the Assistant Secretary of the Northern Pacific Ry. Co. at Saint Paul, Minnesota.

5. <u>Chain of Title</u>

	From	To	Date	Form of Transfer
A.S.Doc. 10058	U.D.St.Ry.&Tfr.Co.	F.M.Prince	May 28, 1888	Deed
A.S.Doc. 10058	F.M.Prince	S.U.D.&Tfr. Co.	May 28, 1888	Deed
A.S.Doc. 10058	S.U.D.&Tfr.Co. by Edward Simonton, Master in Chancery	Stephen M. Crosby, Trustee	May 25, 1896	Deed
A.S.Doc. 10058	Stephen M. Crosby, Trustee	U.D.&Tfr.Co. of Stillwater	Dec. 1, 1896	Deed
A.S.Doc. 1240	U.D.&T.Co. of S.	N.P.Ry.Co.	June 21, 1902	Deed

SCHEDULE OF INSTRUMENTS AND RECORDS

File Ref.	Description
A.S.Doc. 10014	Articles of Incorporation of the U.D.& Tfr.Co. of Stillwater.
A.S.Doc. 1240	Deed of June 21, 1902, by which Union Depot & Transfer Company of Stillwater conveyed its entire property to N.P.Ry.Co.
A.S.Doc. 10058	Deed dated May 28, 1888, by which the Union Depot Street Ry.& Tfr. Co. property and rights were conveyed to F. M. Prince.
A.S.Doc. 10058	Deed dated May 28, 1888, by which F.M.Prince conveyed the above property to the Stillwater Union Depot & Tfr. Co. excepting certain real estate.
A.S.Doc. 10058	Deed dated May 25, 1896, by which Edward Simonton, Master in Chancery, conveyed the property of the S.U.D. & Tfr. Co. to Stephen M. Crosby, Trustee.
A.S.Doc. 10058	Deed dated Dec. 1, 1896, by which Stephen M.Crosby, Trustee, conveyed the above property to Union Depot & Transfer Co. of Stillwater.
L.A.File 140	Land Assistant's file "Data used in compiling return to Order No.20 - Corporate History".

SAINT CLOUD,-GRANTSBURG AND ASHLAND RAILWAY COMPANY

Chart No.19
Place No.28
Map No.15

1. Incorporation

A.S.Doc. 1367

Incorporated under the general laws of the State of Wisconsin.

Articles are dated June 10, 1878, and were filed with the Secretary of State June 13, 1878.

Amended articles filed with the Secretary of State May 4, 1885.

Organization effected June 15, 1878.

2. Construction

L.A.File 140

The St.Paul and Duluth Railroad Co. constructed for account of this company the line from Grantsburg, Wis. to the St.Croix River, including the bridge over the River, a total distance of 11.90 miles. Construction was commenced in 1879, ties were distributed and grading completed December 31, 1881. Bridge over the St.Croix River was built in 1881-1883. Rail was laid and the road finally finished January 1884.

3. Operation

A.S.Doc. 358

The line was operated from January 24, 1884 until March 2, 1899 by the S.P.& D. R. R. Co. under a contract dated June 1, 1897, and made retroactive to January 1, 1884.

4. **Present Status of Corporation**

No action has been taken to dissolve the corporation, but having parted with its assets it is not active.

The records are in the custody of Mr. R. H. Relf, the Assistant Secretary of the Northern Pacific Ry.Co. at Saint Paul, Minnesota.

5. **Chain of Title**

	From	To	Date	Form of Transfer
A.S.Doc. 1029	St.C.G.&A.R.Co.	St.P.& D.R.R.Co.	March 2,1899	Deed
A.S.Doc. 300	St.P.&D.R.R.Co.	N.P. Ry. Co.	June 15,1900	Deed

SCHEDULE OF INSTRUMENTS AND RECORDS

File Ref.	Description
A.S.Doc. 1367	Articles of Incorporation of Saint Cloud-Grantsburg and Ashland Railway Company and amendment thereto.
A.S.Doc. 358	Contract of June 1, 1897, under which property was operated by St.Paul and Duluth Railroad Company.
A.S.Doc. 1029	Deed of March 2, 1899, by which St.C.G.& A.Ry.Co. conveyed its entire property to St.P.& D. R.R. Co.
A.S.Doc. 300	Deed of June 15, 1900, by which St.P.& D. R.R. Co. conveyed its entire railway system to the N. P. Ry. Co.
L.A.File 140	Land Assistant's file "Data used in compiling return to Order No.20 - Corporate History".

THE GRANTSBURG, RUSH CITY AND ST. CLOUD RAILROAD COMPANY

Chart No. 21
Place No. 37
Map No. 16

1. Incorporation

A.S.Doc. 10015

Incorporated under the general laws of the State of Minnesota.

Articles are dated November 28, 1878, and were filed with the Secretary of State November 29, 1878.

Organization effected December 1, 1878.

2. Construction

L.A.File 140

The St. Paul and Duluth Railroad Co. partly constructed for account of this company a line from Rush City, Minn. to the St. Croix River, 5.14 miles. June 14, 1881 a lease was entered into, by the terms of which the St.P.& D. R.R. Co. completed the construction and operated the line. The work of construction began in 1880. December 31, 1881 grading was about finished. Rail was laid and road was completed in January 1884.

3. Operation

A.S.Doc. 362

The line, 5.14 miles in length, was operated by the St.P.& D. R. R. Co. under the lease of June 14, 1881, from Jan. 24, 1884 until March 2, 1899.

4. **Present Status of Corporation**

No action has been taken to dissolve the corporation but having parted with all its property it is not active.

The records are in the custody of Mr. R. H. Relf, the Assistant Secretary of the Northern Pacific Ry.Co. at Saint Paul, Minnesota.

5. **Chain of Title**

	From	To	Date	Form of Transfer
A.S.Doc. 8857	G.R.C.&St.C.R.R. Co.	St.P.& D.R.R.Co.	March 2,1899	Deed
A.S.Doc. 300	St.P.& D.R.R.Co.	N.P. Ry. Co.	June 15,1900	Deed

SCHEDULE OF INSTRUMENTS AND RECORDS

File Ref.	Description
A.S.Doc. 10015	Articles of Incorporation of G.R.C. and St.C.R.R.Co.
A.S.Doc. 362	Lease of June 14, 1881, from The G.R.C. and St.C. R.R.Co. to St.P. and D. R.R. Co.
A.S.Doc. 8857	Deed of March 2, 1899, by which the G.R.C. & St.C. Ry. Co. conveyed its entire property to St.P.& D. R.R. Co
A.S.Doc. 300	Deed of June 15, 1900, by which St.P.& D. R.R. Co. conveyed its entire railway system to the N.P.Ry.Co. (Land Grant excepted).
L.A.File 140	Land Assistant's file "Data used in compiling return to Order No.20 - Corporate History".

THE LITTLE FALLS AND DAKOTA RAILROAD COMPANY

Chart No.22 & 25
Place No.97 & 88
Map No.17

1. Incorporation

A.S.Doc. 10006

Incorporated under the general laws of the State of Minnesota.

Articles are dated January 24, 1879, and were filed with the Secretary of State February 10, 1879.

Organization effected March 26, 1879.

A.S.Doc. 10006

Amended Articles filed with the Secretary of State June 28, 1880, making some changes in the routes of the lines authorized and eliminating the word "The" from the corporate name.

A.S.Doc. 10006

Amended Articles filed with the Secretary of State July 11, 1881, limiting the amount of liability which the company may incur.

2. Construction and Purchases

The N.P.R.R.Co. constructed for account of this company a main line from Little Falls, Minn. to Morris, Minn., 87.85 miles, between July 1881 and November 1882, including a branch to the falls at Little Falls, 6200 feet long, constructed in 1882.

A.S.Doc. R.R.67

This company acquired the right of way and grade of the St.Cloud and Lake Traverse Railway Company from

Morris to a point within 3 miles of the west end of Lake Whipple, but as it paralleled this company's line to Morris no use has been made of it.

3. Operation

A.S.Doc. R.R.125

A.S.Doc. Rec.40

The property of this company was operated by the N.P.R.R.Co. from November 1, 1882 to August 15, 1893 under contract of October 20, 1882; by the Receivers of the N.P.R.R.Co. from August 15, 1893 until August 31, 1896 under lease of November 7, 1894, and by the N.P. Ry. Co. without formal contract from September 1896 until June 5, 1900.

File 82
Compt.
Box 17
M.B.379
p.227

Receivers for this company were appointed October 18, 1893 and they were dismissed October 31, 1894.

4. Present Status of Corporation

A.S.Doc. 10006

No action has been taken to dissolve this corporation but having parted with its assets it is not active.

The records are in the custody of Mr. R. H. Relf, the Assistant Secretary of the Northern Pacific Railway Co. at Saint Paul, Minnesota.

5. Chain of Title

	From	To	Date	Form of Transfer
A.S.Doc. 490	L.F.& D.R.R.Co.	N.P.Ry.Co.	June 5, 1900	Deed

SCHEDULE OF INSTRUMENTS AND RECORDS

File Ref.	Description
A.S.Doc. 10006	Articles of Incorporation of The Little Falls and Dakota Railroad Company.
A.S.Doc. 10006	Amended Articles dated June 28, 1880.
A.S.Doc. 10006	Amended Articles dated June 11, 1881.
A.S.Doc. R.R.125	Lease of Oct. 20, 1882, by which the property was operated by N.P.R.R.Co.
A.S.Doc. 490	Deed of June 5, 1900, by which the L.F.& D.R.R.Co. conveyed its entire property to the N.P.Ry.Co.
L.A.File 140	Land Assistant's file "Data used in compiling return to Order No.20 - Corporate History".
A.S.Doc. R.R.67	Contract of October 1, 1882, by which the L.F.& D. R.R.Co. acquired the right of way and grade of the St.Cloud and Lake Traverse Railway Company, Morris to Lake Whipple.
A.S.Doc. Rec.40	Lease of November 7, 1894, under which the Receivers of the N.P.R.R.Co. operated the property.
File 82 Compt. Box 17	Order appointing Receivers of L.F.& D. R.R. October 2, 1893.

M.B.379   Order dismissing Receivers of L.F.& D.R.R. October
p.227
            31, 1894.

MILL CREEK FLUME AND MANUFACTURING COMPANY

Chart No. 24
Place No. 109
Map No. 18

1. **Incorporation**

A.S.Doc.
9968

Incorporated under the general laws of the Territory of Washington.

Articles are dated February 24, 1880, and were filed with the Secretary of Territory March 1, 1880.

Date of organization is unknown.

Amended Articles changing objects of corporation were filed with the Secretary of Territory October 28, 1880.

Amended Articles further changing objects and increasing capital stock were filed with the Secretary of Territory March 31, 1882.

2. **Construction**

L.A.File
140

This company constructed the following narrow-gauge lines:

	From	To	Miles	Date
Main Line	Walla Walla, Wash.	Dixie, Wash.	11.86	1880 to 1882
Br. Line	Dudley Jct. Wash.	Tracy (formerly Dudley) Wash.	1.65	1880 to 1882

3. **Operation**

L.A.File
140

This company operated its property from 1882 until

176

about June 14, 1887, when the entire capital stock was sold to the Oregon Railway and Navigation Co., who thereafter operated the property as part of its system with no formal contract. In 1896 the O.Ry. and N. Co. was reorganized as The Oregon Railroad and Navigation Co. and continued the operation of this road until it was conveyed to them October 26, 1903.

4. Present Status of Corporation

A.S.Doc. 9968

The name of this company was stricken from the records of the Secretary of State of Washington August 23, 1909, for failure to pay annual license fees.

The N.P. Ry. Co. is not in possession of the records of this company and does not know who is their custodian.

5. Chain of Title

	From	To	Date	Form of Transfer
A.S.Doc. 10094	M.C.F.&Mfg.Co.	The O.R.R.&N.Co.	Oct.26,1903	Deed
A.S.Doc. 2390	The O.R.R.&N Co.	M.C.R.R.Co.	Nov.23,1903	Deed
A.S.Doc. 2678	M.C.R.R.Co.	The W.&C.R. Ry.Co.	Sept.8,1905	Deed
A.S.Doc. 3575	The W.&C.R. Ry.Co.	N.P.Ry.Co.	June 18,1907	Deed

SCHEDULE OF INSTRUMENTS AND RECORDS

File Ref.   **Description**

A.S.Doc. 9968   Articles of Incorporation of M.C.F. and M.Co. and Amendments thereto.

A.S.Doc. 10094   Deed of October 26, 1903, by which M.C.F. and M. Co. conveyed its railroad to The O.R.R.& N.Co.

A.S.Doc. 2390   Deed of Nov. 27, 1903, by which The O.R.R. and N.Co. conveyed to Mill Creek Railroad Company its lines from Walla Walla to Dixie and Tracy, 12.44 miles (excepting a mile of track in Walla Walla used as terminal.)

A.S.Doc. 2678 and 9368   Deed of Sept. 8, 1905, by which M.C.R.R.Co. conveyed to The Washington and Columbia River Railway Company that portion of its line from Mill Creek Jct. to Dudley (Tracy), 6.13 miles.

A.S.Doc. 3575   Deed of June 18, 1907, by which The W.& C.R.Ry.Co. conveyed its entire property to the N.P.Ry.Co.

L.A.File 140   Land Assistant's file "Data used in compiling return to Order No. 20 - Corporate History".

THE OREGON RAILROAD AND NAVIGATION COMPANY

Chart No.99
Place No.99
Map No.18

1. Incorporation

L.A.File 140

Incorporated under the general laws of the State of Oregon.

Articles are dated July 15, 1896, and were filed with the Secretary of State of Oregon July 16, 1896, and with the Secretary of State of Washington November 21, 1898.

Date of organization is unknown.

This company is a reorganization of the Oregon Railway and Navigation Co.

2. Construction and Purchases

A.S.Doc. 10094

This company constructed no lines which are herein reported but purchased October 26, 1903, from the Mill Creek Flume & Manufacturing Co. the following lines:

	From	To	Miles
Main Line	Walla Walla, Wash.	Dixie, Wash.	11.86
Br. Line	Dudley Jct., Wash.	Tracy (formerly Dudley, Wash.)	1.65

3. Operation

L.A.File 140

The O.R.R.& N. Co. operated this property from July 16, 1896 with no formal contract until January 16,

1905, when operation ceased to permit reconstruction of
line. The operation after the title passed to the

M.B.530
p.27

Mill Creek Railroad Company was carried on by the
O.R.R.& N. Co. under a lease dated December 10, 1903.

4. **Present Status of Corporation**

The corporation is still in existence.

L.A.File
140

The records are in the custody of Mr. Alex.Millar,
Secretary, Union Pacific System, 165 Broadway, New York
City.

5. **Chain of Title**

	From	To	Date	Form of Transfer
A.S.Doc. 10094	M.C.F.& M.Co.	The O.R.R.&N.Co.	Oct.26,1903	Deed
A.S.Doc. 2390	The O.R.R.&N. Co.	M.C.R.R.Co.	Nov.23,1903	Deed
A.S.Doc. 2678	M.C.R.R.Co.	The W.&C.R.Ry. Co.	Sept.8,1905	Deed
A.S.Doc. 3575	The W.&C.R. Ry.Co.	N.P.Ry.Co.	June 18,1907	Deed

180

SCHEDULE OF INSTRUMENTS AND RECORDS

File Ref.	Description
A.S.Doc. 10094	Deed of October 26, 1903, by which the M.C.F.& M. Co. conveyed to The O.R.R.& N. Co. its lines from Walla Walla to Dixie and Tracy, 12.44 miles.
A.S.Doc. 2390	Deed of November 23, 1903, by which The O.R.R. and N.Co. conveyed to Mill Creek Railroad Company its lines from Walla Walla to Dixie and Tracy, 12.44 miles, (excepting one mile of track in Walla Walla for terminal use).
A.S.Doc. 2678	Deed of Sept. 8, 1905, by which Mill Creek Railroad Company conveyed to The Washington and Columbia River Railway Company its line from Mill Creek Jct. to Tracy, 6.13 miles.
A.S.Doc. 3575	Deed of June 18, 1907, by which The W.& C.R.Ry. Co. conveyed its entire property to the N.P. Ry. Co.
L.A.File 140	Land Assistant's file "Data used in compiling return to Order No.20 - Corporate History".
M.B.530 p.27	Lease of December 10, 1903, by which The O.R.R.& N. Co. operated the property of the M.C.R.R.Co.

THE SAINT PAUL, MINNEAPOLIS AND MANITOBA RAILWAY COMPANY

Chart No.23
Place No.43
Map No.19

1. Incorporation

L.A.File 140

This company was organized May 23, 1879, for the purpose of purchasing St.Paul and Pacific Railroad Company property sold under foreclosure. The purchases and organization were ratified and confirmed by an Act of the Legislature of the State of Minnesota, approved March 7, 1881, and entitled "An Act confirming the organization and certain purchases of the Saint Paul, Minneapolis and Manitoba Railway Company, and in relation to the Charter, powers, franchises and property of said Company".

Chap.412 Spl.Laws Minn. p.960

2. Construction and Purchases

L.A.File 140

This company acquired the right of way for and partially constructed the grade for a line extending from Wahpeton, North Dakota to Milnor, North Dakota, 39.50 miles, the grading being done between August 1881 and October 1882.

A.S.Doc. 54

This company purchased the branch line of the Northern Pacific, Fergus and Black Hills Railroad Company extending from Fergus Falls, Minn. to Pelican Rapids, Minn.

22.20 miles, November 28, 1882.

3. <u>Operation</u>

This company operated no lines of interest in connection with this report.

4. <u>Present Status of Corporation</u>

This corporation is still in existence.

The records are in the custody of Mr. L. E. Katzenbach, Secretary Great Northern Railway Co., St. Paul, Minnesota.

5. <u>Chain of Title</u>

	From	To	Date	Form of Transfer
A.S.Doc. 1202	St.P.M.&M.Ry.	N.P.F.&B.H. R.R.Co.	April 12, 1883	Deed
A.S.Doc. 130	N.P.F.&B.H. R.R.Co.	N.P.Ry.Co.	April 21, 1898	Deed

SCHEDULE OF INSTRUMENTS AND RECORDS

File Ref.   Description

A.S.Doc. 67   Agreement dated October 1, 1882 between St.P.M.& M. Ry.Co. and Northern Pacific, Fergus and Black Hills Railroad Company covering exchange of property.

A.S.Doc. 130   Deed of April 21, 1898, by which the N.P.F.& B.H. R.R.Co. conveyed its entire property to the N.P.Ry.Co.

A.S.Doc. 54   Deed of Nov. 28, 1882, by which N.P.F.& B.H.R.R.Co. conveyed its Pelican Rapids Branch to St.P.M.& M. Ry.Co.

A.S.Doc. 1202   Deed of April 12, 1883, by which St.P.M.& M. Ry.Co. conveyed its line from Wahpeton to Milnor to N.P.F.& B.H. R.R.Co.

L.A.File 140   Land Assistant's file "Data used in compiling return to Order No.20 - Corporate History".

ROCKY MOUNTAIN RAILROAD COMPANY OF MONTANA

Chart No. 29
Place No. 70
Map No. 20

1. **Incorporation**

File A.S.
599-27

Incorporated under the general laws of the Territory of Montana.

Articles are dated July 11, 1881 and were filed with the Secretary of Territory July 18, 1881.

Organization effected August 31, 1881.

2. **Construction**

L.A.File
140

This company did no actual construction but the N.P.R.R.Co. constructed for account of this company a line from Livingston, Montana to Cinnabar, Montana, 51.70 miles, between December 20, 1882 and September 22, 1883, and partly constructed a line from Cinnabar to Gardiner, Montana, 2.90 miles in 1883.

3. **Operation**

A.S.Doc.
R.R.213

A.S.Doc.
Rec.34

The line was operated by the N.P.R.R. Co. from September 16, 1883 to August 15, 1893 under contract of August 1, 1883; by the Receivers of the N.P.R.R.Co. from August 15, 1893 until August 31, 1896 under contract of November 12, 1894, retroactive for the receivership period, and by the N.P. Ry.Co. without formal contract from September 1, 1896 until April 21, 1898, on which date the property was conveyed to the N.P.Ry.Co.

File 82
Compt.
Box 17
M.B.361
p.97

Receivers for this company were appointed October 4, 1893 and dismissed October 31, 1894.

4. Present Status of Corporation

A.S.File
599-27

No action has been taken to dissolve this corporation but having parted with its assets it is not active.

The records are in the custody of Mr. R. H. Relf, the Assistant Secretary of the Northern Pacific Railway Co. at Saint Paul, Minnesota.

5. Chain of Title

	From	To	Date	Form of Transfer
A.S.Doc. 137	R.M.R.R.Co.of M.	N.P.Ry.Co.	April 21, 1898	Deed

SCHEDULE OF INSTRUMENTS AND RECORDS

File Ref.   **Description**

A.S.File   Articles of Incorporation of Rocky Mountain Rail-
599-27
road Company of Montana.

A.S.Doc.   Lease dated Aug. 1, 1883, by which N.P.R.R.Co.
R.R.213
operated the property.

A.S.Doc.   Deed of April 21, 1898, by which R.M.R.R.Co. of
137
Mont. conveyed its entire property to N.P.Ry.Co.

L.A.File   Land Assistant's file "Data used in compiling
140
return to Order No.20 - Corporate History".

A.S.Doc.   Lease of November 12, 1894, by which the Receivers
Rec.34
of the N.P.R.R.Co. operated the property.

File 82   Order appointing Receivers of R.M.R.R.Co. of M.
Compt.
Box 17   October 4, 1893.

M.B.361   Order dismissing Receivers of R.M.R.R.Co. of M.
p.97
October 31, 1894.

FARGO AND SOUTHWESTERN RAILROAD COMPANY

Chart No.31
Place No.53
Map No.21

1. **Incorporation**

A.S.Doc.
9918

Incorporated under the general laws of the Territory of Dakota.

Articles are dated August 16, 1881, and were filed with the Secretary of Territory August 20, 1881.

Organization effected December 17, 1881.

2. **Construction**

L.A.File
140

This company constructed no lines but the N.P.R.R. Co. constructed for account of this company the following lines:

From	To	Miles	Date
Fargo, N.Dak.	Lisbon, N.Dak.	60.00	May 12,1881 to July 5,1883
Lisbon, N.Dak.	LaMoure, N.D.	27.40	August 15,1882 to Aug.1,1883

3. **Operation**

A.S.Doc.
R.R.96

A.S.Doc.
Rec.34

Operated by the N.P.R.R.Co. until August 15, 1893 under lease of July 1, 1882; by the receivers of the N.P.R.R.Co. from August 15, 1893 until August 31, 1896 under lease of November 12, 1894 and by the N.P.Ry.Co. without formal contract from August 31, 1896 until April 21, 1898, on which date the property was conveyed to the N.P.Ry.Co.

File 83
Compt.
Box 17
M.B.318
p.173

Receivers for this company were appointed October 2, 1893 and dismissed October 31, 1894.

Operation as follows:

From	To	Miles	Date
Fargo, N.D.	Lisbon, N.D.	60.00	July 1, 1883 to April 21, 1898
Lisbon, N.D.	LaMoure, N.D.	27.40	Aug. 25, 1883 to April 21, 1898

4. Present Status of Corporation

A.S.Doc.
9918

No action has been taken to dissolve the corporation but having parted with its assets it is not active.

The records are in the custody of Mr. R. H. Relf, the Assistant Secretary of the Northern Pacific Ry.Co. at Saint Paul, Minnesota.

5. Chain of Title

A.S.Doc.
124

From	To	Date	Form of Transfer
F.& S.W.R.R.Co.	N.P.Ry.Co.	April 21, 1898	Deed

SCHEDULE OF INSTRUMENTS AND RECORDS

File Ref.   **Description**

A.S.Doc.   Articles of Incorporation of Fargo and Southwestern
9918   Railroad Company.

A.S.Doc.   Lease of July 1, 1882, by which the N.P.R.R.Co.
R.R.96   operated the property.

A.S.Doc.   Deed of April 21, 1898, by which F.& S.W. R.R. Co.
124   conveyed its entire property to N.P.Ry.Co.

L.A.File   Land Assistant's file "Data used in compiling re-
140   turn to Order No.20 - Corporate History".

A.S.Doc.   Lease of November 12, 1894, by which the receivers
Rec.34   of the N.P.R.R. Co. operated the property.

File 82   Order appointing Receivers of F.& S.W.R.R.Co. Octo-
Compt.   ber 2, 1892.
Box 17
M.B.318
p.173   Order dismissing Receivers of F.& S.W. R.R. Co.
                  October 31, 1894.

THE JAMESTOWN & NORTHERN RAILROAD COMPANY

Chart No.32
Place No.52
Map No.22

1. Incorporation

A.S.Doc. 9919

Incorporated under the general laws of the Territory of Dakota.

Articles are dated August 31, 1881, acknowledged September 13, 1881, and were filed with the Secretary of Territory September 17, 1881.

A.S.Doc. 9919

Amended Articles filed with the Secretary of Territory October 13, 1883.

Organization effected December 17, 1881.

2. Construction

L.A.File 140

This company did no actual construction but the N.P.R.R.Co. constructed for account of this company the following lines:

	From	To	Miles	Date
Main Line	Jamestown, N.D.	Melville, N.D.	32.80	Sept.5,1881 to Dec.10,1882
Main Line	Melville, N.D.	New Rockford, N.D.	25.10	Sept.1,1882 to Oct.20,1883
Main Line	New Rockford, N.D.	Minnewaukan, N.D.	31.70	June 1883 to June 25,1885
Br. Line	Carrington, N.D.	Sykeston, N.D.	12.90	May 5,1883 to Sept.22,1883

3. __Operation__

A.S.Doc. 97

This company's lines were operated by the N.P.R.R.Co. under contract of July 1, 1882 until August 15, 1893; by the receivers of the N.P.R.R.Co. from August 15, 1893 to August 31, 1896 under lease of November 12, 1894, retroactive for the receivership period, and by the N.P. Ry. Co. from September 1, 1896 to April 21, 1898.

A.S.Doc. Rec.34

File 82
Compt.
Box 17
M.B.356
p.177

Receivers were appointed for this company October 2, 1893 and they were dismissed October 31, 1894.

Details of operation as follows:

Main Line	Jamestown	Melville	32.80	July 1, 1883 to April 21,1898
Main Line	Melville	New Rockford	25.10	Dec. 1,1883 to April 21,1898
Main Line	New Rockford	Minnewaukan	31.70	Aug. 6,1885 to April 21,1898
		Main Line Total -	89.60	
Br. Line	Carrington	Sykeston	12.90	Dec. 1,1883 to April 21,1898

4. __Present Status of Corporation__

A.S.Doc. 9919

No action has been taken to dissolve this corporation but having parted with its assets it is not active.

The records are in the custody of Mr. R. H. Relf, the Assistant Secretary of the Northern Pacific Ry.Co. at Saint Paul, Minnesota.

5. <u>Chain of Title</u>

	From	To	Date	Form of Transfer
A.S.Doc. 128	J.& N.R.R.Co.	N.P.Ry.Co.	April 21, 1898	Deed

SCHEDULE OF INSTRUMENTS AND RECORDS

File Ref.   Description

A.S.Doc. 9919   Articles of Incorporation of Jamestown and Northern Railroad Company.

A.S.Doc. 9919   Amended Articles dated Oct. 13, 1883.

A.S.Doc. R.R.97   Lease of July 1, 1882, by which the N.P.R.R.Co. operated the property.

A.S.Doc. 128   Deed of April 21, 1898, by which J.& N. R.R. Co. conveyed its entire property to N.P.Ry.Co.

L.A.File 140   Land Assistant's file "Data used in compiling return to Order No.20 - Corporate History".

A.S.Doc. Rec.34   Lease of November 12, 1894, by which the Receivers of the N.P.R.R.Co. operated the property.

File 82 Compt. Box 17 M.B.356 p.177   Order appointing Receivers of J.& N. R.R.Co. October 2, 1893.

Order dismissing Receivers of J.& N. R.R. Co. October 31, 1894.

MONTANA RAILWAY COMPANY

Chart No. 34
Place No. 71
Map No. 23

1. Incorporation

A.S.Doc. 9931

Incorporated under the general laws of the Territory of Montana.

Articles are dated December 15, 1881, and were filed with the Secretary of Territory December 17, 1881.

Organization effected February 21, 1882.

2. Construction

L.A.File 140

This company constructed the following lines:

From	To	Miles	Date
# Stuart, Mont.	Anaconda, Mont.	9.00	April to August 1884
Walkerville, Mont.	High Ore, Mont.	1.36	May to October 1887
Anaconda Mine Mont.	Walkerville, Mont.	2.81	Oct. 1886 to Oct 1887
Haggins Mine Spur		1.66	Jan. to Sept. 1887

Originally narrow gauge; standardized in 1886 and 1887.

3. Operation

L.A.File 140

The lines have been operated as follows:

	From	To	Miles	Date
(1)	Stuart	Anaconda	9.00	Aug. 1884 to Aug. 1, 1886

	From	To	Miles	Date
(2)	Stuart	Anaconda	9.00	Aug. 1, 1886 to May 17, 1898
(3)	Stuart	Anaconda	9.00	May 17, 1898 to Oct. 31, 1898
(4)	Walkerville	High Ore	1.36	1887 to Oct. 31, 1898
	Anaconda Mine	Walkerville	2.81	1887 to Oct. 31, 1898
	Haggins Mine Spur		1.66	

(1) Operated by Union Pacific Railway Company without formal agreement.

A.S.Doc. 222

(2) Operated by Montana Union Railway Company under a lease dated August 1, 1886.

A.S.Doc. 97

(3) Operated by the Butte, Anaconda and Pacific Railway Company under a lease dated May 5, 1898 and effective May 17, 1898.

A.S.Doc. 222

(4) Operated by the Montana Union Ry. Co. under lease dated August 1, 1886.

M.B.393

Receivers were appointed for this company October 13, 1893 and they were discharged about March 25, 1898.

4. **Present Status of Corporation**

A.S.Doc. 9931

No action has been taken to dissolve this corporation, but having parted with its assets it is not active.

The records are in the custody of Mr. R. H. Relf, the Assistant Secretary of the Northern Pacific Ry.Co. at Saint Paul, Minnesota.

5. Chain of Title

	From	To	Date	Form of Transfer
A.S.Doc. 159	M.Ry.Co.	N.P.Ry.Co.	Oct.7,1898	Deed

SCHEDULE OF INSTRUMENTS AND RECORDS

File Ref.   Description

A.S.Doc. 9931   Articles of Incorporation of Montana Railway Company.

A.S.Doc. 222   Lease dated August 1, 1886, by which M.U.Ry.Co. operated the property.

A.S.Doc. 97   Lease dated May 5, 1898, by which Butte Anaconda and Pacific Railway Company operated the property.

A.S.Doc. 159   Deed of October 7, 1898, by which M. Ry. Co. conveyed its entire property to the N.P. Ry. Co.

L.A.File 140   Land Assistant's file "Data used in compiling return to Order No.20 - Corporate History".

SANBORN, COOPERTOWN AND TURTLE MOUNTAIN RAILROAD COMPANY

Chart No. 36
Place No. 122
Map No. 24

1. Incorporation

A.S.Doc. 9917

Incorporated under the general laws of the Territory of Dakota.

Articles are dated July 18, 1882, and were filed with the Secretary of Territory July 22, 1882.

Organization effected July 28, 1882.

2. Construction

L.A.File 140

This company did no actual construction but the N.P.R.R.Co. constructed for account of this company a main line from Sanborn, North Dakota to Cooperstown, North Dakota, 36.78 miles, between September 10, 1882 and September 22, 1883.

3. Operation

A.S.Doc. R.R.120

A.S.Doc. Rec.34

The property of this company was operated by the N.P.R.R.Co. from December 1, 1883 to August 15, 1893 under contract of April 18, 1883; by the Receivers of the N.P.R.R.Co. from August 15, 1893 until August 31, 1896 under lease of November 12, 1894, retroactive for the receivership period, and by the N.P.Ry.Co. without formal contract from September 1, 1896 until April 21, 1898.

\# Title as shown in Articles of Incorporation

File 82
Compt.
Box 17
M.B.298

Receivers for this company were appointed October 2, 1893 and they were dismissed October 31, 1894.

4. <u>Present Status of Corporation</u>

A.S.Doc.
9917

No action has been taken to dissolve this corporation, but having parted with its assets it is not active.

The records are in the custody of Mr. R. H. Relf, the Assistant Secretary of the Northern Pacific Ry.Co. at Saint Paul, Minnesota.

5. <u>Chain of Title</u>

	<u>From</u>	<u>To</u>	<u>Date</u>	<u>Form of Transfer</u>
A.S.Doc. 139	S.C.& T.M.R.R.Co.	N.P.Ry.Co.	April 21, 1898	Deed

SCHEDULE OF INSTRUMENTS AND RECORDS

File Ref.	Description
A.S.Doc. 9917	Articles of Incorporation of Sanborn, Coopertown and Turtle Mountain Railroad Company.
A.S.Doc. R.R.120	Lease of April 18, 1883, by which the N.P.R.R.Co. operated the property.
A.S.Doc. 139	Deed of April 21, 1898, by which the S.C.& T.M. R.R.Co. conveyed its entire property to N.P. Ry. Co.
L.A.File 140	Land Assistant's file "Data used in compiling return to Order No.20 - Corporate History".
A.S.Doc. Rec.34	Lease of November 12, 1894, by which the Receivers of the N.P.R.R.Co. operated the property.
File 82 Compt. Box 17 M.B.298	Order appointing Receivers for the S.C.& T.M. R.R. Co. October 2, 1893. Order dismissing Receivers for the S.C.& T.M.R.R. Co. October 31, 1894.

THE PUGET SOUND SHORE RAILROAD COMPANY

Chart No.37
Place No.60
Map No.25

1. **Incorporation**

A.S.Doc. 9969

Incorporated under the general laws of the Territory of Washington.

Articles are dated August 15, 1882, and were filed with the Secretary of Territory August 19, 1882.

A.S.Doc. 9969

Amended Articles, providing for the construction of some additional lines, were filed with the Secretary of Territory July 19, 1889.

Organization effected September 1, 1882.

2. **Construction and Purchases**

L.A.File 140

This company constructed a main line from Stuck Junction, Wash. to Black River Junction, Wash., 13.85 miles, between January 1883 and October 1, 1883.

A.S.Doc. R.R.583

Under an agreement dated September 2, 1882, this company constructed a standard-gauge railroad on the right of way and road-bed of the Columbia and Puget Sound Railroad Co., from Black River Jct. to Seattle, 10.10 miles, relaying the narrow-gauge track of the C. and P.S.R.R.Co. between the rails of the standard-gauge. This work was done between August 1883 and July 1884. In 1883 the trestle and tracks were built on what is known as the "Broad Gauge Strip", in Seattle.

3. Operation

L.A.File 140

This company operated the line Stuck Jct. to Seattle, 23.95 miles, from July 6, 1884 to January 17, 1890, although the property was conveyed to the Northern Pacific and Puget Sound Shore Railroad Co. by deed dated October 31, 1889.

4. Present Status of Corporation

A.S.Doc. 9969

The name of this company was stricken from the records of the Secretary of State of Washington August 23, 1909, for failure to pay annual license fees.

The records are in the custody of Mr. R. H. Relf, Assistant Secretary of the Northern Pacific Ry.Co. at Saint Paul, Minnesota.

5. Chain of Title

	From	To	Date	Form of Transfer
A.S.Doc. R.R.357	P.S.S.R.R.Co.	N.P.&P.S.S.R.R.Co.	Oct.31,1889	Deed
A.S.Doc. 134	N.P.&P.S.R.R.Co.	N.P.Ry.Co.	April 21,1898	Deed

SCHEDULE OF INSTRUMENTS AND RECORDS

File Ref.	Description
A.S.Doc. 9969	Articles of Incorporation of Puget Sound Shore Railroad Co. and Amendments dated August 15, 1882.
A.S.Doc. R.R.583	Agreement dated Sept. 2, 1882, under which P.S.S.R.R.Co. acquired right to reconstruct line of Columbia & Puget Sound Railroad Company from Black River Jct. to Seattle 10.10 miles.
A.S.Doc. R.R.357	Deed of October 31, 1889, by which P.S.S.R.R.Co. conveyed its entire property to Northern Pacific and Puget Sound Shore Railroad Co.
A.S.Doc. R.R.134	Deed of April 21, 1898, by which N.P.& P.S.S.R.R. Co. conveyed its entire property to Northern Pacific Railway Co.
L.A.File 140	Land Assistant's File "Data used in compiling return to Order 20, Corporate History."

HELENA AND JEFFERSON COUNTY RAILROAD COMPANY

Chart No.40
Place No.114
Map No.26

1. **Incorporation**

A.S.File 599-8

Incorporated under the general laws of the Territory of Montana.

Articles are dated July 30, 1883, and were filed with the Secretary of Territory August 10, 1883.

Organization effected August 15, 1883.

2. **Construction**

L.A.File 140

This company constructed no lines but the N.P.R.R.Co. constructed for account of this company a main line from East Helena, (formerly Prickley Pear Junction) Montana to Wickes, Montana, 20.10 miles, between September and December 18, 1883.

3. **Operation**

A.S.Doc. R.R.470

The line was operated by the N.P.R.R.Co. from Dec.18, 1883 to August 15, 1893 under contract of August 1, 1883. The receivers of the N.P.R.R.Co. only partially recognized this contract and operated the road from August 15, 1893 to August 31, 1896 on the same general terms in effect with the other branch line companies. From September 1, 1896 to April 21, 1898 road was operated by the N.P.Ry.Co. with no formal agreement.

4. <u>Present Status of Corporation</u>

A.S.File
599-8

No action has been taken to dissolve this corporation, but having parted with its assets it is not active.

The records are in the custody of Mr. R. H. Relf, the Assistant Secretary of the Northern Pacific Ry.Co. at Saint Paul, Minnesota.

5. <u>Chain of Title</u>

From	To	Date	Form of Transfer
H.&J.C.R.R.Co.	N.P.Ry.Co.	April 21, 1898	Deed

A.S.Doc. 126

SCHEDULE OF INSTRUMENTS AND RECORDS

File Ref.	Description
A.S.File 599-8	Articles of Incorporation of Helena and Jefferson County Railroad Company.
A.S.Doc. 470	Contract of Aug. 1, 1883, by which the N.P.R.R.Co. operated the property.
A.S.Doc. 126	Deed of April 21, 1898, by which the H.& J.C.R.R. Co. conveyed its entire property to N.P.Ry.Co.
L.A.File 140	Land Assistant's file "Data used in compiling return to Order No.20 - Corporate History".

JAMES RIVER VALLEY RAILROAD COMPANY

Chart No.39
Place No.123
Map No.27

1. **Incorporation**

A.S.File
599-11

Incorporated under the general laws of the Territory of Dakota.

Articles are dated August 2, 1883, and were filed with the Secretary of Territory August 2, 1883.

Organization effected August 6, 1883.

2. **Construction**

L.A.File
140

This company constructed the following road:

From		To	Miles	Date
Main Line Jamestown,N.D.		LaMoure,N.D.	48.55	Sept.3,1883 to Dec.2, 1885

The N.P.R.R.Co. constructed for account of this company the line:

# Independence (formerly Valley Jct.) N.D.	Oakes,N.D.	15.20	July 20,1886 to Dec.10, 1886

This includes 326 feet of track at Oakes which is owned jointly with Chicago and Northwestern Railway Company.

3. **Operation**

A.S.Doc.
R.R.165

The property of this company was operated by the

A.S.Doc. Rec.36

N.P.R.R.Co. until August 15, 1893 under lease of January 1, 1886; by the receivers of the N.P.R.R.Co. from August 15, 1893 to August 31, 1896 under lease of November 8, 1894, retroactive for the receivership period, and by the N.P.Ry.Co. from September 1, 1896 to April 21, 1898.

A.S.Doc. R.R.192

Under contract dated November 18, 1886 this company acquired trackage rights over the Fargo and Southwestern Railroad Co. from Independence to LaMoure, N.Dak.

Details of operation as follows:

	From	To	Miles	Date
Main Line	Jamestown	LaMoure	48.51	Dec.14,1885 to April 21,1898
Main Line	Independence	Oakes	15.16	Dec.15,1886 to April 21,1898

File 82
Compt.
Box 17
M.B.334
p.239

Receivers for this company were appointed October 2, 1893 and they were dismissed October 31, 1894.

4. Present Status of Corporation

A.S.File 599-11

No action has been taken to dissolve the corporation but having parted with its assets it is not active.

The records are in the custody of Mr. R. H. Relf, the Assistant Secretary of the Northern Pacific Ry.Co. at Saint Paul, Minnesota.

5. Chain of Title

	From	To	Date	Form of Transfer
A.S.Doc. 127	J.R.V.R.R. Co.	N.P.Ry.Co.	April 21,1898	Deed

SCHEDULE OF INSTRUMENTS AND RECORDS

File Ref.	Description
A.S.File 599-11	Articles of Incorporation of James River Valley Railroad Company.
A.S.Doc. R.R.165	Lease of Jan. 1, 1886, by which the N.P.R.R.Co. operated the property.
A.S.Doc. R.R.192	Contract of November 18, 1886, by which J.R.V.R.R. Co. acquired trackage rights over F.& S.W.R.R.Co., LaMoure to Independence.
A.S.Doc. 127	Deed of April 21, 1898, by which J.R.V.R.R.Co. conveyed its entire property to N.P.Ry.Co.
L.A.File 140	Land Assistant's file "Data used in compiling return to Order No.20 - Corporate History".
File 82 Comp. Box 17	Order appointing Receivers of J.R.V.R.R.Co. October 2, 1893.
M.B.334 p.239	Order dismissing Receivers of J.R.V.R.R.Co. October 31, 1894.
A.S.Doc. Rec.36	Lease of November 8, 1894, under which the receivers of the N.P.R.R.Co. operated the property of the J.R.V.R.R.Co.

DULUTH AND MANITOBA RAILWAY COMPANY

Chart No. 41 & 46
Place No. 121 & 112
Map No. 28

1. Incorporation

A.S.
Doc.10007

Incorporated under the general laws of the State of Minnesota.

Articles are dated May 27, 1884, and were filed with the Secretary of State June 3, 1884.

M.B.353
p.31

Organization effected July 9, 1885.

M.B.353
p.40

Amended Articles limiting the term of the corporation to 50 years from June 3, 1884 and changing name to The Duluth and Manitoba Railroad Company were filed with the Secretary of State November 19, 1885.

2. Construction

L.A.File
140

The N.P.R.R.Co. constructed for account of this company the following lines:

	From	To	Miles	Date
Main Line	Manitoba Jctn.(formerly Winnipeg Jct) Minn.	Red Lake Falls	)	June 15, 1886 to Sept. 1, 1886
Main Line	Red Lake Falls	Grand Forks	) 105.00	Sept. 15, 1886 to Jan. 5, 1887
Main Line	Grand Forks, N.D.	Pembina, N.D.	96.30	May 16, 1887 to Oct. 21, 1887
		Main Line Total - -	201.30	

	From	To	Miles	Date
Br. Line	Key West, Minn.	Omera, Minn.	3.38	June 1886 to Jan. 1887
Br. Line	Omera, Minn.	Sherack, Minn.	2.95	Sept.1 to Oct. 10, 1895
Br. Line	Beyond Sherack-Graded only		0.81	Sept. 1895
Br. Line	Red Lake Falls Jct.	Red Lake Falls	1.06	June 1886 to Jan. 1887

Branch Line Total - 8.20

3. Operation

A.S.Doc. 286

A.S.Docs. 433-143 and 433-145

The lines were operated by the N.P.R.R.Co. until August 15, 1893 under a lease dated June 1, 1887; by the receivers of the N.P.R.R.Co. from August 15, 1893 to August 31, 1896 under lease of November 8, 1894, retroactive for the receivership period, and an extension granted to July 1, 1897. The N.P.Ry.Co. operated the property under a lease dated December 19, 1896 from September 1, 1896 to July 1, 1897 and thereafter with no formal agreement until April 21, 1898.

Details of operation as follows:

	From	To	Miles	Date
Main Line	Manitoba Jctn.	East Grand Forks	105.00	Apr.1,1887 to April 21,1898
Main Line	Grand Forks	Pembina	96.30	Oct.7,1887 to April 21,1898
Br. Line	Key West	Omera	3.38	April 1,1887 to April 21,1898

212

	From	To	Miles	Date
Br. Line	Omera	Sherack	2.95	Oct. 1895 to April 21, 1898
Br. Line	Red Lake	Red Lake Falls	1.06	April 1, 1887 to April 21, 1898

4. <u>Present Status of Corporation</u>

No action has been taken to dissolve this corporation but having parted with its assets it is not active.

The records are in the custody of Mr. R. H. Relf, the Assistant Secretary of the Northern Pacific Ry. Co. at Saint Paul, Minnesota.

5. <u>Chain of Title</u>

	From	To	Date	Form of Transfer
A.S.Doc. 122	D.& M.R.R.Co.	N.P.Ry.Co.	Apr. 21, 1898	Deed

SCHEDULE OF INSTRUMENTS AND RECORDS

File Ref. **Description**

A.S.Doc. 10007 — Articles of Incorporation of Duluth and Manitoba Railway Company.

M.B.353 p.40 — Amended Articles dated Nov. 19, 1885.

A.S.Doc. 286 — Lease of June 1, 1887, by which N.P.R.R.Co. operated the property.

A.S.Doc. 122 — Deed of April 21, 1898, by which D& M.R.R.Co. conveyed its entire property to N.P.Ry.Co.

A.S.Doc. 433-143 — Lease of November 8, 1894, under which the receivers of the N.P.R.R.Co. operated the property until July 1, 1896.

A.S.Doc. 433-145 — Agreement of June 30, 1896 extending lease of Nov.8, 1894 to July 1, 1897.

A.S.Doc. Ry.18 — Lease of Dec. 19, 1896, under which the N.P.Ry.Co. operated the property until July 1, 1897.

L.A.File 140 — Land Assistant's file "Data used in compiling return to Order No.20 - Corporate History".

NORTHERN PACIFIC AND CASCADE RAILROAD COMPANY

Chart No.42
Place No.12
Map No.29 & 3½

1. Incorporation

A.S.
599-18

Incorporated under the general laws of the Territory of Washington.

Articles are dated August 12, 1884, and were filed with the Secretary of Territory August 23, 1884.

Organization effected August 23, 1884.

2. Construction and Purchases

A.S.Doc.
10230

This company purchased from the N.P.R.R.Co. July 1, 1885, the following lines:

	From	To	Miles
Br.line	Cascade Jctn., Wash.	Burnett, Wash.	1.87
"	Cascade Jctn.	Wilkeson, Wash.	5.23
"	Wilkeson	Carbonado, Wash.	3.60

L.A.File
140

This company did no actual construction, but the N.P.R.R.Co. constructed for account of this company, the following lines:

	From	To	Miles	Date
Br.Line	Extension beyond Wilkeson		0.93	Aug.1889
"	Crocker, Wash.	Wingate (formerly Douty) Wash.	5.30	May 1888 to Apr.1889
"	Burnett	Spiketon (formerly Pittsburg) Wash.	2.18	Jan. to July 1890

3. Operation

A.S.Doc. 181

This company's lines were operated from October 1, 1887 to August 15, 1893 by the N.P.R.R.Co; from August 15, 1893 to August 31, 1896 by the receivers of the N.P.R.R.Co. and from September 1, 1896 to April 21, 1898 by the N.P.Ry.Co. under a contract dated October 1, 1887. Prior to that time they were operated by the N.P.R.R.Co. without a formal contract. The details of operation were as follows:

A.S.Doc. 10230

and

L.A.File 140

	From	To	Miles	Date
Br. line	Cascade Jctn.	Burnett	1.87	July 1, 1885 to April 21, 1898.
"	Burnett	Spiketon	2.18	Oct. 6, 1890 to April 21, 1898
"	Cascade Jctn.	Wilkeson	5.23	July 1, 1885 to April 21, 1898
"	Wilkeson	Carbonado	3.60	July 1, 1885 to April 21, 1898
"	Crocker	Wingate	5.30	May 6, 1889 to April 21, 1898
"	Extension beyond Wilkeson		0.93	Aug. 1889 to April 21, 1898

4. Present Status of Corporation

A.S.File 599-18

The name of this corporation was stricken from the records of the State of Washington August 23, 1909, for failure to pay annual license fees

The records are in the custody of Mr. R.H.Relf, the Assistant Secretary of the Northern Pacific Ry.Co.

at Saint Paul, Minnesota.

5. <u>Chain of Title</u>

	<u>Line</u>	<u>From</u>	<u>To</u>	<u>Date</u>	Form of Transfer
A.S.Doc. 10230	Cascade Jct. to Burnett, Wilkeson and Carbonado	N.P.R.R. Co.	N.P.and C.R.R.Co.	July 1, 1885	Deed
A.S.Doc. 135	All	N.P.and C.R.R.Co.	N.P.Ry. Co.	April 21, 1898	Deed

SCHEDULE OF INSTRUMENTS AND RECORDS

File Ref.	Description
A.S. 599-18	Articles of Incorporation of Northern Pacific and Cascade Railroad Company.
A.S.Doc. 10230	Deed of July 1, 1885, by which the Northern Pacific Railroad Company conveyed to N.P. & C. R.R. Co. lines from Cascade Jct. to Burnett, Wilkeson and Carbonado.
A.S.Doc. 181	Contract of October 1, 1887, by which N.P. R.R. Co. et al operated the property.
A.S.Doc. 135	Deed of April 21, 1898, by which N.P. & C. R.R. Co. conveyed all its lines to N.P. Ry. Co.
L.A.File 140	Land Assistant's file "Data used in compiling return under Order No.20 - Corporate History".

NORTHERN PACIFIC AND PUGET SOUND SHORE RAILROAD COMPANY

                                Chart No.43
                                Place No.51
                                Map No.30

1. **Incorporation**

A.S.File 599-22

Incorporated under the general laws of the Territory of Washington.

Articles are dated August 12, 1884, and were filed with the Secretary of Territory August 23, 1884.

Organization effected August 23, 1884.

2. **Construction and Purchases**

L.A.File 140

This company constructed the following lines:

	From	To	Miles	Date
Br. Line	Black River Jct. Wash.	Kennydale, Wash.	6.50	Aug.1890 to July 4,1891
Br. Line	Woodinville, Wash.	Kirkland, Wash.	5.60	Aug.1890 to March 1891
(1)	Kennydale, Wash.	Kirkland Wash.	10.70	Aug.1890 to July 4,1891
(2)	West City Limits, Seattle,Wn.	South City Limits, Seattle,Wn.	2.60	June 20,1890 to July 6, 1891

(1) Graded only.

(2) Trestle work, which was later abandoned, owing to changes in streets and the harbor line.

This company purchased the following lines:

	From	To	Miles	Purchased From	Date
A.S.Doc. 616	Meeker(formerly Puyallup Jct) Wash.	Stuck Jct. Wash.	7.00	N.P.R.R. Co.	July 1, 1885
	Stuck Jct.	Black Riv. Jct., Wn.	13.85	P.S.S. R.R.Co.	Oct.31,1889
A.S.Doc. R.R.357	# Black River Jct.	Seattle, Wash.	10.10	P.S.S. R.R.Co.	Oct.31,1889

Single track standard gauge road constructed on the right of way of the Columbia and Puget Sound Railroad Co.

3. **Operation**

A.S.Docs. R.R.182A, R.R.182 and R.R.362

This company operated no lines, its property being operated by the N.P.R.R.Co. until August 15, 1893 under contracts dated respectively August 1, 1885, October 1, 1887 and November 1, 1889; operated from August 15, 1893 to August 31, 1896 by the receivers of the N.P.R.R.Co., and from September 1, 1896 until April 21, 1898 by the N.P.Ry.Co. October 10, 1893, Henry Stanton, C. H. Prescott and L.S.J.Hunt were appointed as receivers for this company but they did not operate the property.

Details of operation:

	From	To	Miles	Date
L.A.File 140	Main Line Meeker	Stuck Jct.	7.00	July 1,1885 to April 21,1898
	Main Line Stuck Jct.	Black River Jct.	13.85	Jan.17,1890 to April 21,1898
	Main Line Black Riv.Jct.	Seattle	10.10	Jan.17,1890 to April 21,1898

	From	To	Miles	Date
Br. Line	Black Riv.	Renton	5.50	1893(approx.) to Aug.31,1896,(approx.)
Br. Line	Renton	Kennydale	1.00	Not operated
Br. Line	Woodinville (formerly Jacobson)	Kirkland	5.60	1893 (approx.) to Aug.31,1896,(approx.)

4. Present Status of Corporation

L.A.File 140

The name of this company was stricken from the records of the Secretary of State of Washington August 23, 1909, for failure to pay annual license fees.

The records are in the custody of Mr. R. H. Relf, the Assistant Secretary of the Northern Pacific Railway Company at Saint Paul, Minnesota.

5. Chain of Title

	From	To	Date	Form of Transfer
A.S.Doc. 616	N.P.R.R.Co.	N.P.& P.S.R.R. Co.	July 1,1885	Deed
A.S.Doc. R.R.357	P.S.S.R.R. Co.	N.P.&P.S.S.R.R. Co.	Oct.31,1889	Deed
A.S.Doc. 134	N.P.& P.S.S. R.R.Co.	N.P. Ry. Co.	April 21,1898	Deed

221

SCHEDULE OF INSTRUMENTS AND RECORDS

File Ref.   Description

A.S.File   Articles of Incorporation of Northern Pacific and
599-22   Puget Sound Shore Railroad Company.

A.S.Doc.   Deed of July 1, 1885, by which the Northern Pacific
616   Railroad Company conveyed to N.P. & P. S. S. R. R. Co.
                 line from Meeker to Stuck Jct., 7.00 miles.

A.S.Doc.   Deed of October 31, 1889, by which Puget Sound Shore
R.R.357   Railroad Co. conveyed its entire property to N.P. & P.S.S
                 R.R.Co.

A.S.Docs.   Contracts of August 1, 1885, October 1, 1887 and
R.R.182A,
R.R.182   November 1, 1889, under which N.P.R.R.Co. operated the
and
R.R.362   property.

A.S.Doc.   Deed of April 21, 1898, by which N.P.& P.S.S. R.R.
134   Co. conveyed its entire property to Northern Pacific
                 Railway Co.

L.A.File   Land Assistant's file "Data used in compiling re-
140   turn to Order No.20 - Corporate History".

THE COUER D'ALENE STEAM NAVIGATION AND TRANSPORTATION COMPANY

Chart No.44
Place No.80
Map No.31

1. **Incorporation**

A.S.Doc. 11058

Incorporated under the general laws of the Territory of Washington.

Articles are dated February 3, 1885, and were filed with the Secretary of Territory February 6, 1885.

Date of organization is unknown.

2. **Construction**

L.A.File 140

The N.P.Ry. Co. has no knowledge of any construction by this company, but it is known to have operated a boat line between Coeur d'Alene City on Lake Coeur d'Alene and Mission, on the Coeur d'Alene River, a distance of about 45 miles.

3. **Operation**

L.A.File 140

The record of operation by this company is indefinite, but available information indicates that it was being operated as early as July 31, 1886, and it is known positively to have been in operation November 28, 1886, and the assumption is that operation continued until sale of the property to the Coeur d'Alene Ry.& Navigation Co. about March 1887.

4. **Present Status of Corporation**

L.A.File 140

The name of this corporation was stricken from the records of the Secretary of State of Washington August 23, 1909, for failure to pay annual license fees.

The N.P.Ry.Co. is not in possession of the records of this company and does not know who is their custodian.

5. **Chain of Title**

L.A.File 140

and

M.B.367 p.15

June 7, 1887, the Coeur d'Alene Railway and Navigation Company arranged for an increase in its capital stock to provide, among other things, for the purchase of the property and franchises of The Coeur d'Alene Steam Navigation & Transportation Co. A thorough search of the public records of Kootenai and Shoshone Counties and of the railway records fails to show that any deed or bill of sale was ever made to cover the transaction but the records show that the Coeur d'Alene Railway & Navigation Co. did purchase this property and sale was confirmed by its Board of Directors September 8, 1888.

SCHEDULE OF INSTRUMENTS AND RECORDS

File Ref.	Description
A.S.Doc. 11058	Articles of Incorporation of the Coeur d'Alene Steam Navigation & Transportation Co.
M.B.367 p.15	Minutes of Coeur d'Alene Ry.& Navigation Co. Board of Directors' meeting Sept. 8, 1888. "Resolved that the purchase of the property and franchises of the Coeur d'Alene Steam Navigation & Transportation Co., heretofore made in behalf of this company by the President thereof, under authority from this board, be, and the same is hereby ratified."
L.A.File 140	Land Assistant's file "Data used in compiling return to Order No.20 - Corporate History".

SEATTLE, LAKE SHORE AND EASTERN RAILWAY COMPANY

Chart No. 45 & 100
Place No. 58 & 49
Map No. 32 & 32$\frac{1}{2}$

1. Incorporation

A.S.Doc.
9972

Incorporated under the general laws of the Territory of Washington.

Articles are dated April 25, 1885 and were filed with the Secretary of State April 28, 1885.

Supplementary Articles, providing for some additional lines were filed with the Secretary of State August 10, 1886.

M.B.326
p.25

Organization effected April 29, 1885.

2. Construction and Purchases

	From	To	Miles	Date
L.A.File 140	Seattle	Woodinville	24.30	Feb. 1887 to Oct. 1887
	Woodinville	Sallal Prairie	39.02	May 1887 to Oct. 9, 1887
#	Woodinville	Snohomish	14.40	June 1887 to July 1888
	Snohomish	Sumas	88.50	Sept. 1888 to March 1891
	Spokane	Davenport	50.05	May 1888 to August 1889

A.S.Doc.
10095

\# Partly constructed line of the Seattle & West Coast Ry. Co. purchased March 24, 1888 and its construction completed by this company.

3. **Operation**

L.A.File
140-82

This company operated its lines as follows:

	From	To	Miles	Date
Main Line	Spokane	Wheatdale	47.45	Oct.15,1888 to June 30,1893
Main Line	Wheatdale	Davenport		July 1,1889 to June 30,1893
Main Line	Seattle	Woodinville	24.30	Mar.19,1888 to June 30,1893
Main Line	Woodinville	Issaquah (Gilman)	20.00	Mar.19,1888 to June 30,1893
Main Line	Issaquah	Sallal Prairie	19.02	Dec.1889 to June 30,1893
Br. Line	Woodinville	Snohomish	14.40	July 3,1888 to June 30,1893
Br. Line	Snohomish	Arlington	22.00	June 1,1890 to June 30,1893
Br. Line	Arlington	Sedro Woolley	26.00	Nov.15,1890 to June 30,1893
Br. Line	Sedro Woolley	Sumas	40.50	May 1,1891 to June 30,1893

A.S.Doc. 567½

September 18, 1889, the line from Spokane to the Spokane River, 2.60 miles, was leased for 99 years to Seattle and Eastern Construction Company, which company

A.S.Doc. 567½

September 25, 1889, assigned the lease to Union Depot Company of Spokane Falls. The lease has since come into

L.A.File 140

possession of the Oregon-Washington Railroad and Navigation Company, who now operate the property.

A.S.Doc. R.R.324

In a contract dated June 5, 1890 it was provided

that the lines of this company should be turned over to the Oregon and Trans. Continental Co. for operation as of July 25, 1890. The interest of the O. and T. Co. was assigned to the N. P. R. R. Co., who virtually operated this property until July 1, 1893. The Spokane Division being taken over September 23, 1890 and the rest of the system in March 1892.

L.A.File 140

A.S.Doc. R.R.454 and 78

The S.L.S.& E. Ry. Co. failed and receivers were appointed June 26, 1893, who had charge of the entire property from July 1, 1893 to June 30, 1896. The Spokane division was not operated after June 30, 1893 except 1.50 miles leased to the Great Northern Ry. Co.

The property of this company was sold under foreclosure May 16, 1896, being purchased by a Committee of Bondholders represented by Morton S. Paton, et al, to whom conveyance was made June 19, 1896 by deed from Eben Smith, Special Master, and Thomas R. Brown and John H. Bryant, Receivers. In the meantime the Committee of Bondholders had organized the Seattle and International Ry. Co. and the Spokane and Seattle Railway Company and the property was taken over by them as shown in the chain of title below.

4. **Present Status of Corporation**

A.S.Doc. 9972

The name of this company was stricken from the records of the Secretary of State of Washington, August 23,

1909, for failure to pay annual license fees.

The records are in the custody of Mr. R. H. Relf, the Assistant Secretary of the Northern Pacific Railway Co. at Saint Paul, Minnesota.

5. <u>Chain of Title</u>

	Line	From	To	Date	Form of Transfer
A.S.Doc. 10095	Woodinville to Snohomish	S.&W.C.Ry. Co.	S.L.S.&E.Ry.	Mar. 24, 1886	Deed
A.S.Doc. 567½	Spokane to Spokane Riv.	S.L.S.&E. Ry.Co.	S.&E.Const.	Sept. 18, 1889	99 yr. lease
A.S.Doc. 1336	All	Eben Smith, Spl. Master & Receivers S.L.S.&E. Ry.Co.	Morton S. Paton, et al, Committee of Bondholders	June 19, 1896	Deed
A.S.Doc. 1336	Spokane to Davenport	Morton S. Paton, et al	S.&S.Ry.Co.	July 28, 1896	Deed
A.S.Doc. 1336	Seattle to Sallal Prairie and Woodinville to Sumas	Morton S. Paton, et al	S.&I.Ry.Co.	July 28, 1896	Deed
A.S.Doc. 198	Medical Lake to Davenport	S.&S.Ry.Co.	N.P.Ry.Co.	Mar. 17, 1899	Deed
A.S.Doc. 402	Spokane to Medical Lake	S.&S.Ry.Co.	N.P.Ry.Co.	Oct. 3, 1900	Deed
A.S.Doc. 310	Seattle to Sallal Prairie & Woodinville to Sumas	S.&I.Ry.Co.	N.P.Ry.Co.	Mar. 21, 1901	Deed

SCHEDULE OF INSTRUMENTS AND RECORDS

File Ref.	Description
A.S.Doc. 9972	Articles of Incorporation of Seattle, Lake Shore and Eastern Railway Company.
A.S.Doc. 10095	Deed of Mar. 24, 1888, by which the Seattle and West Coast Railway Company conveyed its property to S.L.S.& E. Ry. Co.
A.S.Doc. 567½	Lease dated Sept. 18, 1889, by which Seattle and Eastern Construction Company operated the property between Spokane and Spokane River, 2.6 miles.
A.S.Doc. 567½	Assignment of lease to Union Depot Company of Spokane Falls.
A.S.Doc. R.R.324	Contract of June 5, 1890 between S.L.S.& E.Ry.Co. and O. and T. Co., under which N.P.R.R. Co. controlled the property.
A.S.Doc. 1336	Deed of July 28, 1896, by which S.L.S. and E.Ry.Co. conveyed to Spokane and Seattle Railway Company the line from Spokane to Davenport.
A.S.Doc. R.R.454 and A.S.Doc. 78	Portion of Spokane division of S.L.S.& E.Ry.Co. leased to G.N.Ry.Co. Reference to leases.

A.S.Doc. 402 — Deed of Oct. 3, 1900, by which S.& S. Ry. Co. conveyed its line between Spokane and Medical Lake to N.P. Ry.Co.

A.S.Doc. 1336 — Deed of July 28, 1896, by which S.L.S.& E.Ry.Co. conveyed to Seattle and International Railway Company the lines from Seattle to Sallal Prairie and Sumas.

A.S.Doc. 310 — Deed of Mar. 21, 1901, by which S.& I. Ry. Co. conveyed its entire property to N.P. Ry. Co.

A.S.Doc. 198 — Deed of Mar. 17, 1899, by which S.& S. Ry. Co. conveyed its line between Medical Lake and Davenport to N.P. Ry. Co.

L.A.File 140 — Land Assistant's file "Data used in compiling return to Order No. 20 - Corporate History".

SPOKANE AND SEATTLE RAILWAY COMPANY

Chart No. 97
Place No. 50
Map No. 32½

1. Incorporation

A.S.Doc. 9973

Incorporated under the general laws of the State of Washington.

Articles are dated June 22, 1896 and were filed with the Secretary of State June 30, 1896.

Organization effected June 30, 1896.

2. Construction and Purchases

A.S.Doc. 1336

This company constructed no lines but acquired July 28, 1896, the portion of the main line of the Seattle Lake Shore and Eastern Railway Company's lines between Spokane, Washington and Davenport, Washington, 50.05 miles.

3. Operation

L.A.File 140

A.S.Doc. 567½

The portion of the property between Spokane and the Spokane River, 2.60 miles, has been operated under a lease for 99 years made by the Seattle, Lake Shore and Eastern Railway Company to Seattle and Eastern Construction Company September 18, 1889, and assigned September 25, 1889 to Union Depot Company of Spokane Falls. The Depot Company has come into the possession of the Oregon-

Washington Railroad & Navigation Company, which continued to operate under the lease.

L.A.File 140
A.S.Doc. R.R.454
A.S.Doc. 78

The balance of the line between Spokane River and Davenport, 47.45 miles, was not operated while owned by the Spokane and Seattle Railway Company, except 1.50 miles leased to the G.N. Ry. Co. July 1, 1892 and July 1, 1897.

4. Present Status of Corporation

A.S.Doc. 9973

The name of this company was stricken from the records of the Secretary of State of Washington August 23, 1909, for failure to pay annual license fees.

The records are in the custody of Mr. R. H. Relf, the Assistant Secretary of the Northern Pacific Railway Co. at Saint Paul, Minnesota.

5. Chain of Title

Ref	Line	From	To	Date	Form of Transfer
A.S.Doc. 1336	Entire Property of S.L.S.&E.Ry.Co.	Eben Smith, Spl.Master and Recvr. S.L.S.&E.Ry.Co.	Morton S.Paton, et al, Committee of Bondholders	June 19, 1896	Deed
A.S.Doc. 1336	Spokane to Davenport	Morton S.Paton, et al	S.&S.Ry.Co.	July 28, 1896	Deed
A.S.Doc. 198	Medical Lake to Davenport	S.&S.Ry.Co.	N.P.Ry.Co.	Mar. 17, 1899	Deed
A.S.Doc. 402	Spokane to Medical Lake	S.&S.Ry.Co.	N.P.Ry.Co.	Oct. 3, 1900	Deed

SCHEDULE OF INSTRUMENTS AND RECORDS

File Ref.	Description

A.S.Doc. 9973 — Articles of Incorporation of Spokane and Seattle Railway Company.

A.S.Doc. 1336 — Deed of June 19, 1896, by which property of Seattle Lake Shore and Eastern Ry. Co. was purchased by a Committee of Bondholders.

A.S.Doc. 1336 — Deed of July 28, 1896, by which Committee of Bondholders of S.L.S.& E. Ry. Co. conveyed the line Spokane to Davenport to S.& S. Ry. Co.

A.S.Doc. 567½ — Lease dated September 18, 1889, by which Seattle and Eastern Construction Company et al operate the property between Spokane and Spokane River, 2.6 miles.

A.S.Doc. 402 — Deed of October 3, 1900, by which S.& S. Ry. Co. conveyed its line between Spokane and Medical Lake to N.P. Ry.Co.

A.S.Doc. 198 — Deed of March 17, 1899, by which S.& S. Ry. Co. conveyed its line between Medical Lake and Davenport to N. P. Ry. Co.

A.S.Doc. R.R.454 and A.S.Doc. 78 — Leases of July 1, 1892 and July 1, 1897, by which the G.N. Ry. Co. operated 1.50 miles of this company's line in Spokane.

L.A.File 140   Land Assistant's file "Data used in compiling return to Order No. 20 - Corporate History".

235

SPOKANE AND PALOUSE RAILWAY COMPANY

Chart No. 48 & 47
Place No. 111 & 120
Map No. 33

1. Incorporation

A.S.File 599-5

The Eastern Washington Railway Company incorporated under the general laws of the Territory of Washington.

Articles are dated November 15, 1885, filed with the Secretary of Territory December 3, 1885 and were recorded December 21, 1885.

A.S.File 599-31

Amended Articles changing the name of the company to Spokane and Palouse Railway Company were filed with the Secretary of Territory March 1, 1886.

A.S.File 599-31

Amended Articles providing for the construction of some additional lines were filed with the Secretary of Territory June 13, 1887.

Eastern Washington Railway Company was never organized; Spokane and Palouse Railway Company effected its organization March 9, 1886.

2. Construction

L.A.File 140

This company constructed the following lines:

	From	To	Miles	Date
Main Line	Marshall, Wash.	Belmont, Wash.	43.00	April 9, 1886 to March 1, 1887
Main Line	Belmont, Wash.	Wash.-Ida. Line	53.51	May 1, 1887 to June 30, 1888

	From	To	Miles	Date
Main Line	Wash.-Ida. Line	Genesee, Ida.	7.15	May 1, 1887 to June 30, 1888

Main Line Total - - - 103.66

	From	To	Miles	Date
Br. Line	Pullman Jct. Wash.	Juliaetta, Ida.	40.05	May 12, 1890 to July 31, 1891
Br. Line	Belmont	Farmington	6.09	Aug. 28, to Dec. 4, 1890
Br. Line	2½ Miles South of Juliaetta, Ida.	8 Miles South of Lewiston-Ida.	29.55	Partly graded in 1890

Branch Line Total - - 75.69

3. Operation

A.S.Docs.
R.R.177 &
R.R.604

M.B.307
p.146

The lines were operated by the N.P.R.R.Co. until August 15, 1893 under leases dated May 1, 1886 and June 1, 1887 respectively; by the receivers of N.P.R.R. from August 15, 1893; to August 31, 1896 under lease dated November 17, 1894, retroactive for the receivership period, and by the N.P.Ry.Co. without formal contract from September 1, 1896 to February 21, 1899.

Details of operation as follows:

	From	To	Miles	Date
Main Line	Marshall	Belmont	43.00	Oct. 15, 1886 to Feb. 21, 1899
Main Line	Belmont	Wash-Ida. Line	53.51	July 1, 1888 to Feb. 21, 1899

		From	To	Miles	Date
Main Line		Wash.-Ida. Line	Genesee, Ida.	7.15	July 1, 1888 to Feb. 21, 1899
Br. Line		Pullman Jct.	Juliaetta	40.05	Sept. 15, 1891 to Feb. 21, 1899
Br. Line		Belmont	Farmington	6.09	Dec. 10, 1890 to Feb. 21, 1899

4. **Present Status of Corporation**

A.S.File 599-5

The name of this company was stricken from the records of the Secretary of State of Washington August 23, 1909, for failure to pay annual license fees.

The records are in the custody of Mr. R. H. Relf, the Assistant Secretary of the Northern Pacific Railway Co. at Saint Paul, Minnesota.

5. **Chain of Title**

	From	To	Date	Form of Transfer
A.S.Doc. 203	S.& P.Ry.Co.	N.P.Ry.Co.	Feb. 21, 1899	Deed

SCHEDULE OF INSTRUMENTS AND RECORDS

File Ref.   Description

A.S.File
599-5
Articles of Incorporation of Eastern Washington Railway Company.

A.S.File
599-31
Amended Articles of Mar. 1, 1886 changed name to Spokane and Palouse Railway Company.

A.S.Docs.
R.R.177
and
R.R.604
M.B.307
p.146
Leases of May 1, 1886, June 1, 1887 and November 17, 1894, by which N.P.R.R.Co. et al operated the property.

A.S.Doc.
203
Deed of February 21, 1899, by which Spokane and Palouse Ry. Co. conveyed its entire property to N.P. Ry.Co.

L.A.File
140
Land Assistant's file "Data used in compiling return to Order No.20 - Corporate History".

THE OREGON AND WASHINGTON TERRITORY RAILROAD COMPANY

Chart No. 49 & 90
Place No. 98 & 89
Map No. 34

1. **Incorporation**

A.S.Doc. 9978

Incorporated under the general laws of the State of Oregon.

Articles are dated March 1, 1886 and were filed with the Secretary of State March 4, 1886.

Date of organization is unknown.

Supplémentary Articles eliminating the word "The" from the corporate name and increasing the capital stock were filed with the Secretary of State May 26, 1887.

Supplementary Articles of Incorporation again increasing the capital stock were filed with the Secretary of State April 20, 1888.

2. **Construction**

L.A.File 140

	From	To	Miles	Date
Main Line	Hunts Jct. Wash.	Smeltz (formerly Killian Jct. Ore.)	20.10	May 20, 1887 to Jan. 15, 1888
Main Line	Smeltz	Fulton, Ore.	14.00	July 10, 1887 to Oct. 25, 1888
Main Line	Fulton	Pendleton, Ore.	7.00	May 1889 to Sept. 1889
Main Line	Hunts Jct.	Walla Walla, Wash.	53.54	Dec. 1888 (completed)

	From	To	Miles	Date
Main Line	Walla Walla	Dayton, Wash.	33.86	July to Dec.1889

Main Line Total - - 128.50

	From	To	Miles	Date
Br. Line	Smeltz (formerly Killian Jct.)	Athena, Ore. (formerly Centerville)	14.39	1887 and 1888
Br. Line	Eureka Jct. Wash.	Pleasant View, Wash.	19.73	1888

Branch Line Total - 34.12

3. Operation

L.A. File 140

The available records of this company indicate that it was operating as early as July 1888; date of opening for operation of the various lines is not known and dates shown are final construction dates.

This company operated its lines until December 1891 when property passed to Receiver W.D.Tyler, in whose hands it remained until the Washington and Columbia River Ry. Co. took over its operation November 5, 1892.

Details of operation as follows:

	From	To	Miles	Date
Main Line	Pendleton	Ore.-Wash. Line	30.42	Oct.1888 to Nov.4,1892
Main Line	Ore.-Wash. Line	Dayton	98.08	1888(approx.) to Nov.4,1892
Br. Line	Eureka Jct.	Pleasant View	19.73	1888(approx.) to Nov.4,1892
Br. Line	Smeltz	Athena	14.39	1888(approx.) to Nov.4,1892

A.S.Docs.
8858
and
8859

April 20, 1892, C. B. Wright purchased the entire property at sale held by Master in Chancery under a court decree of February 12, 1892, and deed conveying the property to him was executed by the Master Geo.H. Durham October 1, 1892. October 5, 1892 C. B. Wright made conveyance to W. & C. R. Ry. Co.

4. Present Status of Corporation

A.S.Doc.
9978

Dissolved by Proclamation of the Governor of Oregon January 20, 1906.

The N.P. Ry. Co. is not in possession of the records and does not know who is their custodian.

5. Chain of Title

	From	To	Date	Form of Transfer
A.S.Doc. 8862	Farmers Loan & Trust Co.	C.B.Wright	July 29, 1892	Deed
A.S.Doc. 8858	O.&W.T.R.R. Co.	C.B.Wright	Aug. 18, 1892	Deed
A.S.Doc. 8859	Geo.H.Durham, Master in Chancery	C.B.Wright	Oct. 1, 1892	Deed
A.S.Doc. 8858	C.B.Wright	The W.&C.R. Ry.Co.	Oct. 5, 1892	Deed
A.S.Doc. 3575	The W.&C.R. Ry.Co.	N.P.Ry.Co.	June 18, 1907	Deed

SCHEDULE OF INSTRUMENTS AND RECORDS

File Ref.	Description
A.S.Doc. 9978	Articles of Incorporation and Amendments thereto of The Oregon and Washington Territory Railroad Company.
A.S.Doc. 8862	Deed of July 29, 1892, by which The F.L.& T. Co. as trustee conveyed the entire property of the O.& W. T. R. R. Co. to C. B. Wright.
A.S.Doc. 8858	Deed of Aug. 18, 1892, by which the O.& W. T. R. R. Co. conveyed its entire property to C. B. Wright.
A.S.Doc. 8859	Deed of Oct. 1, 1892, by which the Master in Chancery conveyed the entire property of Oregon and Washington Territory Railroad Company to C. B. Wright.
A.S.Doc. 8858	Deed of Oct. 5, 1892, by which C. B. Wright conveyed the O.& W.T. R.R. Co's. lines to The Washington and Columbia River Railway Company.
A.S.Doc. 3575	Deed of June 18, 1907, by which The W. & C. R. Ry. Co. conveyed its entire property to N. P. Ry. Co.
L.A.File 140	Land Assistant's file "Data used in compiling return to Order No.20 - Corporate History".

PUGET SOUND AND GRAYS HARBOR RAILROAD AND TRANSPORTATION CO.

Chart No. 50
Place No. 126
Map No. 35

1. Incorporation

A.S.Doc. 9957

Incorporated under the general laws of the Territory of Washington.

Articles are dated March 13, 1886, filed with the Secretary of Territory March 22, 1886, and were recorded March 23, 1886.

Date of organization is unknown.

2. Construction

L.A.File 140

This company was the owner of a railroad extending from Kamilche, Wash. to Montesano. That portion of the line extending from Montesano to Simpson, Wash. was sold to the Tacoma, Olympia and Grays Harbor Railroad Co. by deed dated February 16, 1891, and was constructed as shown below:

	From	To	Miles	Date
L.A.File 140	Montesano, Wash.	Sec.1, Twp.18-N Range 5-W	18.30	May 15, 1889 to Dec. 10, 1889
	Sec.1, Twp.18-N Range 5-W	Simpson, Wash. (formerly Summit)	1.20	Prior to July 1890
	Montesano, Wash.	Chehalis River	1.30	July to September 1890
		Total -	20.80	

3. Operation

A.S.Doc.
R.R.450

This company operated its property until conveyance was made to the T.O.& G.H.R.R.Co. on February 16, 1891.

4. Present Status of Corporation

A.S.Doc.
9957

The name of this company was stricken from the records of the Secretary of State of Washington August 23, 1909, for failure to pay annual license fees.

The N.P.Ry.Co. is not in possession of the records of this company and does not know who is their custodian.

5. Chain of Title

	From	To	Date	Form of Transfer
A.S.Doc. R.R.450	P.S.& G.H.R.R. & T.Co.	T.O.& G.H.R.R.Co.	Feb.16,1891	Deed
A.S.Doc. R.R.450	T.O.& G.H.R.R. Co.	U.R.R. of W.	Feb.13,1892 #	Deed
A.S.Doc. 132	U.R.R. of W.	N.P.Ry.Co.	April 21,1898	Deed

\# This deed is dated February 13, 1892, but is retroactive to August 5, 1890.

SCHEDULE OF INSTRUMENTS AND RECORDS

File Ref.   **Description**

A.S.Doc. 9957
Articles of Incorporation of the Puget Sound and Grays Harbor Railroad and Transportation Company.

A.S.Doc. R.R.450
Deed of February 16, 1891, by which Puget Sound and Grays Harbor Railroad and Transportation Co. conveyed its line from Montesano to Simpson, Washington to Tacoma, Olympia and Grays Harbor Railroad Company.

A.S.Doc. R.R.450
Deed of February 13, 1892, by which T.O.& G.H.R.R. Co. conveyed its entire property to The United Railroads of Washington.

A.S.Doc. 132
Deed of April 21, 1898, by which U.R.R. of W. conveyed its entire property to N.P.Ry.Co.

L.A.File 140
Land Assistant's file "Data used in compiling return to Order No.20 - Corporate History".

HELENA AND RED MOUNTAIN RAILROAD COMPANY

Chart No.52
Place No.124
Map No.36

1. Incorporation

A.S.599-10

Incorporated under the general laws of the Territory of Montana.

Articles are dated June 19, 1886, and were filed with the Secretary of Territory June 19, 1886.

Amended Articles increasing amount of capital stock dated November 13, 1886 were filed with the Secretary of Territory November 15, 1886.

Organization effected June 19, 1886.

2. Construction

L.A.File 140

This company did no actual construction but the N.P. R.R. Co. constructed for account of this company the following lines:

	From	To	Miles	Date
Main Line	Helena, Mont.	Rimini, Mont.	16.37	June 19,1886 to Dec.15, 1886

3. Operation

A.S.Doc. 216
and
A.S.Doc. Rec.35

The line was operated by the N.P.R.R.Co. from Dec.15, 1886 until August 15, 1893 under a lease dated March 1, 1887; by the Receivers of the N.P. R.R. Co. from Aug.15, 1893 until August 31, 1896 under a lease dated Nov.12,

1894, retroactive for the receivership period; by the N.P. Ry. Co. from September 1, 1896 until Dec. 15, 1899 without formal contract.

Details of operation as follows:

	From	To	Miles	Date
Main Line	Helena	Rimini	16.37	Dec.15,1886 to Dec. 15,1899

4. <u>Present Status of Corporation</u>

A.S.File 599-10

No action has been taken to dissolve this corporation but having parted with its assets it is not active.

The records are in the custody of Mr. R. H. Relf, the Assistant Secretary of the Northern Pacific Railway Co. at Saint Paul, Minnesota.

5. <u>Chain of Title</u>

From	To	Date	Form of Transfer
H.&R.M.R.R.Co.	N.P.Ry.Co.	Dec.15,1899	Deed

A.S.Doc. 238

SCHEDULE OF INSTRUMENTS AND RECORDS

File Ref.	Description
A.S.File 599-10	Articles of Incorporation of Helena and Red Mountain Railroad Company.
A.S.Doc. 216	Lease of March 1, 1887, by which N.P. R.R. Co. operated the property.
A.S.Doc. Rec.35	Lease of November 12, 1894, by which the receivers of the N.P. R.R. Co. operated the property.
A.S.Doc. 238	Deed of December 15, 1899, by which H. & R. M. R.R. Co. conveyed its entire property to N. P. Ry. Co.
L.A.File 140	Land Assistant's File "Data used in compiling return to Order 20, Corporate History."

DULUTH SHORT LINE RAILWAY COMPANY

Chart No.54
Place No.46
Map No.37

1. **Incorporation**

A.S.599-4 Incorporated under the general laws of the State of Minnesota.

A.S.Doc. 1374 Articles are dated July 1, 1886, and were filed with Secretary of State July 2, 1886.

Organization effected August 21, 1886.

M.B.122 p.44 Amended Articles filed with the Secretary of State June 8, 1889.

2. **Construction**

L.A.File 140 This company constructed a main line from Thomson, Minnesota to a connection with the St.Paul and Duluth Railroad Co. at West End Jct. (Oneota) and from connection at West Duluth Jct. to West Superior, Wis. Details of construction as follows:

From	To	Miles	Date
Thomson, Minn.	Minn-Wis. Line	16.21	Dec.1,1886 to Jan.16,1888
Minn.-Wis.Line	West Superior, Wis.	1.54	1888

L.A.File 140

Main Line Total - 17.75

3. **Operation**

A.S.Doc. 363 The line was operated by the Saint Paul and Duluth

Railroad Company from Jan. 16, 1888 to November 11, 1898, under a lease dated September 1, 1886.

4. <u>Present Status of Corporation</u>

No action has been taken to dissolve this corporation, but having parted with all its assets it is not active.

The records are in the custody of Mr. R. H. Relf, the Assistant Secretary of the Northern Pacific Railway Co. at Saint Paul, Minnesota.

5. <u>Chain of Title</u>

	From	To	Date	Form of Transfer
A.S.Doc. 712	D.S.L.Ry.Co.	S.P.& D.R.R.Co.	Nov.11,1898	Deed
A.S.Doc. 300	St.P.& D.R.R. Co.	N. P. Ry. Co.	June 15,1900	Deed

SCHEDULE OF INSTRUMENTS AND RECORDS

File Ref.	Description
A.S.599-4 A.S.Doc. 1374	Articles of Incorporation of Duluth Short Line Railway Company.
M.B.122 p.44	Amended Articles.
A.S.Doc. 363	Lease of September 1, 1886, by which Saint Paul and Duluth Railroad Company operated the property.
A.S.Doc. 712	Deed of November 11, 1898, by which D.S.L.Ry. Co. conveyed its entire property to St.P.& D. R.R.Co.
A.S.Doc. 300	Deed of June 15, 1900, by which St.P.& D. R.R. Co. conveyed its entire railroad system to N.P. Ry. Co. (Except Land Grant)
L.A.File 140	Land Assistant's file "Data used in compiling return to Order No.20 - Corporate History".

THE COEUR D'ALENE RAILWAY AND NAVIGATION COMPANY

Chart No. 55
Place No. 72
Map No. 38

1. **Incorporation**

A.S.File 599-3

Incorporated under the general laws of the Territory of Montana.

Articles are dated July 1, 1886, and were filed with the Secretary of Territory July 6, 1886.

M.B.367 p.1

Organization effected July 14, 1886.

2. **Construction and Purchases**

L.A.File 140

This company constructed the following lines:

	From	To	Miles	Date
Main Line	Old Mission	Wardner, Ida.	15.00	June 1, 1886 to 1887
Main Line	Wardner	Wallace, Ida.	9.71	April 1887 to April 1888 Approx.
Main Line	Wallace	Mullan, Ida.	7.05	Nov. 12, 1888 to June 16, 1889
Main Line	Mullan	Ida-Mont. State Line	11.10	Oct. 23, 1889 to May 5, 1891

Lines from Wallace to Mullan and from Wallace to Burke were standardized in 1890.

A.S.Doc. 8861

This company purchased the graded road-bed of the Canyon Creek Railroad Company extending from Wallace to Burke, Idaho, 6.83 miles, and laid a narrow gauge track upon it, which was in operation prior to April 20, 1888, although conveyance was not made until August 29, 1888.

M.B.367 p.24

The property of The Coeur d'Alene Steam Navigation and Transportation Company of Idaho Territory, which consisted of a boat line operating on Lake Coeur d'Alene and the Coeur d'Alene River between Coeur d'Alene City, Idaho and Old Mission was also acquired, about March 1887.

3. Operation

L.A.File 140

The property was operated by Coeur d'Alene Ry.& Nav. Co. as follows:

	From	To	Miles	Date
Main Line	Old Mission	Wardner	15.00	Mar.20,1887 to Oct.1,1888
Main Line	Wardner	Wallace	9.71	April 20,1888 to Oct.1,1888
Steamboat Line	Coeur d'Alene City	Old Mission	45.00	Mar.20,1887 to Oct.1,1888
Br. Line	Wallace	Burke	6.83	Approx.April 20, 1888 to Oct.1, 1888

A.S.Doc. 270

On September 14, 1888 all of the property was leased to the Northern Pacific Railroad Company and that company operated it until August 15, 1893. The

A.S.Doc. Rec.10

receivers of the N.P.R.R.Co. operated the property from August 15, 1893 to September 1, 1896.

A.S.Doc. 1A

October 10, 1893, the property passed to receivers,

and on September 1, 1896, they leased it to Northern Pacific Railway Company. Operation continued under this lease until January 26, 1897.

Details of operation as follows:

	From	To	Miles	Date
Main Line	Old Mission	Wallace	24.71	Oct.1,1888 to Jan.26,1897
Main Line	Wallace	Mullan	7.05	June 1889 to Jan.26,1897
Main Line	Mullan	Ida-Mont. Line	11.10	Aug.15,1891 to Jan.26,1897
Br. Line	Wallace	Burke	6.83	Oct. 1,1888 to Jan.26,1897
Steamboat Line	Coeur d' Alene City	Mission	45.00	Oct. 1,1888 to Jan.26,1897

4. Present Status of Corporation

No action has been taken to dissolve this corporation, but having parted with its assets it is not active.

The records are in the custody of Mr. R. H. Relf, the Assistant Secretary of the Northern Pacific Railway Co. at Saint Paul, Minnesota.

5. Chain of Title

	From	To	Date	Form of Transfer
M.B.367 p.24	C.d'A.S.N.&T.Co.	C.d'A.Ry.&Nav.Co.	Approx.Mar.1887	Unknown
A.S.Doc. 8861	C.C.R.R.Co.	C.d'A.Ry.&Nav.Co.	Aug. 29, 1888	Deed
A.S.Doc. 22	C.d'A.Ry.&Nav.Co. J.P.M.Richards Special Master	N.P.Ry.Co.	Jan. 26, 1897	Deed

SCHEDULE OF INSTRUMENTS AND RECORDS

File Ref.	Description
A.S. 599-3	Articles of Incorporation of The Coeur d'Alene Railway and Navigation Company.
A.S.Doc. 270	Lease of Sept. 14, 1888 effective October 1, 1888, by which N.P.R.R.Co. operated the property.
A.S.Doc. Rec.10	Agreement of April 25, 1894, under which receivers of N.P.R.R.Co. operated the property.
A.S.Doc. 1a	Reference to operation by receivers from October 10, 1893 to September 1, 1896, and by N.P.Ry.Co. from September 1, 1896 to January 26, 1897.
A.S.Doc. 22	Deed of January 26, 1897, by which C.d'A.Ry.& Nav. Co. conveyed its entire property to N.P.Ry.Co.
L.A.File 140	Land Assistant's file "Data used in compiling return to Order No. 20 - Corporate History".
A.S.Doc. 8861	Deed dated Aug. 29, 1888, by which the C.C.R.R.Co. conveyed its property to the C.d'A.Ry..& Nav. Co.
M.B.367 p.24	Reference in Minute Book to purchase of the property of the C.d'A.S.N.& T.Co.

HELENA, BOULDER VALLEY AND BUTTE RAILROAD COMPANY

Chart No.56
Place No.61
Map No.39

1. Incorporation

A.S.Doc.
9933

Incorporated under the general laws of the Territory of Montana.

Articles are dated August 10, 1886, and were filed with the Secretary of Territory August 10, 1886.

M.B.358

Organization effected September 9, 1886.

Certificate of Increase of Capital Stock filed with the Secretary of Territory, April 26, 1887.

2. Construction

This company did no actual construction but the N.P.R.R.Co. constructed for account of this company a main line from Jefferson City, Montana, to Calvin, Montana, 30.00 miles, between October 1, 1886 and September 14, 1887.

3. Operation

L.A.File
140
and
A.S.Doc.
217

This company did not operate the property but the line was operated by the N.P.R.R.Co. under contract of May 1, 1887 from December 1887 to September 7, 1888, on which date the property was conveyed to the Northern Pacific and Montana Railroad Company.

4. **Present Status of Corporation**

A.S.Doc. 9933

No action has been taken to dissolve this corporation but having parted with its assets it is not active.

The records are in the custody of Mr. R. H. Relf, the Assistant Secretary of the Northern Pacific Railway Co. at Saint Paul, Minnesota.

5. **Chain of Title**

	From	To	Date	Form of Transfer
A.S.Doc. R.R.275	H.B.V.& B.R.R.Co.	N.P.& M.R.R.Co.	Sept. 7, 1888	Deed
A.S.Doc. 133	N.P.& M.R.R.Co.	N.P.Ry.Co.	April 21, 1898	Deed

SCHEDULE OF INSTRUMENTS AND RECORDS

File Ref.	Description
A.S.Doc. 9933	Articles of Incorporation of Helena Boulder Valley and Butte Railroad Company.
A.S.Doc. R.R.217	Contract of May 1, 1887, under which the N.P.R.R.Co. operated the property.
A.S.Doc. R.R.275	Deed of Sept. 7, 1888, by which H.B.V.& B. R.R. Co. conveyed its entire property to Northern Pacific and Montana Railroad Company.
A.S.Doc. 133	Deed of April 21, 1898, by which N.P.& M.R.R.Co. conveyed its entire property to N.P.Ry.Co.
L.A.File 140	Land Assistant's file "Data used in compiling return to Order No.20 - Corporate History".

CLEALUM RAILROAD COMPANY

Chart No.57
Place No.23
Map No.40

1. **Incorporation**

A.S.File 599-2

Incorporated under the general laws of Territory of Washington.

Articles are dated August 31, 1886, and were filed with the Secretary of Territory September 17, 1886.

A.S.File 599-2

Supplementary articles dated November 25, 1887 were filed with the Secretary of Territory December 19, 1887.

Organization effected November 4, 1886.

2. **Construction**

This company did no actual construction but the N.P.R.R.Co. constructed for account of this company a line from Clealum to Roslyn, 3.42 miles, from September to December 1886, and extended it to Ronald, 1.86 miles, from January to November 1887.

3. **Operation**

L.A.File 140

This line was operated as follows:

	From	To	Miles	Date
(1)	Clealum	Roslyn	3.42	Dec.21,1886 to Oct.1896 (approx)
	Roslyn	Ronald	1.86	Dec. 1887 to Oct.1896 (approx)
(2)	Clealum	Ronald	5.28	Oct.1896 to April 21,1898

(1) Operated by Northern Pacific Coal Company without a formal contract.

(2) Operated by the N.P.Ry.Co. without a formal contract.

4. **Present Status of Corporation**

A.S. 599-2

The name of this corporation was stricken from the records of the State of Washington August 23, 1909, for failure to pay annual license fees.

The records are in the custody of Mr. R. H. Relf, the Assistant Secretary of the Northern Pacific Ry.Co. at Saint Paul, Minnesota.

5. **Chain of Title**

	From	To	Date	Form of Transfer
A.S.Doc. 121	C.R.R.Co.	N.P.Ry.Co.	April 21, 1898	Deed

SCHEDULE OF INSTRUMENTS AND RECORDS

File Ref.   Description

A.S.   Articles of Incorporation of Clealum Railroad
599-2   Company.

A.S.   Supplementary articles.
599-2

A.S.Doc.
121   Deed of April 21, 1898, by which Clealum Railroad
          Company conveyed its entire property to N.P.Ry.Co.

L.A.File   Land Assistant's file 140 "Data used in compiling
140   return to Order No.20 - Corporate History".

SOUTH - EASTERN DAKOTA RAILROAD COMPANY

Chart No. 60
Place No. 132
Map No. 41

1. Incorporation

A.S. File
599-29

Incorporated under the general laws of the Territory of Dakota.

Articles are dated October 1, 1886, and were filed with the Secretary of Territory November 10, 1886.

Organization effected February 7, 1888.

2. Construction

L.A. File
140

The Northern Pacific Railroad Co. constructed for account of this company the following lines:

	From	To	Miles	Date
Main Line	Adams (formerly Fairview, N.D.) now Mathews	Great Bend, N.D.	5.74	April to Oct. 1887
Br. Line	Keystone Jct.	Bayne, N.D.	6.04	April 1, 1889 to Aug. 1890

L.A. File
140

The Northern Pacific Railroad Co. constructed a line known as Judd's Spur from Fairview Jct. to Mathews (formerly Adams and Fairview) from July to September 1884. It was considered as a part of the Northern Pacific Fergus and Black Hills Railroad until the first section of this company's line was opened for operation, after which time it was operated as part of the South-Eastern Dakota

Railroad Co.

3. **Operation**

L.A.File 140

A.S.Doc. 368

M.B.315 p.67

This property was operated by the N.P.R.R.Co. without a formal agreement until November 1, 1889, when a contract was entered into under which operation continued until August 15, 1893; by the Receivers of the N.P.R.R.Co. from August 15, 1893 until August 31, 1896 under lease of November 17, 1894, retroactive for the receivership period, and by the N.P.Ry.Co. from August 31, 1896 until April 21, 1898, on which date the property was conveyed to the N.P.Ry.Co.

File 82
Compt.
Box 17
M.B.315
p.65

Receivers for this company were appointed October 2, 1893 and dismissed October 31, 1894.

Details of operation as follows:

		From	To	Miles	Date
Main Line		Fairview Jct.	Mathews (formerly Fairview & Adams)	3.06	Oct.19,1887 to April 21,1898
Main Line		Mathews	Great Bend	5.74	Oct.19,1887 to April 21,1898
Br. Line		Keystone Jct.	Bayne	6.04	Aug.1,1890 to April 21,1898

4. **Present Status of Corporation**

A.S.File 599-29

No action has been taken to dissolve this corporation, but having parted with its assets it is not active.

The records are in the custody of Mr. R. H. Relf,

the Assistant Secretary of the Northern Pacific Ry.Co. at Saint Paul, Minnesota.

5. Chain of Title

	From	To	Date	Form of Transfer
A.S.Doc. 138	S.-E.D.R.R.Co.	N.P.Ry.Co.	April 21, 1898	Deed

SCHEDULE OF INSTRUMENTS AND RECORDS

File Ref.	Description
A.S.File 599-29	Articles of Incorporation of South-Eastern Dakota Railroad Company.
A.S.Doc. 368	Contract of Nov. 1, 1889, by which N.P.R.R.Co. operated the property.
A.S.Doc. 138	Deed of April 21, 1898, by which S.E.D.R.R.Co. conveyed its entire property to N.P.Ry.Co.
L.A.File 140	Land Assistant's file "Data used in compiling return to Order No.20 - Corporate History".
M.B.315 p.67	Lease of November 17, 1894, by which the Receivers of the N.P.R.R. Co. operated the property.
File 82 Compt. Box 17	Order appointing Receivers for S.E.D.R.R.Co. October 2, 1893.
M.B.315 p.65	Order dismissing Receivers of S.E.D.R.R.Co. October 31, 1894.

SPOKANE FALLS AND IDAHO RAILROAD COMPANY

Chart No. 58
Place No. 128
Map No. 42

1. Incorporation

A.S.File
599-30

Incorporated under the general laws of the Territory of Washington.

Articles are dated October 23, 1886, and were filed with the Secretary of Territory October 25, 1886.

Organization effected November 1, 1886.

2. Construction

L.A.File
140

This company did no actual construction, but the N.P.R.R.Co. constructed for account of this company a main line from Hauser Jct., Idaho to Coeur d'Alene City, Idaho, 13.61 miles, between September 1, 1886 and Oct. 24, 1886.

3. Operation

A.S.Doc.
250

The line was operated by the N.P.R.R.Co. from October 24, 1886 to September 30, 1887 without a contract; and from Oct. 1, 1887 to Aug. 15, 1893 under a contract dated October 1, 1887. From Aug. 15, 1893 to Aug. 31, 1896 line was operated by the Receivers of the N.P.R.R.Co. and from Aug. 31, 1896 to April 21, 1898 it was operated by the N.P.Ry.Co.

4. **Present Status of Corporation**

A.S.
599-30

The name of this corporation was stricken from the records of the State of Washington for failure to pay annual license fees, August 23, 1909.

The records are in the custody of Mr. R. H. Relf, the Assistant Secretary of the Northern Pacific Railway Co. at Saint Paul, Minnesota.

5. **Chain of Title**

	From	To	Date	Form of Transfer
A.S.Doc. 140	S.F.& I.R.R.Co.	N.P.Ry.Co.	April 21, 1898	Deed

SCHEDULE OF INSTRUMENTS AND RECORDS

File Ref.	Description
A.S. 599-30	Articles of Incorporation of Spokane Falls and Idaho Railroad Company.
A.S.Doc. 250	Contract of October 1, 1887, by which N.P. R.R. Co. et al operated the property.
A.S.Doc. 140	Deed of April 21, 1898, by which S.F.& I. R.R. Co. conveyed its entire property to N.P. Ry. Co.
L.A.File 140	Land Assistant's file "Data used in compiling return to Order No.20 - Corporate History".

HELENA AND NORTHERN RAILROAD COMPANY

Chart No. 59
Place No. 62
Map No. 43

1. **Incorporation**

A.S.
599-9

Incorporated under the general laws of the Territory of Montana.

Articles are dated October 30, 1886, and were filed with the Secretary of Territory October 30, 1886.

Organization effected November 11, 1886.

2. **Construction**

L.A.File
140

This company did no actual construction but the N.P.R.R.Co. constructed for account of the company a main line from Clough Junction (formerly Birdseye) Montana to Marysville, Montana, 12.58 miles, between March 28, 1887 and October 18, 1887.

3. **Operation**

A.S.Doc.
R.R.229

This company did not operate the property, but the line was operated by the N.P.R.R.Co. under contract of June 1, 1887 from November 20, 1887 to September 7, 1888, on which date the property was conveyed to the Northern Pacific and Montana Railroad Company.

A.S.Doc.
599-9

4. **Present Status of Corporation**

No action has been taken to dissolve this corporation

but having parted with its assets it is not active.

The records are in the custody of Mr. R. H. Relf, the Assistant Secretary of the Northern Pacific Ry.Co. at Saint Paul, Minnesota.

5. <u>Chain of Title</u>

	From	To	Date	Form of Transfer
A.S.Doc. R.R.274	H.& N.R.R.Co.	N.P.& M.R.R.Co.	Sept.7, 1888	Deed
A.S.Doc. 133	N.P.&M.R.R.Co.	N.P.Ry.Co.	April 21, 1898	Deed

SCHEDULE OF INSTRUMENTS AND RECORDS

File Ref.	Description
A.S. 599-9	Articles of Incorporation of Helena and Northern Railroad Company.
A.S.Doc. R.R.229	Contract of June 1, 1887, under which the N.P.R.R. Co. operated the property.
A.S.Doc. R.R.274	Deed of September 7, 1888, by which H.& N. R.R. Co. conveyed its entire property to Northern Pacific and Montana Railroad Company.
A.S.Doc. 133	Deed of April 21, 1898, by which N.P.& M.R.R.Co. conveyed its entire property to N.P. Ry. Co.
L.A.File 140	Land Assistant's file "Data used in compiling return to Order No.20 - Corporate History".

NORTHERN PACIFIC, LAMOURE AND MISSOURI RIVER RAILROAD COMPANY

Chart No. 61
Place No. 14
Map No. 44

1. Incorporation

A.S. File 599-20

Incorporated under the general laws of the Territory of Dakota.

Articles are dated November 10, 1886, and were filed with the Secretary of Territory December 10, 1886. Organization effected July 21, 1887.

2. Construction

L.A. File 140

The N.P.R.R. Co. constructed for account of this company a main line from LaMoure, North Dakota to Edgeley, North Dakota, 21.30 miles, between June 15, 1887 and October 15, 1887.

3. Operation

A.S. Doc. 230

M.B. 317 p.91

A.S. Doc. 131

The property of this company was operated by the N.P.R.R. Co. from November 1, 1887 to August 15, 1893, under contract of June 1, 1887; by the receivers of the N.P.R.R. Co. from August 15, 1893 to August 31, 1896 under lease of November 17, 1894, retroactive for the receivership period, and by the N.P.Ry. Co. from September 1, 1896 to April 21, 1898, without a formal contract.

File 82
Compt.
Box 17
M.B.317
p.89

Receivers for this company were appointed October 2, 1893 and dismissed October 31, 1894.

4. <u>Present Status of Corporation</u>

A.S.File
599-20

No action has been taken to dissolve this corporation but having parted with its assets it is not active.

The records are in the custody of Mr. R. H. Relf, the Assistant Secretary of the Northern Pacific Ry.Co. at Saint Paul, Minnesota.

5. <u>Chain of Title</u>

	From	To	Date	Form of Transfer
A.S.Doc. 131	N.P.L.M.&M.R.R.R. Co.	N.P.Ry.Co.	April 21, 1898	Deed

SCHEDULE OF INSTRUMENTS AND RECORDS

File Ref.	Description
A.S.File 599-20	Articles of Incorporation of Northern Pacific, LaMoure and Missouri River Railroad Company.
A.S.Doc. 230	Contract of June 1, 1887, by which N.P.R.R.Co. operated the property.
A.S.Doc. 131	Deed of April 21, 1898, by which N.P.L.M.& M.R. R.R. Co. conveyed its entire property to N.P.Ry.Co.
L.A.File 140	Land Assistant's file "Data used in compiling return to Order No.20 - Corporate History".
M.B.317 p.91	Contract of November 17, 1894, by which the Receivers of the N.P.R.R.Co. operated the property.
File 82 Compt. Box 17	Order appointing Receivers for N.P.L.M.& M.R. R.R. Co. October 2, 1893.
M.B.317 p.89	Order dismissing Receivers of N.P.L.M.& M.R. R.R. Co. October 31, 1894.

ROCKY FORK AND COOKE CITY RAILWAY COMPANY

Chart No.62
Place No.129
Map No.45

1. **Incorporation**

A.S.File
599-27

Incorporated under the general laws of the Territory of Montana.

Articles are dated December 10, 1886, and were filed with Secretary of Territory December 30, 1886.

Organization effected March 28, 1887.

A.S.File
599-27

Amended Articles, increasing the amount of capital stock were filed with the Secretary of Territory June 4, 1888.

M.B.338
p.138

Amended Articles increasing capital stock adopted May 4, 1889. No record of filing.

2. **Construction**

L.A.File
140

This company constructed a main line from Laurel, Montana to Red Lodge, Montana, 44.37 miles, between October 10, 1887 and March 1, 1889.

3. **Operation**

L.A.File
140

This company operated its property from June 1889 until July 31, 1890.

Operated by the N.P.R.R.Co. without formal contract from August 1, 1890 to August 15, 1893; by the Receivers of the N.P. R. R. Co. without formal contract from August 15, 1893 to August 31, 1896, and by the N.P.Ry. Co. without formal contract from Sept. 1, 1896 to April 21, 1898, on which date the property was conveyed to the N.P. Ry. Co.

4. **Present Status of Corporation**

A.S.File 599-27

No action has been taken to dissolve this corporation, but having parted with its assets it is not active.

The records are in the custody of Mr. R. H. Relf, the Assistant Secretary of the Northern Pacific Ry.Co. at Saint Paul, Minnesota.

5. **Chain of Title**

	From	To	Date	Form of Transfer
A.S.Doc. 136	R.F.& C.C.Ry.Co.	N.P.Ry.Co.	April 21,1898	Deed

SCHEDULE OF INSTRUMENTS AND RECORDS

File Ref.	Description
A.S.File 599-27	Articles of Incorporation of Rocky Fork and Cooke City Railway Company.
A.S.File 599-27	Amended Articles increasing capital stock.
M.B.338 p.138	Amended Articles increasing capital stock.
A.S.Doc. 136	Deed of April 21, 1898, by which R.F.& C.C. Ry.Co. conveyed its entire property to N. P. Ry. Co.
L.A.File 140	Land Assistant's file "Data used in compiling return to Order No.20 - Corporate History".

THE MISSOULA AND BITTER ROOT VALLEY RAILROAD COMPANY

Chart No. 63
Place No. 63
Map No. 46

1. Incorporation

A.S. 599-17

Incorporated under the general laws of the Territory of Montana.

Articles are dated January 4, 1887, and were filed with the Secretary of Territory January 17, 1887.

M.B. 316

Organization effected January 17, 1887.

2. Construction

L.A. File 140

This company did no actual construction but the N.P.R.R.Co. constructed for account of this company a main line, 50.85 miles in length, as follows:

From	To	Date
Missoula, Montana	M.P. 40	May 25, 1887 to Jan. 10, 1888
M.P. 40	Grantsdale, (formerly Skalkaho, Mont.)	Nov. 15, 1887 to May 1, 1888

3. Operation

A.S.Doc. R.R. 239

This company did not operate the property but the lines were operated by the N.P.R.R.Co. under contract of June 1, 1887 as follows:

From	To	Miles	Date
Missoula	Victor	35.85	June 1, 1888 to Sept. 7, 1888
Victor	Grantsdale	15.00	Aug. 1, 1888 to Sept. 7, 1888

On September 7, 1888 this property was conveyed to the Northern Pacific and Montana Railroad Company.

4. Present Status of Corporation

A.S.Doc. 599-17

No action has been taken to dissolve this corporation, but having parted with its assets it is not active.

The records are in the custody of Mr. R. H. Relf, the Assistant Secretary of the Northern Pacific Ry.Co. at Saint Paul, Minnesota.

5. Chain of Title

	From	To	Date	Form of Transfer
A.S.Doc. R.R.276	M.& B.R.V. R.R.Co.	N.P.& M.R.R.Co.	Sept. 7, 1888	Deed
A.S.Doc. 133	N.P.& M. R.R.Co.	N.P. Ry. Co.	April 21, 1898	Deed

SCHEDULE OF INSTRUMENTS AND RECORDS

File Ref.	Description
A.S. 599-17	Articles of Incorporation of The Missoula and Bitter Root Valley Railroad Company.
A.S.Doc. R.R.239	Contract of June 1, 1887 under which the N.P.R.R.Co. operated the property.
A.S.Doc. R.R.276	Deed of September 7, 1888, by which M.& B. R.V. R.R.Co. conveyed its entire property to Northern Pacific and Montana Railroad Company.
A.S.Doc. 133	Deed of April 21, 1898, by which N.P.& M.R.R. Co. conveyed its entire property to Northern Pacific Railway Company.
L.A.File 140	Land Assistant's file "Data used in compiling return to Order No.20 - Corporate History".

THE DRUMMOND AND PHILIPSBURG RAILROAD COMPANY

Chart No. 64
Place No. 64
Map No. 47

1. Incorporation

A.S.Doc. 9934

Incorporated under the general laws of the Territory of Montana.

Articles are dated January 4, 1887, and were filed with the Secretary of Territory January 17, 1887.

Organization effected January 17, 1887.

2. Construction

L.A.File 140

This company did no actual construction but the N.P.R.R. Co. constructed for account of this company a main line from Drummond, Montana to Philipsburg, Montana, 25.80 miles, between April 15, 1887 and September 12, 1887.

3. Operation

A.S.Doc. R.R.227

This company did not operate the property but the line was operated by the N.P.R.R.Co. under contract of June 1, 1887 from November 20, 1887 to September 7, 1888, on which date the property was conveyed to the Northern Pacific and Montana Railroad Company.

4. Present Status of Corporation

A.S.Doc. 9934

No action has been taken to dissolve this corporation,

but having parted with its assets it is not active.

The records are in the custody of Mr. R.H.Relf, the Assistant Secretary of the Northern Pacific Ry.Co. at Saint Paul, Minnesota.

5. <u>Chain of Title</u>

	From	To	Date	Form of Transfer
A.S.Doc. R.R.273	D.& P.R.R.Co.	N.P.& M.R.R.Co.	Sept.7,1888	Deed
A.S.Doc. 133	N.P.& M.R.R.Co.	N.P.Ry.Co.	April 21,1898	Deed

SCHEDULE OF INSTRUMENTS AND RECORDS

File Ref.	Description
A.S.Doc. 9934	Articles of Incorporation of The Drummond and Philipsburg Railroad Company.
A.S.Doc. R.R.227	Contract of June 1, 1887, under which the N.P.R.R.Co operated the property.
A.S.Doc. R.R.273	Deed of Sept. 7, 1888, by which D.& P. R.R. Co. conveyed its entire property to Northern Pacific and Montana Railroad Company.
A.S.Doc. 133	Deed of April 21, 1898, by which N.P.& M. R.R. Co. conveyed its entire property to N.P. Ry. Co.
L.A.File 140	Land Assistant's file "Data used in compiling return to Order No.20 - Corporate History".

VANCOUVER, KLICKITAT AND YAKIMA RAILROAD COMPANY

Chart No.65, 107 & 106
Place No.101, 92 & 83
Map No.48

1. Incorporation

A.S.Doc. 9970

Incorporated under the general laws of the Territory of Washington.

Articles are dated January 27, 1887, filed with the Secretary of Territory January 29, 1887 and recorded Jan. 30, 1887.

Date of organization is unknown.

2. Construction

L.A.File 140

This company constructed a main line extending northeasterly from Vancouver, Washington, 13.50 miles, to Salmon Creek, beyond Brush Prairie. The line from Vancouver to Brush Prairie was built in 1888 and 1889 and extended to Salmon Creek in 1895.

3. Operation

This company operated its line from March 1889 to November 30, 1897. A receiver was appointed about 1895 but details of the receivership are not available.

4. Present Status of Corporation

A.S.Doc. 9970

The name of this corporation was stricken from the records of the Secretary of State of Washington, August 23,

1909, for failure to pay annual license fees. The records are in the custody of Mr. R. H. Relf, Assistant Secretary of the N.P.Ry.Co., St. Paul, Minnesota.

5. <u>Chain of Title</u>

L.A.File 140

This company failed and the property was sold under foreclosure November 20, 1897, being conveyed by Sheriff's deed of November 30, 1897 to R. L. Durham, Trustee, who on the same date conveyed the property to Louis Gerlinger and he conveyed it to the Portland Vancouver & Yakima Railway Co.

	From	To	Date	Form of Transfer
A.S.Doc. 8863	J.Miller, Sheriff of Clarke County	R.L.Durham, Trustee	Nov.30,1897	Sheriff's Deed
A.S.Doc. 8863	R.L.Durham, Trustee	Louis Gerlinger	Nov.30,1897	Deed
A.S.Doc. 8863	Louis Gerlinger et ux	P.V.&Y.Ry. Co.	Nov.30,1897	Deed
A.S.Doc. 1395	P.V.& Y.Ry.Co.	W.Ry.& Nav. Co.	July 3,1903	Articles of Consolidation
A.S.Doc. 1517	W.Ry.& Nav.Co.	N.P.Ry.Co.	Oct.19,1903 #	Deed

\# An error was discovered in this deed and a corrected deed was executed December 10, 1903.

SCHEDULE OF INSTRUMENTS AND RECORDS

File Ref.	Description
A.S.Doc. 9970	Articles of Incorporation of the V.K.& Y. R.R. Co.
A.S.Doc. 8863	Sheriff's Deed of Nov. 30, 1897, by which Vancouver, Klickitat and Yakima Railroad Company conveyed its entire property to R. L. Durham, Trustee.
A.S.Doc. 8863	Deed of Nov. 30, 1897, by which R.L.Durham, Trustee conveyed the property to Louis Gerlinger.
A.S.Doc. 8863	Deed of Nov. 30, 1897, by which Louis Gerlinger conveyed the property to Portland, Vancouver & Yakima Railway Company.
A.S.Doc. 1395	Articles of July 3, 1903 consolidating the P.V.& Y. Ry. Co. and Washington & Oregon Railway Co. to form the Washington Railway & Navigation Co.
A.S.Doc. 1517	Deed of Oct. 19, 1903, by which W.Ry.& Nav. Co. conveyed its entire property to N. P. Ry. Co.
L.A.File 140	Land Assistant's file "Data used in compiling return to Order No.20 - Corporate History."

SEATTLE AND WEST COAST RAILWAY COMPANY

          Chart No.66
          Place No.65
          Map No.49

1. Incorporation

A.S.Doc. 9958

Incorporated under the general laws of the Territory of Washington.

Articles are dated February 7, 1887 and were filed with the Secretary of Territory April 13, 1887.

M.B.674 p.8

Organization effected April 14, 1887.

2. Construction

L.A.File 140

This company completed the grade for a main line of railroad between Woodinville, Washington and Snohomish, Washington, 14.40 miles, between June 1887 and January 1888.

3. Operation

This company operated no lines.

4. Present Status of Corporation

L.A.File 140

The name of this company was stricken from the records of the Secretary of State of Washington August 23, 1909, for failure to pay annual license fees.

The N. P. Ry. Co. is not in possession of the records of this company and does not know who is their custodian.

5. **Chain of Title**

	From	To	Date	Form of Transfer
A.S.Doc. 10095	S.& W.C.Ry.Co.	S.L.S.& E.Ry.Co.	Mar. 24, 1888	Deed
A.S.Doc. 1336	Eben Smith, Special Master, and Receivers of the S.L.S. & E.Ry.Co.	Morton S. Paton, et al, Comm. of Bondholders	June 19, 1896	Deed
A.S.Doc. 1336	Morton S. Paton, et al, Comm. of Bondholders	S. & I. Ry.Co.	July 28, 1896	Deed
A.S.Doc. 310	S. & I. Ry.Co.	N. P. Ry. Co.	Mar. 21, 1901	Deed

SCHEDULE OF INSTRUMENTS AND RECORDS

File Ref.	Description
A.S.Doc. 10095	Deed of March 24, 1888, by which Seattle and West Coast Railway Company conveyed its entire property to Seattle Lake Shore and Eastern Railway Company.
A.S.Doc. 1336	Deed of June 19, by which the entire property of the S.L.S.& E. Ry. Co. was conveyed to a Committee of Bondholders.
A.S.Doc. 1336	Deed dated July 28, 1896, by which the Committee of Bondholders conveyed that portion of the S.L.S.& E. Ry. Co's. lines lying between Seattle, Sumas and Sallal Prairie to the S. & I. Ry. Co.
A.S.Doc. 310	Deed of March 21, 1901, by which S. & I. Ry. Co. conveyed its entire property to N. P. Ry. Co.
L.A.File 140	Land Assistant's file "Data used in compiling return to Order NO. 20 - Corporate History".

CANYON CREEK RAILROAD COMPANY

Chart No. 67
Place No. 81
Map No. 50

1. Incorporation

A.S.Doc. 9994

Incorporated under the general laws of the Territory of Idaho.

Articles are dated July 6, 1887, and were filed with the Secretary of Territory July 14, 1887.

Date of organization is unknown.

2. Construction

L.A.File 140

This company graded a line between Wallace, Idaho, and Burke (formerly Custer) 6.83 miles in Idaho, between July and November 1887, but had laid no track on it when property was sold.

3. Operation

L.A.File 140

This company operated no lines.

4. Present Status of Corporation

L.A.File 140

The charter of this corporation was declared forfeited by the Secretary of State of Idaho, December 1, 1912, because of failure to comply with Idaho corporation tax law

The N.P.Ry.Co. has no knowledge as to the location

of the records of this company and does not know who is their custodian.

5. Chain of Title

	From	To	Date	Form of Transfer
A.S.Doc. 8861	C.C.R.R.Co.	C.d'A.Ry.& N.Co.	Aug. 29, 1888	Deed
A.S.Doc. 22	C.d'A.Ry.& N.Co.	N.P.Ry.Co.	Jan. 26, 1897	Deed

SCHEDULE OF INSTRUMENTS AND RECORDS

File Ref.	Description
A.S.Doc. 9994	Articles of Incorporation of Canyon Creek Railroad Co.
A.S.Doc. 8861	Deed of Aug. 29, 1888, by which Canyon Creek Railroad Company conveyed its entire property to Coeur d'Alene Railway and Navigation Company.
A.S.Doc. 22	Deed of Jan. 26, 1897, by which C.d'A. Ry.& N.Co. conveyed its entire property to N.P. Ry. Co.
L.A.File 140	Land Assistant's file "Data used in compiling return to Order No.20 - Corporate History".

THE CENTRAL WASHINGTON RAILROAD COMPANY

Chart No.69 & 111
Place No.125 & 115
Map No.51

1. Incorporation

A.S.Doc. 9962

Incorporated under the general laws of the Territory of Washington.

Articles are dated February 1, 1888, and were filed with the Secretary of Territory March 2, 1888.

Organization effected March 5, 1888.

2. Construction

L.A.File 140

This company did no actual construction but the N.P.R.R.Co. constructed for account of this company a main line as follows:

From	To	Miles	Date
Cheney, Wash.	Davenport, Wash.	41.40	July 10, 1888 to April 1889
Davenport, Wash.	Almira, Wash.	46.10	July 16 to Nov. 25, 1889
Almira, Wash.	Coulee City, Wash.	21.16	Nov. 10, 1889 to Dec. 10, 1890
	Total - -	108.66	

Maps were filed for a line extending northwesterly from Coulee City and this was graded for 8.00 miles in 1890. No right of way was acquired and the line was abandoned.

3. **Operation**

A.S.Doc. 282

and

L.A.File 140

The line was operated as follows:

Cheney, Wash.	Davenport, Wash.	41.40	July 1, 1889 to June 1, 1898
Davenport, Wash.	Almira, Wash.	46.10	June 14, 1890 to June 1, 1898
Almira, Wash.	Coulee City, Wash.	21.16	Nov. 1, 1890 to June 1, 1898

Operated by Northern Pacific Railroad Company under lease dated November 1, 1888 from July 1, 1889 to Aug. 15, 1893.

Receivers were appointed for the Central Wash. R.R.Co. Oct. 6, 1893 but they did not operate the property and were discharged Oct. 31, 1894.

Operated by Receivers of N.P.R.R.Co. under lease of Nov. 1, 1888 from Aug. 15, 1893 to Oct. 31, 1895.

Chas. P. Chamberlin was appointed receiver for the Cent. Wash. R.R.Co. and road turned over to him Oct. 31, 1895. Operation under this receivership was from Nov. 1, 1895 to June 1, 1898.

A.S.Doc. 7

By agreement dated Oct. 1, 1896 The C.W.R.R.Co. was permitted to operate over the N.P.Ry.Co's tracks from Cheney, Wash. to Spokane, Wash.

4. **Present Status of Corporation**

A.S.Doc. 9962

The name of this corporation was stricken from the records of the Secretary of State of Washington, Aug. 23,

1909, for failure to pay annual license fees.

The records are in the custody of Mr. R. H. Relf, the Assistant Secretary of the Northern Pacific Railway Co. at Saint Paul, Minnesota.

5. Chain of Title

The company failed and the property was sold under decree of foreclosure January 18, 1898, and conveyed by deed dated June 1, 1898 from W.J.C.Wakefield, Master in Chancery, to Charles T.Barney, et al, who by deed dated June 1, 1898 conveyed the property to the Washington Central Ry.Co.

	From	To	Date	Form of Transfer
A.S.Doc. 498	W.J.C.Wakefield Master in Chancery	Charles T.Barney et al	June 1, 1898	Master's Deed
	Chas.T.Barney et al	W.C.Ry.Co.	June 1, 1898	Deed
A.S.Doc. 7940	W.C.Ry.Co.	N.P.Ry.Co.	June 29, 1914	Deed

SCHEDULE OF INSTRUMENTS AND RECORDS

File Ref.   **Description**

A.S.Doc. 9962   Articles of Incorporation of The Central Washington Railroad Company.

A.S.Doc. 282   Lease of November 1, 1888, by which N.P.R.R.Co. et al operated the property.

A.S.Doc. 498   Master's Deed of June 1, 1898, from W.J.C.Wakefield to Charles T.Barney, et al and deed of June 1, 1898 from Charles T.Barney, et al to Washington Central Railway Company covering entire property.

A.S.Doc. 7940   Deed of June 29, 1914, by which W.C.Ry.Co. conveys its entire property to N.P.Ry.Co.

L.A.File 140   Land Assistant's file "Data used in compiling return to Order No.20 - Corporate History".

A.S.Doc. 7   Contract of Oct. 1, 1895 between N.P.Ry.Co. and C.P.Chamberlin, Receiver Cent. Wash. R.R.Co., permitting Cent.Wash. trains to run over N.P.Ry.Co's track Cheney to Spokane.

NORTHERN PACIFIC AND MONTANA RAILROAD COMPANY

Chart No. 71
Place No. 55
Map No. 52

1. **Incorporation**

A.S. 599-21

Incorporated under the general laws of the Territory of Montana.

Articles are dated April 18, 1888, and were filed with Secretary of Territory April 23, 1888.

M.B. 342

Organization effected May 2, 1888.

2. **Construction and Purchases**

L.A. File 140

This company constructed the following lines:

	From	To	Miles	Date
Main Line	Logan, Mont.	Butte, Mont.	71.00	
	First Section		27.00	Mar. 3, 1889 to Jan. 30, 1890
	Second Section		20.00	June 12, 1889 to April 15, 1890
	Third Section		24.00	May 27, 1889 to April 25, 1890
	Main Line Total		71.00	
Br. Line	Philipsburg, Mont.	Rumsey, Mont.	6.37	June 10, 1888 to Dec. 1, 1888
Br. Line	Sappington, Mont.	Norris, Mont.	20.64	Sept. 23, 1889 to June 14, 1890
Br. Line	Harrison, Mont.	Pony, Mont.	7.08	Nov. 18, 1889 to July 1, 1890
Br. Line	Boulder, Mont.	Elkhorn, Mont.	20.43	Sept. 18, 1889 to June 10, 1890

	From	To	Miles	Date
Br.Line	De Smet, Mont.	Lookout, Mont.	109.54	
	First Section		20.00	Sept. 24, 1889 to April 5, 1890
	Second Section		20.00	Nov. 15, 1889 to July 28, 1890
	Third Section		20.04	Jan. 15, 1890 to Sept. 4, 1890
	Fourth Section		20.00	Feb. 1, 1890 to Oct. 18, 1890
	Fifth Section		29.50	May 28, 1890 to Dec. 12, 1890
Br.Line	Whitehall, Mont.	Parrott, Mont. (formerly Gaylord now Renova)	5.75	July 3, 1895 to Sept. 3, 1895
	Branch Lines Total		169.81	

September 7, 1888, this company purchased the following lines:

A.S.Doc. R.R.274 Main Line of Helena and Northern Railroad Company from Clough Jctn. (formerly Birdseye) Montana, to Marysville, Montana, 12.58 miles.

A.S.Doc. R.R.275 Main Line of Helena, Boulder Valley and Butte Railroad Company from Jefferson City, Montana to Calvin, Montana, 30.00 miles.

A.S.Doc. R.R.273 Main Line of The Drummond and Philipsburg Railroad Company from Drummond, Montana to Philipsburg, Montana, 25.80 miles.

A.S.Doc. R.R.276 Main Line of The Missoula and Bitter Root Valley Railroad Company from Missoula, Montana to Grantsdale (formerly Skalkaho) Montana, 50.85 miles.

3. Operation

This company operated no lines, but its lines were operated by the N.P.R.R.Co., the receivers of the N.P.R.R Co. and the N.P.Ry. Co. as follows:

A.S.Doc.
R.R.283

N.P.R.R.Co. under lease of October 1, 1888 until August 15, 1893.

A.S.Doc.
Rec.37

Receivers of the N.P.R.R.Co. under lease of November 12, 1894, retroactive for the receivership period, from August 15, 1893 to August 31, 1896.

N.P.Ry.Co. from September 1, 1896 to April 21, 1898 without a formal contract.

Details of operation as below:

		From	To	Miles	Date
Main Line		Logan	Butte	71.00	June 14, 1890 to April 21, 1898
Br.	Line	Clough Jcth.	Marysville	12.58	Sept. 7, 1888 to April 21, 1898
Br.	Line	Jefferson City	Calvin	30.00	Sept. 7, 1888 to April 21, 1898
Br.	Line	Drummond	Philipsburg	25.80	Sept. 7, 1888 to April 21, 1898
Br.	Line	Philipsburg	Rumsey	6.37	Dec. 15, 1888 to April 21, 1898
Br.	Line	Missoula	Grantsdale	50.85	Sept. 7, 1888 to April 21, 1898
Br.	Line	Sappington	Norris	20.64	July 10, 1890 to April 21, 1898
Br.	Line	Harrison	Pony	7.08	July 10, 1890 to April 21, 1898

		From	To	Miles	Date
	Br. Line	Boulder	Elkhorn	20.43	July 10, 1890 to Apr. 21, 1898
	Br. Line	De Smet	St. Regis	71.40	Jan. 1, 1891 to April 21, 1898
	Br. Line	St. Regis	Lookout	38.14	Aug. 15, 1891 to April 21, 1898
	Br. Line	Whitehall	Parrott	5.75	Sept. 1, 1895 to April 21, 1898

L.A. File 140

This company went into a receivership October 4, 1893, Henry Stanton, S.T. Hauser of Helena, Mont. and E.L. Bonner of Missoula Mont. being appointed as receivers. Receivers were discharged October 31, 1894.

4. Present Status of Corporation

No action has been taken to dissolve this corporation but having parted with its assets it is not active.

The records are in the custody of Mr. R. H. Relf, the Assistant Secretary of the Northern Pacific Railway Co. at Saint Paul, Minnesota.

5. Chain of Title

	From	To	Date	Form of Transfer
A.S. Doc. R.R. 275	H.B.V.& B.R.R.Co.	N.P.& M.R.R.Co.	Sept. 7, 1888	Deed
A.S. Doc. 274	H. & N. R.R.Co.	N.P.& M.R.R.Co.	Sept. 7, 1888	Deed
A.S. Doc. 273	D. & P. R.R.Co.	N.P.& M.R.R.Co.	Sept. 7, 1888	Deed

	From	To	Date	Form of Transfer
A.S.Doc. 276	M.& B.R.V.R.R.Co.	N.P.& M. R.R.Co.	Sept.7,1888	Deed
A.S.Doc. 133	N.P.& M.R.R.Co.	N.P.Ry.Co.	April 21,1898	Deed

SCHEDULE OF INSTRUMENTS AND RECORDS

File Ref.	Description
A.S. 599-21	Articles of Incorporation of Northern Pacific and Montana Railroad Company.
A.S.Doc. P.R.274	Deed of Sept. 7, 1888, by which Helena and Northern Railroad Company conveyed its entire property to N.P.& M.R.R.Co.
A.S.Doc. R.R.275	Deed of Sept. 7, 1888, by which Helena Boulder Valley and Butte Railroad Company conveyed its entire property to N.P. & M.R.R.Co.
A.S.Doc. R.R.273	Deed of Sept. 7, 1888, by which The Drummond and Phillipsburg Railroad Company conveyed its entire property to N.P.& M.R.R.Co.
A.S.Doc. R.R.276	Deed of Sept. 7, 1888, by which The Missoula and Bitter Root Valley Railroad Company conveyed its entire property to N.P.& M.R.R.Co.
A.S.Doc. R.R.283	Lease of Oct. 1, 1888, by which the N.P.R.R.Co. operated the entire property of N.P.& M.R.R.Co.
A.S.Doc. Rec.37	Lease of November 12, 1894, by which the Receivers of the N.P.R.R.Co. operated the entire property of the N.P.& M.R.R.Co.

A.S.Doc. 133   Deed of April 21, 1898, by which N.P.& M.R.R.Co. conveyed its entire property to N.P.Ry.Co.

L.A.File 140   Land Assistant's file "Data used in compiling return to Order No.20 - Corporate History".

WASHINGTON SHORT LINE RAILWAY COMPANY

Chart No.72
Place No.134
Map No.53

1. Incorporation

A.S.File 599-41

Incorporated under the general laws of the Territory of Washington.

Articles are dated May 10, 1888, and were filed with the Secretary of Territory May 21, 1888.

Organization effected June 1, 1888.

2. Construction

L.A.File 140

This company constructed no lines. The road authorized by its charter was partially constructed by Allen C. Mason, between April 5, 1888 and June 1888 under an arrangement with the Northern Pacific R.R. Co., who took over the property and practically reconstructed it. The work of reconstruction commenced in June 1888 and was completed in December 1888. The road was delivered to the operating department February 8, 1889. This line extended from the Tacoma Mill to the smelter at Ruston, 3.08 miles.

3. Operation

No operation by this company. This line was operated as part of the Northern Pacific system from February 8, 1889 until August 22, 1900, when formal conveyance was made of this company's apparent interest.

4. <u>Present Status of Corporation</u>

A.S.File
599-41

The name of this corporation was stricken from the records of the State of Washington August 23, 1909, for failure to pay annual license fees.

The records are in the custody of Mr. R. H. Relf, the Assistant Secretary of the Northern Pacific Railway Co. at Saint Paul, Minnesota.

5. <u>Chain of Title</u>

A.S.Doc.
426

From	To	Date	Form of Transfer
W.S.L.Ry.Co.	N.P.Ry.Co.	Aug.22,1900	Deed

SCHEDULE OF INSTRUMENTS AND RECORDS

File Ref.   Description

A.S.599-41   Articles of Incorporation of Washington Short Line Railway Company.

A.S.Doc. 426   Deed of Aug. 22, 1900, by which W.S.L. Ry.Co. conveyed its entire property to N.P. Ry. Co.

L.A.File 140   Land Assistant's file 140 - "Data used in compiling return to Order No.20 - Corporate History".

THE TACOMA, ORTING & SOUTHEASTERN RAILROAD COMPANY

Chart No.74
Place No.24
Map No.54

1. Incorporation

A.S.Doc. 9963

Incorporated under the general laws of the Territory of Washington.

Articles are dated June 25, 1888, and were filed with the Secretary of Territory June 27, 1888.

Organization effected August 2, 1888.

2. Construction

L.A.File 140

This company did no actual construction but the N.P.R.R.Co. constructed for account of this company a main line from Orting, Washington to Puyallup River, Washington, 7.64 miles, between September 25, 1888 and June 12, 1889.

3. Operation

L.A.File 140

The line was operated by the N.P.R.R.Co. from June 24, 1889 to August 15, 1893; from August 15, 1893 to August 31, 1896 by the receivers of the N.P. R.R.Co. and from Sept. 1, 1896 to April 21, 1898 by the N.P.Ry. Co., without a formal contract.

4. Present Status of Corporation

The name of this corporation was stricken from the records of the State of Washington August 23, 1909 for failure to pay annual license fees.

The records are in the custody of Mr. R. H. Relf, the Assistant Secretary of the Northern Pacific Railway Co. at Saint Paul, Minnesota.

5. <u>Chain of Title</u>

	From	To	Date	Form of Transfer
A.S.Doc. 141	T.O.& S.E.R.R.Co.	N.P.Ry.Co.	April 21,1898	Deed

SCHEDULE OF INSTRUMENTS AND RECORDS

File Ref.   Description

A.S.Doc. 9963   Articles of Incorporation of Tacoma, Orting and Southeastern Railroad Company.

A.S.Doc. 141   Deed of March 21, 1898, by which T.O.& S.E. R.R. Co. conveyed its entire property to N.P.Ry. Co.

L.A.File 140   Land Assistant's file "Data used in compiling return to Order No.20 - Corporate History".

THE DULUTH, CROOKSTON AND NORTHERN RAIL ROAD COMPANY

Chart No.75
Place No.42
Map No.55

1. Incorporation

A.S.Doc. 10008

Incorporated under the general laws of the State of Minnesota.

Articles are dated February 16, 1889, and were filed with the Secretary of State March 4, 1889.

Organization effected March 12, 1889.

2. Construction

L.A.File 140

		From	To	Miles	Date
#	Main Line	Fertile, Minn.	Crookston, Minn.	22.40	Aug.10,1889 to Nov.15,1889
##	Main Line	Crookston, Minn.	Carthage Jct., Minn.	22.10	May 15 to Sept.5,1890

\# Constructed by the D.C.& N.R.R.Co.

\## Constructed by the N.P.R.R.Co. for account of the D.C.& N. R.R.Co.

3. Operation

A.S.Doc. R.R.354

The line was operated by the N.P.R.R.Co. under a contract dated August 1, 1890 until August 15, 1893; by the receivers of the N.P.R.R. Co. from August 15, 1893 to August 31, 1896 with no formal agreement, and from September 1, 1896 to April 21, 1898 by the N.P.Ry.Co.

with no formal agreement. Details follow:

	From	To	Miles	Date
Main Line	Fertile	Crookston	22.40	Dec. 2, 1889 to April 21, 1898
Main Line	Crookston	Carthage Jct.	22.10	Sept. 6, 1890 to April 21, 1898

4. **Present Status of Corporation**

No action has been taken to dissolve this corporation but having parted with its property it is not active.

The records are in the custody of Mr. R. H. Relf, the Assistant Secretary of the Northern Pacific Railway Co. at Saint Paul, Minnesota.

5. **Chain of Title**

	From	To	Date	Form of Transfer
A.S.Doc. 123	D.C.& N.R.R.Co.	N.P.Ry.Co.	April 21, 1898	Deed

SCHEDULE OF INSTRUMENTS AND RECORDS

File Ref.   Description

A.S.Doc. 10008   Articles of Incorporation of The Duluth Crookston and Northern Rail Road Company.

A.S.Doc. R.R.354   Contract of Aug. 1, 1890, by which N.P.R.R.Co. operated the property.

A.S.Doc. 123   Deed of April 21, 1898, by which D.C.& N. R.R. Co. conveyed its entire property to N.P.Ry.Co.

L.A.File 140   Land Assistant's file "Data used in compiling return to Order No.20 - Corporate History".

THE SNOHOMISH, SKYKOMISH AND SPOKANE RAILWAY AND TRANSPORTATION COMPANY

Chart No. 76
Place No. 57
Map No. 56

1. **Incorporation**

A.S.Doc. 9971

Incorporated under the general laws of the State of Washington.

Articles are dated April 15, 1889, and were filed with the Secretary of State April 19, 1889.

Supplementary Articles of Incorporation were filed with the Secretary of State April 23, 1891.

Date of organization is unknown.

2. **Construction**

L.A.File 140

This company constructed a main line from Snohomish Washington to Lowell, Washington, 8.00 miles, between July and September 1891.

3. **Operation**

L.A.File 140

This company operated no lines.

4. **Present Status of Corporation**

A.S.Doc. 9971

The name of this corporation was stricken from the records of the State of Washington for failure to pay annual license fees, August 23, 1909.

The N.P.Ry.Co. has no knowledge as to the location of this company.

5. **Chain of Title**

	From	To	Date	Form of Transfer
A.S.Doc. 8860	S.S.& S.Ry.& T.Co.	E.& M.C.Ry.Co.	Dec.15,1892	Deed
A.S.Doc. 10093	Sheriff of Snohomish County	E.V.Cary	Aug.18,1900 " 19,1901	Cert. Deed
A.S.Doc. 247	E.& M.C.Ry.Co.	S.& I.Ry.Co.	Jan.31,1900	Deed
A.S.Doc. 247	E.V.Cary	S.& I.Ry.Co.	Aug.18,1900	Deed
A.S.Doc. 310	S.& I.Ry.Co.	N.P.Ry.Co.	Mar.21,1901	Deed

SCHEDULE OF INSTRUMENTS AND RECORDS

File Ref.	Description
A.S.Doc. 9971	Articles of Incorporation of the Snohomish, Skykomish and Spokane Railway and Transportation Company.
A.S.Doc. 247	Deed of Jan. 31, 1900 by which E. and M.C.Ry.Co. conveyed its line, Snohomish to Everett, to Seattle & International Railway Co.
A.S.Doc. 247	Deed from E.V.Cary to the S.& I. Ry.Co. conveying Snohomish to Everett line.
A.S.Doc. 310	Deed of Mar. 21, 1901 by which S. & I. Ry.Co. conveyed its entire property to N.P. Ry. Co.
A.S.Doc. 8860	Deed of Dec. 15, 1892 by which Snohomish, Skykomish & Spokane Railway & Transportation Co. conveyed its entire property to Everett and Monte Cristo Ry.Co.
A.S.Doc. 10093	Certificate of Sale dated Aug. 18, 1900 and deed dated Aug. 19, 1901, from the Sheriff of Snohomish County to E.V.Cary, covering all the property of the E. & M. C. Ry. Co., sold under foreclosure proceedings.
L.A.File 140	Land Assistant's file "Data used in compiling return under Order No.20 - Corporate History".

JAMESTOWN AND NORTHERN EXTENSION RAILROAD COMPANY

Chart No.77
Place No.15
Map No.57

1. Incorporation

A.S.Doc. 9916

Incorporated under the general laws of the Territory of Dakota.

Articles are dated June 3, 1889, and were filed with the Secretary of Territory June 8, 1889.

Organization effected June 12, 1889.

Amended Articles changing route filed October 11, 1889.

2. Construction

L.A.File 140

The N.P.R.R.Co. constructed for account of this company a main line from Minnewaukan, North Dakota to Leeds, North Dakota, 18.03 miles, between July 1, 1889 and November 1, 1889.

3. Operation

A.S.Doc. 311

M.B.296 p.85

The property of this company was operated by the N.P.R.R.Co. from December 1, 1889 to August 15, 1893 under contract of September 2, 1889; by the receivers of the N.P.R.R.Co. from August 15, 1893 to August 31, 1896 under lease of November 17, 1894, retroactive for the receivership period, and from September 1, 1896 to April 21, 1898 by the N.P.Ry.Co. with no formal contract.

4. **Present Status of Corporation**

A.S.Doc. 9916

No action has been taken to dissolve this corporation but having parted with its assets it is not active.

The records are in the custody of Mr. R. H. Relf, the Assistant Secretary of the Northern Pacific Railway Co. at Saint Paul, Minnesota.

5. **Chain of Title**

From	To	Date	Form of Transfer
J.& N.E.R.R.Co.	N.P.Ry.Co.	April 21,1898	Deed

A.S.Doc. 129

SCHEDULE OF INSTRUMENTS AND RECORDS

File Ref.	Description
A.S.Doc. 9916	Articles of Incorporation of Jamestown and Northern Extension Railroad Company.
A.S.Doc. R.R.311	Lease of September 2, 1889, by which N.P.R.R.Co. operated the property.
M.B.296 p.85	Lease of November 17, 1894, by which Receivers of N.P. R.R. Co. operated the property.
A.S.Doc. 129	Deed of April 21, 1898, by which J.& N.E. R.R. Co. conveyed its entire property to N.P. Ry. Co.
L.A.File 140	Land Assistant's File "Data used in compiling return to Order No.20 - Corporate History".
File 82 Compt. Box 17	Order appointing Receivers of J.& N.E. R.R. October 2, 1893.
M.B.296 p.83	Order dismissing Receivers of J.& N.E. R.R. October 31, 1894.

SEATTLE TERMINAL RAILWAY AND ELEVATOR COMPANY

Chart No.79
Place No.102
Map No.58

1. Incorporation

A.S.Doc. 9959

Incorporated under the general laws of the State of Washington.

Articles are dated March 27, 1890, and were filed with the Secretary of State March 31, 1890.

A.S.File 1054

Organization effected March 29, 1890. (According to ruling of Interstate Commerce Commission any meeting held prior to date Articles of Incorporation are filed is illegal.)

2. Construction

L.A.File 140

This company constructed a railway line from Seattle, Washington to West Seattle, 3.20 miles, with a wharf and elevator at West Seattle, during the year 1890.

3. Operation

L.A.File 140

This company operated the property from the time of construction until April 20, 1893, when it was leased to the Seattle Terminal Ry. & Warehouse Co. for a period of one year. In June 1894 G.B.Nicoll was appointed receiver for the S.T.Ry. & Elevator Co. and he operated the property until the receivership was terminated, in May 1895. On May 24, 1895 the property passed to the

Philadelphia Mortgage and Trust Co. through sheriff's sale, the Trust Co. conveying it to the Seattle Warehouse and Terminal Co. July 3, 1895. The records indicate that the latter company operated the property throughout the Trust Co's. ownership.

No details of above operation are available.

4. <u>Present Status of Corporation</u>

A.S.Doc. 9959

The name of this corporation was stricken from the records of the Secretary of State of Washington August 23, 1909, for failure to pay annual license fees.

The N. P. Ry. Co. is not in possession of the records of this company and does not know who is their custodian.

5. <u>Chain of Title</u>

	From	To	Date	Form of Transfer
R.W.Deed 118	Sheriff of King Co.Wash.	Phila.Mtg.& Trust Co.	May 24, 1895	Cert.of Purchase
R.W.Deed 118-C	Phila.Mtg.& Trust Co.	S.W.&Ter.Co.	July 3, 1895	Deed
A.S.Doc. 3486	S.W.& Ter.Co.	S.& S.F.Ry. & Nav.Co.	Oct.12,1899	Deed
R.W.Deed 118	Sheriff of King Co.	S.& S.F.Ry. & Nav.Co.	Mar.26,1903	Deed
A.S.Doc. 1558	Sheriff of King Co.Wn.	N.W.I.Co.	Oct.10,1903	Cert.of Purchase.

	From	To	Date	Form of Transfer
A.S.Doc. 1516	N.W.I.Co.	N.P.Ry.Co.	Oct.21,1903	Deed
A.S.Doc. 1558	Sheriff of King Co.	N.W.I.Co.	Nov. 2, 1904	Deed

SCHEDULE OF INSTRUMENTS AND RECORDS

File Ref.   **Description**

A.S.Doc.
9959
Articles of Incorporation of Seattle Terminal Railway and Elevator Company.

R.W.Deed
118
Certificate of Purchase dated May 24, 1895, under which Seattle Terminal Railway and Elevator Company property was sold by the Sheriff of King County to Philadelphia Mortgage and Trust Company.

R.W.Deed
118-C
Deed of July 3, 1895, by which Philadelphia Mortgage and Trust Company conveyed the former property of the S.T.Ry. & Elev. Co. to Seattle Warehouse and Terminal Company.

A.S.Doc.
3486
Deed of October 12, 1899, by which S.W.& Term. Co. conveyed its entire property to The Seattle and San Francisco Railway and Navigation Company.

R.W.Deed
118
Deed of March 26, 1903, by which Sheriff of King County conveyed to S.& S.F.R.& N.Co. the S.T.Ry.& Elevator Co's. property.

A.S.Doc.
1558
Certificate of Purchase dated October 10, 1903, under which the Sheriff of King County, Wash. sold the entire property of the S.& S.F.Ry. & N. Co. to North-

western Improvement Company.

A.S.Doc. 1516   Deed of October 21, 1903, by which N.W.I.Co. conveyed the former property of the Seattle Ter.Ry.& Elev. Co. to N.P.Ry.Co.

A.S.Doc. 1558   Deed of Nov. 2, 1904, by which Sheriff of King County conveyed to N.W.I.Co. the property covered by Certificate of Purchase dated Oct. 10, 1903.

L.A.File 140   Land Assistant's file "Data used in compiling return to Order No.20 - Corporate History".

PHILADELPHIA MORTGAGE AND TRUST COMPANY

Chart No. 51
Place No. 93
Map No. 58

1. Incorporation

L.A. File 140

Incorporated under an Act of the General Assembly of the Commonwealth of Pennsylvania entitled "An Act to provide for the incorporation and regulation of certain corporations", approved April 29, 1874, and its various supplements.

Articles are dated May 19, 1886, and were filed with the Secretary of the Commonwealth on that date.

Date of organization is unknown.

2. Construction and Purchases

L.A. File 140

This company acquired possession of the property of the Seattle Terminal Railway and Elevator Company by purchase under foreclosure proceedings May 24, 1895. The property consisted of a railway extending from Seattle, Washington to West Seattle, 3.20 miles, with a wharf and elevator at West Seattle.

3. Operation

L.A. File 140

In June 1895 the Seattle Warehouse & Terminal Co. was incorporated and the records indicate that the property of the Seattle Terminal Railway and Elevator Company

325

was operated by them during the Trust Co's. ownership, viz: May 24, 1895 to July 3, 1895.

No details of operation are available.

4. Present Status of Corporation

This corporation is still in existence.

The records are in the custody of Mr. L. Gill, Secretary and Treasurer, 106 and 108 Fourth Street, Philadelphia, Pennsylvania.

5. Chain of Title

	From	To	Date	Form of Transfer
R.W.Deed 118	Sheriff of King County	P.M.& Trust Co.	May 24, 1895	Cert. of Purchase
R.W.Deed 118-C	Phila.M.& Trust Co.	S.W.& Ter.Co.	July 3, 1895	Deed
A.S.Doc. 3486	S.W.&Ter.Co.	S.&S.F.Ry.& N.Co.	Oct.12, 1899	Deed
R.W.Deed 118	Sheriff of King County	S.&S.F.Ry.& N.Co.	Mar.26, 1903	Sheriff's Deed
A.S.Doc. 1558	Sheriff of King County	N.W.I.Co.	Oct.10, 1903	Cert. of Purchase
A.S.Doc. 1516	N.W.I.Co.	N.P.Ry.Co.	Oct.21, 1903	Deed
A.S.Doc. 1558	Sheriff of King County	N.W.I.Co.	Nov. 2, 1904	Deed

SCHEDULE OF INSTRUMENTS AND RECORDS

File Ref.   Description

R.W.Deed 118
Sheriff's Certificate of Purchase dated May 24, 1895, by which the P.M.& T. Co. acquired the property of the Seattle Ter.Ry. & Elevator Co.

R.W.Deed 113-C
Deed of July 3, 1895, by which Philadelphia Mortgage and Trust Company conveyed the former property of the Seattle Terminal Railway and Elevator Company to Seattle Warehouse and Terminal Company.

A.S.Doc. 3486
Deed of October 12, 1899, by which S.W.& T.Co. conveyed its entire property to The Seattle and San Francisco Railway and Navigation Company.

R.W.Deed 118
Deed of March 26, 1903, by which Sheriff of King County conveyed to the S.& S.F.R.& N.Co. the S.T.Ry.& E. Co's. property.

A.S.Doc. 1558
Certificate of Purchase dated October 10, 1903, under which the property of the S.& S.F.Ry. & Nav. Co. was conveyed by the Sheriff of King County to Northwestern Improvement Company.

A.S.Doc. 1516
Deed of October 21, 1903, by which N.W.I.Co. conveyed the former property of the S.Ter.Ry.& Elev. Co. to N.P.Ry.Co.

A.S.Doc. 1558   Deed dated Nov. 2, 1904, by which the Sheriff of King County conveyed to the N.W.I.Co. the property covered by Certificate of Purchase dated Oct. 10, 1903.

L.A.File 140   Land Assistant's file "Data used in compiling return to Order No.20 - Corporate History".

SEATTLE WAREHOUSE & TERMINAL COMPANY

Chart No. 94
Place No. 85
Map No. 58

1. **Incorporation**

A.S.Doc. 9955

Incorporated under the general laws of the State of Washington.

Articles are dated June 21, 1895, and were filed with the Secretary of State June 22, 1895.

A.S.Doc. 3486

Organization effected June 26, 1895.

2. **Construction and Purchases**

L.A.File 140

This company purchased July 3, 1895, from the Philadelphia Mortgage & Trust Company, the property formerly owned by the Seattle Terminal Railway and Elevator Company, consisting of a railway extending from Seattle, Washington to West Seattle, 3.20 miles, with a wharf, warehouse and elevator at West Seattle.

3. **Operation**

L.A.File 140

This company operated the property from June 1895 to July 31, 1902, although conveyance was made to the Seattle and San Francisco Ry. and Navigation Co. by deed dated October 12, 1899.

4. **Present Status of Corporation**

L.A.File 140

The name of this corporation was stricken from the

records of the Secretary of State of Washington, Aug. 23, 1909, for failure to pay annual license fees.

The records of this company are in the custody of Mr. R. H. Ralf, Assistant Secretary of the Northern Pacific Ry. Co. at St. Paul, Minn.

5. Chain of Title

	From	To	Date	Form of Transfer
R.W.Deed 118	Sheriff of King Co.Wn.	P.M.& T.Co.	May 24, 1895	Cert. of Purchase
R.W.Deed 118-C	P.M.& T.Co.	S.W.& T.Co.	July 3, 1895	Deed
A.S.Doc. 3486	S.W.& T.Co.	S.& S.F.Ry. & Nav.Co.	Oct.12,1899	Deed
R.W.Deed 118	Sheriff of King Co.	S.& S.F.Ry. & Nav.Co.	Mar.26,1903	Sheriff's Deed
A.S.Doc. 1558	Sheriff of King Co.Wn.	N.W.I.Co.	Oct.10,1903	Cert.of Purchase
A.S.Doc. 1516	N.W.I.Co.	N.P.Ry.Co.	Oct.21,1903	Deed
A.S.Doc. 1558	Sheriff of King Co.	N.W.I.Co.	Nov. 2,1904	Deed

SCHEDULE OF INSTRUMENTS AND RECORDS

File Ref.   Description

A.S.Doc. 9955
Articles of Incorporation of Seattle Warehouse & Terminal Company.

R.W.Deed 118-C
Deed of July 3, 1895, by which P.M.& T.Co. conveyed the property of the S.T.Ry.& E. Co. to the S.W.& T. Co.

A.S.Doc. 3486
Deed of October 12, 1899, by which S.W.& T.Co. conveyed its entire property to Seattle and San Francisco Railway and Navigation Company.

A.S.Doc. 1558
Certificate of purchase dated October 10, 1903, under which the entire property of the S.& S.F.Ry.& N. Co. was sold to Northwestern Improvement Company by the Sheriff of King Co., Wash.

A.S.Doc. 1516
Deed of October 21, 1903, by which N.W.I.Co. conveyed the former property of the Seattle Terminal Railway and Elevator Company to N.P.Ry.Co.

A.S.Doc. 1558
Deed dated Nov. 2, 1904, by which the Sheriff of King County conveyed to the N.W.I.Co. the property covered by Certificate of Purchase dated Oct. 10, 1903.

L.A. File 140   Land Assistant's file "Data used in compiling return to Order No. 20 - Corporate History".

THE SEATTLE AND SAN FRANCISCO RAILWAY AND NAVIGATION COMPANY

Chart No.113
Place No.76
Map No.58

1. **Incorporation**

A.S.Doc. 1193

Incorporated under the general laws of the State of Washington.

Articles are dated March 23, 1899, and were filed with the Secretary of State March 27, 1899.

M.B.489 p.11

Organization effected March 28, 1899.

2. **Construction and Purchases**

L.A.File 140

On March 28, 1899 this company entered into a general contract, which provided for the acquisition or construction of certain properties; the same to be delivered, complete and ready for operation. Contract also made provision for operation by the constructing company prior to delivery. There was no railroad construction under this contract, with the exception of spurs and sidings in Seattle, and a short connection with the Northern Pacific Railway Company's tracks from the coal mines at Leary, Washington (now Ravensdale).

The Seattle Warehouse & Terminal Co., a railroad extending from Seattle, Washington to West Seattle, 3.20 miles, with a wharf, warehouse and elevator at West Seattle was one of the properties acquired under above contract; conveyance being made direct to this company by deed dated Oct. 12, 1899.

3. Operation

L.A.File 140

Having complied with the requirements of the contract of March 28, 1899, the properties acquired were turned over to this company for operation Nov. 1, 1900, and this operation continued until July 31, 1902.

The Seattle Warehouse & Terminal Co's. property, purchased Oct. 12, 1899, operated independently until July 31, 1902. By contract dated August 11, 1902, effective August 1, 1902, both lines came under control of the Northern Pacific Railway Company, but were operated by the S. and S.F.Ry. & Navig. Co. until Oct. 1, 1903. From this date operation was by the N.P.Ry.Co. The property was sold by the sheriff, October 10, 1903 to the N.W.I.Co. and by them conveyed, Oct. 21, 1903, to the N.P.Ry.Co.

A receiver was appointed for the S. and S.F.Ry. and Navig. Co. November 2, 1900 and he was discharged Nov. 20, 1900.

4. Present Status of Corporation

A.S.Doc. 1193

The name of this corporation was stricken from the records of the Secretary of State of Washington July 1, 1913 for failure to pay annual license fees, although it continued to hold meetings until October 8, 1914.

The records are in the custody of Mr. R.H.Relf, Assistant Secretary of the Northern Pacific Railway Company, St. Paul, Minnesota.

5. Chain of Title

	From	To	Date	Form of Transfer
R.W.Deed 118	Sheriff of King Co.Wn.	P.M.& T.Co.	May 24, 1895	Cert. of Purchase
R.W.Deed 118-C	P.M.& T.Co.	S.W.& T.Co.	July 3, 1895	Deed
A.S.Doc. 3486	S.W.& T.Co.	S.& S.F.Ry. & N.Co.	Oct.12, 1899	Deed
R.W.Deed 118	Sheriff of King Co.	S.& S.F.Ry. & N.Co.	Mar.26, 1903	Deed
A.S.Doc. 1558	Sheriff of King Co.	N.W.I.Co.	Oct.10, 1903 Nov. 2, 1904	Cert. of Purchase Deed
A.S.Doc. 1516	N.W.I.Co.	N.P.Ry.Co.	Oct.21, 1903	Deed

SCHEDULE OF INSTRUMENTS AND RECORDS

File Ref.	Description
A.S.Doc. 1193	Articles of Incorporation of The Seattle and San Francisco Railway and Navigation Company.
A.S.Doc. 3486	Deed of Oct. 12, 1899, by which the S.W.& T.Co. conveyed its entire property to the S.& S.F.Ry. & Nav. Co.
A.S.Doc. 1558	Certificate of Purchase dated Oct. 10, 1903, under which the Sheriff of King Co., Wash. sold the entire property of the S.& S.F.Ry. & N. Co. to the Northwestern Improvement Co.
A.S.Doc. 1516	Deed of Oct. 21, 1903, by which N.W.I.Co. conveyed the railroad property of the S. and S.F.Ry. & N. Co. to the N.P.Ry.Co.
A.S.Doc. 1186	Lease of Aug. 11, 1902, effective Aug. 1, 1902, under which the N.P.Ry. Co. controlled operation of the property of the S.& S.F.Ry. & N. Co.
A.S.Doc. 1558	Sheriff's deed of Nov. 2, 1904, by which the Sheriff of King County, conveyed to the N.W.I.Co. the property covered by Certificate of Purchase dated Oct. 10, 1903.
R.W.Deed 118	Certificate of Purchase dated May 24, 1895, under

which the Sheriff of King County sold the property of the Seattle Terminal Ry. & Elevator Co. to the Philadelphia Mtge. & Trust Co.

R.W.Deed 118
Deed dated Mar. 26, 1903, by which the Sheriff of King County conveyed to the S.& S.F.Ry. & N. Co. the property formerly owned by the Seattle Terminal Ry. & Elevator Co. Deed given to clear title.

R.W.Deed 118-C
Deed dated July 3, 1895, by which the Philadelphia Mortgage & Trust Co. conveyed the property of the S.T.Ry. & E. Co. to the S.W.& T.Co.

L.A.File 140
Land Assistant's file "Data used in compiling return to Order No.20 - Corporate History".

NORTHWESTERN IMPROVEMENT COMPANY

Chart No.104
Place No.68
Map No.58

1. Incorporation

A.S.Doc. 1146

Incorporated under the general laws of the State of New Jersey.

Articles are dated October 15, 1897, and were filed with the Secretary of State October 19, 1897.

Amended articles providing for the acquisition and development of mining properties filed with the Secretary of State October 6, 1898.

M.B.392 p.19

Organization effected October 20, 1897.

2. Construction and Purchases

This company did no construction of interest in connection with this report but it acquired at Sheriff's Sale October 10, 1903, the property of The Seattle and San Francisco Railway and Navigation Company. This property consisted of certain coal mines and a railway extending from Seattle, Washington, to West Seattle, 3.20 miles, with a wharf and elevator at West Seattle.

This company retained only the mines and conveyed the railroad property to the N.P. Ry. Co.

3. Operation

This company operated no railroads.

4. **Present Status of Corporation**

The corporation is still in existence and is active.

The records are in the custody of Mr. R. H. Relf, its Assistant Secretary at Saint Paul, Minnesota.

5. **Chain of Title**

	From	To	Date	Form of Transfer
A.S.Doc. 1516	Sheriff of King Co.	N.W.I.Co.	Oct.10, 1903	Cert. of Purchase
A.S.Doc. 1516	N.W.I.Co.	N.P.Ry.Co.	Oct.21, 1903	Deed
A.S.Doc. 1558	Sheriff of King Co.	N.W.I.Co.	Nov. 2, 1904	Deed

SCHEDULE OF INSTRUMENTS AND RECORDS

File Ref.	Description
A.S.Doc. 1146	Articles of Incorporation of Northwestern Improvement Company.
A.S.Doc. 1516	Sheriff's Certificate of Purchase dated Oct. 10, 1903, by which the entire property of the S.& S.F. Ry.& N. Co. was conveyed to the N.W.I.Co.
A.S.Doc. 1516	Deed of October 21, 1903, by which N.W.I.Co. conveyed to N.P. Ry. Co. the former railroad property of The Seattle and San Francisco Railway & Navigation Company.
A.S.Doc. 1558	Sheriff's deed dated Nov. 2, 1904, by which the Sheriff of King County conveyed to the N.W.I. Co. the property covered by Sheriff's Certificate of Purchase dated October 10, 1903.

WALLACE AND SUNSET RAILROAD COMPANY

Chart No. 80
Place No. 33
Map No. 59

1. **Incorporation**

A.S.File
599-39

Incorporated under the general laws of the Territory of Idaho.

Articles are dated April 14, 1890, and were filed with the Secretary of Territory April 22, 1890.

Organization effected May 14, 1890.

2. **Construction**

L.A.File
140

This company completed no lines but the N.P. R.R. Co. for account of this Company acquired some right of way and did about 3.00 miles of grading on a line from Wallace, Idaho to Sunset, Idaho, between June 1890 and May 1891. This line was completed to Custer, Idaho by the N.P.Ry. Co. in 1898 and 1899.

3. **Operation**

None

4. **Present Status of Corporation**

A.S.File
599-39

The charter of this company was declared forfeited by the Secretary of State of Idaho, for failure to comply with the Idaho Corporation Tax Law, December 1, 1912.

The records are in the custody of Mr. R. H. Relf, the Assistant Secretary of the Northern Pacific Railway Co. at Saint Paul, Minnesota.

5. **Chain of Title**

L.A. File 140

A search of the records of the N.P.Ry.Co. and of the public records of Shoshone County, Idaho, fails to reveal any deed by which the W.& S.R.R.Co. disposed of its property. Its holdings were insignificant and were appropriated by the N.P.Ry.Co. about 1898 when the Sunset Branch was completed.

SCHEDULE OF INSTRUMENTS AND RECORDS

File Ref.   **Description**

A.S.599-39   Articles of Incorporation of Wallace and Sunset Railroad Company.

L.A.File 140   Land Assistant's file "Data used in compiling return to Order No. 20 - Corporate History".

YAKIMA AND PACIFIC COAST RAILROAD COMPANY

Chart No. 81
Place No. 117
Map No. 60

1. **Incorporation**

A.S.599-43   Incorporated under the general laws of the State of Washington.

Articles are dated April 28, 1890, and were filed with the Secretary of State May 1, 1890.

M.B.322   Organization effected May 3, 1890.

2. **Construction**

L.A.File 140   This company did no actual construction but the N.P.R.R.Co. constructed for account of this company the following line:

From	To	Miles	Date
Chehalis, Wash.	South Bend, Wash.	56.68	Aug. 19, 1890 to Jan. 23, 1893

Although this company sold its property to The United Railroads of Washington by deed dated February 13, 1892, retroactive to August 5, 1890, the work of construction was completed by the N.P.R.R.Co. under the original account.

3. **Operation**

This company operated no lines.

4. **Present Status of Corporation**

A.S.Doc.
599-43

The name of this company was stricken from the records of the Secretary of State of Washington August 23, 1909, for failure to pay annual license fees.

The records are in the custody of Mr. R. H. Relf, the Assistant Secretary of the Northern Pacific Railway Co. at Saint Paul, Minnesota.

5. **Chain of Title**

	From	To	Date	Form of Transfer
A.S.Doc. 449	Y.& P.C.R.R.Co.	U.R.R.of W.	Feb. 13, 1892	# Deed
A.S.Doc. 132	U.R.R.of W.	N.P.Ry.Co.	April 21, 1898	Deed

This deed is dated February 13, 1892, but is retroactive to August 5, 1890.

SCHEDULE OF INSTRUMENTS AND RECORDS

File Ref.   **Description**

A.S.
599-43
Articles of Incorporation of Yakima and Pacific Coast Railroad Company.

A.S.Doc.
R.R.449
Deed of February 13, 1892, by which Y.& P.C.R.R. Co. conveyed its entire property to The United Railroads of Washington (Retroactive to Aug. 5, 1890.)

A.S.Doc.
132
Deed of April 21, 1898, by which U.R.R.'s of W. conveyed its entire property to N.P.Ry.Co.

L.A.File
140
Land Assistant's file "Data used in compiling return to Order No.20 - Corporate History".

TACOMA, OLYMPIA AND GRAYS HARBOR RAILROAD COMPANY

Chart No. 82
Place No. 116
Map No. 61

1. Incorporation

A.S. File
599-32

Incorporated under the general laws of the State of Washington.

Articles are dated May 7, 1890, and were filed with the Secretary of State on that date.

M.B. 346

Organization effected May 8, 1890.

2. Construction and Purchases

L.A. File
140

The Tacoma, Olympia and Chehalis Valley Railroad Co. was the owner of a right of way for a railroad between Centralia, Washington and Elma, Washington. About 10 miles of this line had been graded prior to entering into a contract for sale of the line to the T.O.& G.H. R.R. Co. Conveyance was made by deed dated September 10, 1890.

The T.O.& G.H. R.R. Co. did no actual construction but the N.P. R.R. Co. constructed for account of this company the following lines:

From	To	Miles	Date
Centralia	Elma	32.57	May 26, 1890 to May 1, 1891
Montesano	Ocosta	24.70	June 26, 1890 to Jan. 28, 1892

From	To	Miles	Date
Lakeview, Wash.	Gate, Wash.	43.50	June 8, 1890 to Aug. 5, 1891
Cosmopolis Jct.	Cosmopolis, Wn.	1.60	July to Sept. 1891
Aberdeen Jct.	Aberdeen, Wash.	2.60	Aug. 1890 to April 1891 Graded only

The T.O.& G.H. R.R. Co. by deed dated February 16, 1891 acquired the portion of the Puget Sound and Grays Harbor Railroad and Transportation Co's. line between Simpson (formerly Summit) and Montesano, Washington, 20.80 miles. This deed included an engine and two coaches.

Although this Company sold its property to the United Railroads of Washington by deed dated February 13, 1892, retroactive to August 1890, construction work on its line was completed by the N.P.R.R.Co. under the original account.

3. Operation

L.A.File 140

This company operated no lines.

Prior to conveyance of its property, February 13, 1892, the road was operated without a formal contract by the N.P.R.R.Co. in the interest of the United Railroads of Washington as follows:

From	To	Miles	Date
Simpson (formerly Summit) Wash.	Montesano, Wash.	20.80	Feb. 16, 1891 to Feb. 13, 1892
Centralia, Wash.	Elma, Wash.	32.57	May 1, 1891 to Feb. 13, 1892
Lakeview, Wash.	Olympia, Wash.	23.85	May 1, 1891 to Feb. 13, 1892
Olympia, Wash.	Gate, Wash.	19.65	Aug. 10, 1891 to Feb. 13, 1892

4. **Present Status of Corporation**

The name of this company was stricken from the records of the Secretary of State of Washington August 23, 1909, for failure to pay annual license fees.

The records are in the custody of Mr. R. H. Relf, the Assistant Secretary of the Northern Pacific Railway Co. at Saint Paul, Minnesota.

5. **Chain of Title**

	From	To	Date	Form of Transfer
R.W. Deed 274	T.O.& C.V.R.R. Co.	T.O.& G.H.R.R. Co.	Sept. 10, 1890	Deed
A.S. Doc. R.R. 450	P.S.& G.H.R.R. & T. Co.	T.O.& G.H.R.R. Co.	Feb. 16, 1891	Deed
A.S. Doc. R.R. 450	T.O.& G.H.R.R. Co.	U.R.R. of Wash.	Feb. 13, 1892	# Deed
A.S. Doc. 132	U.R.R. of Wash.	N.P.Ry. Co.	April 21, 1898	Deed

\# This deed is dated February 13, 1892, but is retroactive to August 5, 1890.

SCHEDULE OF INSTRUMENTS AND RECORDS

File Ref.   **Description**

A.S.599-32   Articles of Incorporation of Tacoma, Olympia and Grays Harbor Railroad Company.

R.W.Deed 274   Deed of September 10, 1890, by which Tacoma, Olympia and Chehalis Valley Railroad Company conveyed to T.O.& G.H.R.R.Co. its line between Centralia and Elma.

A.S.Doc. R.R.450   Deed of February 16, 1891, by which Puget Sound and Gray's Harbor Railroad and Transportation Company conveyed to T.O.& G.H. R.R. Co. its line from Simpson to Montesano.

A.S.Doc. R.R.450   Deed of February 13, 1892, by which T.O.& G.H. R.R. Co. conveyed its entire property to The United Railroads of Washington. (Retroactive to August 5, 1890).

A.S.Doc. 132   Deed of February 14, 1898, by which U.R.R. of W. conveyed its entire property to N.P. Ry. Co.

L.A.File 140   Land Assistant's file "Data used in compiling return to Order No.20 - Corporate History".

DULUTH TRANSFER RAILWAY COMPANY

Chart No. 83
Place No. 30
Map No. 62

1. **Incorporation**

A.S.Doc. 9996

Incorporated under the general laws of the State of Minnesota.

Articles are dated May 21, 1890, and were filed with Secretary of State May 24, 1890.

Amended articles, increasing the capital stock, filed with Secretary of State May 12, 1892.

Organization effected May 31, 1890.

2. **Construction**

L.A.File 140

This company constructed lines serving various industries along the Bay Front of Duluth, Minnesota, its main line extending from Bay Front Division southwesterly via West Duluth and Spirit Lake, about 9.06 miles.

The construction was begun in the year 1891, 3 miles being completed in West Duluth by April of that year. Work was completed in November 1893.

3. **Operation**

L.A.File 140
and
A.S.Doc. 10166

First completed section of 3 miles was put in operation in 1891. The lines were operated by Duluth Transfer Ry.Co. from time of construction until Sept. 28, 1896, when the company passed into a receivership with

John Eliot Bowles as receiver. The property was sold at public auction to a Committee of Bondholders January 2, 1902, who organized a new company called Duluth Transfer Railroad Company. The committee instructed the Special Master in Chancery, Thomas H. Pressnell, to convey the property direct to the new company and the conveyance was made January 21, 1902.

4. <u>Present Status of Corporation</u>

A.S.Doc. 9996

No action has been taken to dissolve this company, but having parted with its assets it is not active.

The records are not in the possession of the Northern Pacific Ry. Co. and their custodian is unknown.

5. <u>Chain of Title</u>

	From	To	Date	Form of Transfer
A.S.Doc. 10166	Thomas H. Pressnell Special Master	D.T.R.R.Co.	Jan. 21, 1902	Deed
A.S.Doc. 1125	D.T.R.R.Co.	N.P.Ry.Co.	May 26, 1902	Deed

SCHEDULE OF INSTRUMENTS AND RECORDS

File Ref.	Description
A.S.Doc. 9996	Articles of Incorporation of the Duluth Transfer Railway Company.
A.S.Doc. 10166	Deed of January 21, 1902, by which Thomas H. Pressnell, Master in Chancery, conveyed the property of the Duluth Transfer Railway Company to the Duluth Transfer Railroad Company.
L.A.File 140	Land Assistant's file "Data used in compiling return to Order No.20 - Corporate History".
A.S.Doc. 1125	Deed of May 26, 1902 by which D.T.R.R. Co. conveyed its entire property to N.P.Ry. Co.

DULUTH TRANSFER RAILROAD COMPANY

Chart No. 117
Place No. 21
Map No. 62

1. **Incorporation**

A.S.Doc. 9996

Incorporated under the general laws of the State of Minnesota.

Articles are dated December 31, 1901, and were filed with Secretary of State January 6, 1902.

Organization effected January 11, 1902.

2. **Construction**

L.A.File 140

This company constructed no lines but acquired on January 21, 1902, the lines of the Duluth Transfer Railway Company, which consisted of about 9.06 miles of main track extending from Bay Front Division in the City of Duluth, Minnesota, southwesterly via West Duluth and Spirit Lake, with tracks leading to various industries along the Bay Front of Duluth.

3. **Operation**

L.A.File 140

This company operated the property from January 21, 1902 until May 26, 1902.

4. **Present Status of Corporation**

A.S.Doc. 9996

No action has been taken to dissolve this corporation

but having parted with its assets it is not active.

The records are not in the custody of the Northern Pacific Ry. Co. and their custodian is unknown.

5. **Chain of Title**

	From	To	Date	Form of Transfer
A.S.Doc. 10166	Thomas H. Pressnell, Special Master	D.T.R.R.Co.	Jan. 21, 1902	Deed
A.S.Doc. 1125	D.T.R.R.Co.	N.P.Ry.Co.	May 26, 1902	Deed

SCHEDULE OF INSTRUMENTS AND RECORDS

File Ref.   **Description**

A.S.Doc.   Articles of Incorporation of the Duluth Transfer
9996   Railroad Company.

A.S.Doc.   Deed of January 21, 1902, by which Thomas H. Press-
10166   nell, Master in Chancery, conveyed the property of the
                Duluth Transfer Railway Company to the Duluth Transfer
                Railroad Company.

L.A.File   Land Assistant's file "Data used in compiling re-
140   turn to Order No. 20 - Corporate History".

THE UNITED RAILROADS OF WASHINGTON

Chart No. 84
Place No. 107
Map No. 63

1. Incorporation

A.S.599-35 Incorporated under the general laws of the State of Washington.

Articles are dated July 25, 1890, and were filed with the Secretary of State on August 2, 1890.

M.B.301 Organization effected August 4, 1890.

2. Construction and Purchases

L.A.File 140 This company constructed no lines.

A.S.Doc. R.R.450 This company acquired from the Tacoma, Olympia and Grays Harbor Railroad Company by deed dated February 13, 1892, and retroactive to August 5, 1890, the following lines:

	From	To	Miles
Main Line	Centralia, Wash.	Elma, Wash.	32.57
Main Line	Montesano, Wash.	Ocosta, Wash.	24.70
Main Line	Elma	Montesano	10.63
Br. Line	Elma	Simpson (formerly Summit) Wash.	10.17
Br. Line	Lake View, Wash.	Gate, Wash.	43.50
# Br. Line	Aberdeen Jctn.	Aberdeen, Wash.	2.60

	From	To	Miles
Br. Line	Cosmopolis Jctn.	Cosmopolis, Wash.	1.60

\# Completed June 8, 1895.

A.S.Doc.
R.R.449

This company acquired from the Yakima and Pacific Coast Railroad Company by deed dated February 13, 1892, and retroactive to August 5, 1890, a partially constructed line extending from Chehalis, Jct., Washington to South Bend, Washington, a distance of 56.68 miles.

The N.P.R.R.Co. finished construction of this line under the original account (Yakima and Pacific Coast Railroad Co.)

3. Operation

L.A.File
140
and
A.S.Doc.
R.R.355

This company's lines were operated by the N.P.R.R. Co. until August 15, 1893 under an agreement dated Aug. 5, 1890.

A.S.Doc.
Rec. 33

Operated by the receivers of the N.P.R.R.Co. from August 15, 1893 to August 31, 1896 under a lease dated November 24, 1894, retroactive for the receivership period.

Operated by the N.P.Ry.Co. from September 1, 1896 to April 21, 1898 without a formal contract.

Details of operation as follows:

	From	To	Miles	Date
Main Line	Elma	Montesano	10.63	Feb.13,1892 to April 21,1898

	From	To	Miles	Date
Main Line	Centralia	Elma	32.57	Feb.13,1892 to April 21,1898
Main Line	Montesano	So.Aberdeen	11.20	April 11,1892 to April 21,1898
Main Line	So.Aberdeen	Ocosta	13.50	June 6, 1892 to April 21,1898
Main Line	Chehalis Jctn.	So.Bend	56.68	June 1, 1893 to April 21,1898
Br. Line	Elma	Simpson	10.17	Feb.13,1892 to April 21,1898
Br. Line	Aberdeen Jctn.	Aberdeen	2.60	June 1, 1895 to April 21,1898
Br. Line	Lake View	Olympia, Wash.	23.85	Feb.13,1892 to April 21,1898
Br. Line	Olympia	Gate	19.65	Feb.13,1892 to April 21,1898
Br. Line	Cosmopolis Jct.	Cosmopolis	1.60	April 11, 1892 to April 21,1898

M.B.301 Receivers were appointed for this company October 6, 1893 and by stipulation of all parties, the receivers were discharged October 31, 1894.

4. <u>Present Status of Corporation</u>

The name of this company was stricken from the records of the Secretary of State of Washington August 23, 1909, for failure to pay annual license fees.

The records are in the custody of Mr. R. H. Relf, the Assistant Secretary of the Northern Pacific Railway Co. at Saint Paul, Minnesota.

5. Chain of Title

	From	To	Date	Form of Transfer
R.W.Deed G.H.Br.274	T.O.&C.V.R.R. Co.	T.O.& G.H.R.R. Co.	Sept. 10, 1890	Deed
A.S.Doc. R.R.450	P.S.& G.H.R.R. & T. Co.	T.O.& G.H.R.R. Co.	Feb. 16, 1891	Deed
A.S.Doc. R.R.450	T.O.& G.H.R.R. Co.	U.R.R's.of Wash.	Feb. 13, 1892	Deed
A.S.Doc. R.R.449	Y.& P.C.R.R.Co.	Y.R.R's.of Wash.	Feb. 13, 1892	Deed
A.S.Doc. 132	U.R.R.of W.	N.P. Ry. Co.	April 21, 1898	Deed

SCHEDULE OF INSTRUMENTS AND RECORDS

File Ref.	Description
A.S. 599-35	Articles of Incorporation of The United Railroads of Washington.
R.W.Deed G.H.Br.274	Deed of September 10, 1890, by which the Tacoma, Olympia and Chehalis Valley Railroad Company conveyed its property between Centralia and Elma, Washington to the Tacoma, Olympia and Grays Harbor Railroad Company.
A.S.Doc. R.R.450	Deed of February 16, 1891, by which the Puget Sound and Grays Harbor Railroad and Transportation Company conveyed its line from Montesano to Simpson, Washington to the Tacoma, Olympia and Grays Harbor Railroad Company.
A.S.Doc. R.R.450	Deed of February 13, 1892, by which Tacoma, Olympia and Grays Harbor Railroad Company conveyed to U.R.R's. of W. its entire property.
A.S.Doc. R.R.449	Deed of February 13, 1892, by which Yakima and Pacific Coast Railroad Company conveyed its entire property to U.R.R's. of W.
A.S.Doc. R.R.355	Contract of August 5, 1890, under which N.P.R.R.Co. operated the property of the U.R.R's. of W.
A.S.Doc. 132	Deed of April 21, 1898, by which U.R.R's. of W. conveyed its entire property to N. P. Ry. Co.

A.S.Doc. Rec.33   Lease of Nov. 17, 1894, under which Receivers of the N.P.R.R.Co. operated the property of the U.R.R. of W. et al.

L.A.File 140   Land Assistant's file "Data used in compiling return to Order No.20 - Corporate History".

GREEN RIVER AND NORTHERN RAILROAD COMPANY

Chart No.85
Place No.5
Map No.64, 29¹

1. **Incorporation**

A.S.
599-7

Incorporated under the general laws of the State of Washington.

Articles are dated September 18, 1890, and were filed with the Secretary of State September 22, 1890.

Organization effected September 23rd, 1890.

2. **Construction**

L.A.File
140

This company did no actual construction but the N.P.R.R.Co. constructed for account of this company the following lines:

	From	To	Miles	Date
Br.Line	Palmer Jct., Wash.	Durham, Wash.	2.90	May to Oct.1888
Br.Line	Durham	Kangley Mine, Wn.	1.50	Aug. to Oct.1889
Br.Line	Kangley Jctn. (formerly Durham) Wash.	M.P.10½	7.50	May to Nov.1890
Br.Line	M.P.10½	Niblock Mine	10.38	May to Nov.1890 (Graded only)

3. **Operation**

L.A.File
140

This company's completed lines were operated without a formal contract by the N.P.R.R.Co. until August 15, 1893 and from August 15, 1893 to August 31, 1896 by the Receivers of the N.P.R.R.Co., and from Sept. 1, 1896 to April 21, 1898 by the N.P.Ry.Co. Details of operation as follows:

	From	To	Miles	Date
Br.Line	Palmer	Durham	2.90	Dec.1,1888 to April 21,1898
Br.Line	Kangley Jct.	Mile Post 10½	7.50	June 30,1893 to April 21,1898
Br.Line	Durham	Kangley Mine	1.50	Jan.1,1891 to April 21,1898.

4. <u>Present Status of Corporation</u>

A.S. 599-7

The name of this corporation was stricken from the records of the State of Washington August 23, 1909, for failure to pay annual license fees.

The records are in the custody of Mr. R. H. Relf, the Assistant Secretary of the Northern Pacific Railway Co. at Saint Paul, Minnesota.

5. <u>Chain of Title</u>

A.S.Doc. 125

From	To	Date	Form of Transfer
G.R.& N.R.R.Co.	N.P.Ry.Co.	April 21, 1898	Deed

SCHEDULE OF INSTRUMENTS AND RECORDS.

File Ref.	Description
A.S. 599-7	Articles of Incorporation of Green River and Northern Railroad Company.
A.S.Doc. 125	Deed of Apr. 21, 1898 by which G.R.& N. R.R. Co. conveyed its entire property to N.P. Ry. Co.
L.A.File 140	Land Assistant's file "Data used in compiling return under Order No.20 - Corporate History".

LITTLE FALLS AND SOUTHERN RAILROAD COMPANY

Chart No.86
Place No.130
Map No.65

1. Incorporation

A.S.Doc.
9506

Incorporated under the general laws of the State of Minnesota.

Articles are dated September 30, 1890, and were filed with the Secretary of State October 1, 1890.

M.B.368
p.8

Organization effected October 16, 1890.

2. Construction

L.A.File
140

This company constructed a line in the City of Little Falls, Minnesota, 1.08 miles in length, extending from a connection with The Little Falls and Dakota Railroad on the west side of the Mississippi River to a point 200 feet south of the main channel of the canal of the Little Falls Water Power Company, between October 1890 and January 1, 1891.

3. Operation

L.A.File
140
and
A.S.Doc.
R.R.501

The railroad of this company was operated by the N.P.R.R.Co. without a formal contract from January 1, 1891 to Oct. 1, 1891, at which time a contract was executed for use of this line. Operation by the N.P.R.R.Co. continued until August 15, 1893; by the receiver of the

N.P.R.R.Co. from August 15, 1893 to August 31, 1896 and by the N.P.Ry.Co. from September 1, 1896 to September 4, 1899.

4. <u>Present Status of Corporation</u>

A.S.Doc. 9506

No action has been taken to dissolve this corporation but having parted with its assets it is not active.

The records are in the custody of Mr. R. H. Relf, the Assistant Secretary of the Northern Pacific Railway Co. at Saint Paul, Minnesota.

5. <u>Chain of Title</u>

A.S.Doc. 220

From	To	Date	Form of Transfer
L.F.& S.R.R.Co.	N.P.Ry.Co.	Sept. 4, 1899	Deed

SCHEDULE OF INSTRUMENTS AND RECORDS

File Ref.   Description

A.S.Doc.   Articles of Incorporation of Little Falls and
9506   Southern Railroad Company.

A.S.Doc.   Contract of October 1, 1891, by which Northern
R.R.501   Pacific Railroad Co. et al operated the property.

A.S.Doc.   Deed of Sept. 4, 1899, by which L.F.& S.R.R.Co.
220   conveyed its entire property to N.P.Ry.Co.

L.A.File   Land Assistant's file "Data used in compiling re-
140   turn to Order No.20 - Corporate History".

THE PORTLAND AND PUGET SOUND RAILROAD COMPANY

Chart No. 78
Place No. 84
Map No. 66

1. **Incorporation**

A.S.Doc. 9993

Incorporated under the general laws of the State of Oregon.

Articles are dated July 15, 1889 and were filed with the Secretary of State August 16, 1889.

Articles were also filed with the Secretary of State of Washington November 8, 1890.

Date of organization is unknown.

2. **Construction**

L.A.File 140

This company acquired the right of way for and partially graded a line between Vancouver, Washington and Tacoma, Washington in 1890, and about August 13, 1891 it acquired from the Oregon Railway Extensions Co. a bridge pier in the Columbia River, about 360 feet from the north bank, at Vancouver, Wash., together with all bridge material and the rights and franchises granted to the O.R.Ex.Co. by Act of Congress dated August 29, 1890.

R.W.Deed 1, 2&3
Vancouver to Yacolt

The portion of this line between Vancouver and Kalama, Washington, 28.90 miles, including the bridge pier, was acquired by the Washington and Oregon Railway

Company by condemnation decrees dated March 19, 1901 and September 26, 1901.

The balance of the line eventually became the property of the Spokane, Portland and Seattle Railway Company.

3. **Operation**

This company operated no lines.

4. **Present Status of Corporation**

L.A.File 140

This corporation was dissolved by proclamation of the Governor of the State of Washington, filed with the Secretary of State, January 20, 1906.

The N.P.Ry. Co. has no knowledge of the status of this company in Oregon.

The N.P.Ry. Co. is not in possession of the records of this company and does not know who is their custodian.

5. **Chain of Title**

	From	To	Date	Form of Transfer
R.W.Deed 2	O.R.Ex.Co.	P.&P.S.R.R.Co.	Aug.13,1891	Deed
R.W.Deeds 1&3	P.&P.S.R.R.Co.	W.& O.Ry.Co.	Mar.19,1901	Condemnation Decree
R.W.Deed 2	P.&P.S.R.R.Co.	"	Sept.26,1901	Condemnation Decree
A.S.Doc. 1395	W.& O.Ry.Co.	W.Ry.&Nav.Co.	July 3, 1903	Articles of Consolidation

	From	To	Date	Form of Transfer
A.S.Doc. 1517	# W.Ry.& Nav.Co.	N.P.Ry.Co.	Oct. 19, 1903	Deed

An error was discovered in this deed and a corrected deed was executed Dec. 10, 1903.

SCHEDULE OF INSTRUMENTS AND RECORDS

File Ref.	Description
A.S.Doc. 9993	Articles of Incorporation of P.& P.S.R.R.Co.
R.W.Deed 1&3	Condemnation Decree of Mar. 18, 1901, by which Washington & Oregon Railway Co. acquired the right of way and grade of the Portland and Puget Sound Railroad Co. between Vancouver and Kalama.
R.W.Deed 2	Condemnation Decree of Sept. 26, 1901, by which the W. & O. Ry. Co. acquired the bridge pier in the Columbia River at Vancouver. Also refers to deed from O. R. Ex. Co. to P. & P.S.R.R.Co.
A.S.Doc. 1395	Articles dated July 3, 1903 consolidating W.& O. Ry. Co. with Portland Vancouver and Yakima Railway Co. to form Washington Railway & Navigation Co.
A.S.Doc. 1517	Deed of Oct. 19, 1903, by which W.Ry.& Nav. Co. conveyed its entire property to N.P. Ry. Co.
L.A.File 140	Land Assistant's file "Data used in compiling return to Order No.20 - Corporate History".

WASHINGTON & OREGON RAILWAY COMPANY

Chart No. 116
Place No. 75
Map No. 66

1. Incorporation

A.S.Doc. 9974

Incorporated under the general laws of the State of Washington.

Articles are dated December 1, 1900, and were filed with the Secretary of State December 3, 1900.

M.B.519 p.34

Amended articles, increasing the capital stock, were filed with the Secretary of State July 19, 1901.

Organization effected December 14, 1900.

2. Construction

R.W.Deeds 1, 2 & 3 Vancouver to Yacolt

This company acquired the portion of the right of way and grade of the Portland and Puget Sound Railroad Company, extending from Kalama, Washington to Vancouver, Washington, 28.90 miles, including a bridge pier in the Columbia River, by condemnation decrees dated March 19, 1901 and September 26, 1901, and constructed a main line on the right of way and grade between March 1901 and March 1903. With the exception of the bridge across the Lewis River and a few buildings, the road was practically complete September 1, 1902.

3. Operation

L.A.File 140

This road was put in operation as soon as a section

was finished, commencing about Dec. 1, 1901 and continuing until Sept. 1, 1902, when the line became part of the Pacific Division of the N.P.Ry.Co., although the two companies maintained their accounts separately.

Regular through train service was not in effect until March 1, 1903, after the completion of the Lewis River bridge.

The line was operated by the N.P.Ry.Co., without a formal contract, from September 1, 1902 to June 30, 1903.

4. Present Status of Corporation

A.S.Doc. 1395

By Articles of Consolidation dated July 3, 1903, and filed with the Secretary of State July 13, 1903, this company was consolidated with the Portland, Vancouver & Yakima Railway Company as a new company called Washington Railway & Navigation Company.

The records are in the custody of Mr. R. H. Relf, the Assistant Secretary of the Northern Pacific Railway Co. at Saint Paul, Minnesota.

5. Chain of Title

	From	To	Date	Form of Transfer
R.W.Deed 2	Oregon Ry. Extensions Co.	P.&P.S.R.R. Co.	Aug.13,1891	Deed

	From	To	Date	Form of Transfer
R.W.Deeds 1&3	P.& P.S.R.R. Co.	W.&O.Ry.Co.	Mar.19,1901	Cond.
R.W.Deed 2	P.& P.S.R.R. Co.	W.&O.Ry.Co.	Sept.26,1901	Decree
A.S.Doc. 1395	W.&O.Ry.Co.	W.Ry.&Nav. Co.	July 3, 1903	Articles of Consolidation
A.S.Doc. 1317	# W.Ry.&Nav. Co.	N.P.Ry.Co.	Oct. 19,1903	Deed

\# An error was discovered in this deed and a corrected deed was executed December 10, 1903.

SCHEDULE OF INSTRUMENTS AND RECORDS

File Ref. **Description**

A.S.Doc. 7794
Articles of Incorporation of Washington & Oregon Railway Company.

M.B.519 p.34
Amended Articles dated July 19, 1901.

R.W.Deeds 1&3 Vancouver to Yacolt
Condemnation decree of March 19, 1901, by which W.& O. Ry. Co. acquired the right of way and grade of the Portland and Puget Sound Railroad Company between Vancouver and Kalama.

R.W.Deed 2
Condemnation decree dated Sept. 26, 1901, by which W. & O. Ry. Co. acquired from P.& P.S. R.R. Co. the bridge pier in the Columbia River at Vancouver; also refers to deed from O.R.Ex.Co. to P.& P.S.R.R.Co.

A.S.Doc. 1395
Articles consolidating W.& O. Ry. Co. and Portland, Vancouver and Yakima Railway Company to form Washington Railway and Navigation Company.

A.S.Doc. 1517
Deed of Oct. 19, 1903, by which Washington Railway and Navigation Company conveyed its entire property to N.P.Ry.Co.

L.A.File 140
Land Assistant's file "Data used in compiling return to Order No.20 - Corporate History".

BELLINGHAM BAY AND EASTERN RAILROAD COMPANY

Chart No. 87
Place No. 135
Map No. 67

1. Incorporation

A.S.Doc.
9975

Incorporated under the general laws of the State of Washington.

Articles are dated December 15, 1891, and were filed with the Secretary of State December 17, 1891.

Organization effected December 24, 1891.

2. Construction

L.A.File
140

This company constructed a main line as follows:

From	To	Miles	Date
Whatcom, Wash. (Coal Bunkers)	New Whatcom (Kentucky St.Jctn.)	2.15	1892
New Whatcom (Kentucky St. Jctn.)	Whatcom Jctn. (Larson)	3.73	1899-1900
Whatcom Jctn. (Larson)	Wickersham, Wash.	16.17	1901-1902
Whatcom (Coal Bunkers)	Fairhaven (now part of Bellingham) Wash.	1.32	1901-1902

3. Operation

L.A.File
140

This company operated the property as follows:

From	To	Miles	Date
Whatcom (Coal Bunkers)	New Whatcom (Kentucky St.Jctn.)	2.15	June 8, 1892 to Oct. 10, 1902
Larson	Wickersham	16.17	Feb. 1, 1902 to Oct. 10, 1902

From	To	Miles	Date
Whatcom (Coal Bunkers)	Fairhaven	1.32	Feb. 1, 1902 to Oct. 10, 1902
New Whatcom (Kentucky St. Jctn.)	Whatcom Jct. (Larson)	3.73	Mar. 15, 1900 (approx.) to Oct. 10, 1902
Bellingham Wash. (New Whatcom)	Wickersham, Wash.	22.82	Oct. 11, 1902 to July 1, 1903

The distance from Bellingham to Wickersham was shortened 0.55 of a mile, owing to portions of track as constructed not being used when entire line was completed.

This company put in and removed numerous logging spurs prior to sale to the N.P.Ry.Co. and these are not detailed.

The ownership of this company passed to the N.P. Ry.Co. the night of Oct. 10, 1902, and operation by the N.P.Ry.Co. is from that date, although the accounts were kept separate and the road not operated as part of the N.P.Ry.Co. until July 1, 1903.

This Company had trackage rights over line of Fairhaven & New Whatcom St.Ry. (name changed Northern Ry. & Improvement Co.) from New Whatcom to Whatcom Jctn. (now Larson) under an agreement dated Jan. 27, 1892.

4. Present Status of Corporation

A.S.Doc. 9975

The name of this corporation was stricken from the records of the State of Washington August 23, 1909, for failure to pay annual license fees.

The records are in the custody of Mr. R.H.Relf, the Assistant Secretary of the Northern Pacific Railway Co. at Saint Paul, Minnesota.

5. <u>Chain of Title</u>

	From	To	Date	Form of Transfer
A.S.Doc. 1362	B.B.& E.R.R.Co.	N.P.Ry.Co.	July 1, 1903	Deed

SCHEDULE OF INSTRUMENTS AND RECORDS

File Ref.	Description
A.S.Doc. 9975	Articles of Incorporation of Bellingham Bay and Eastern Railroad Company.
A.S.Doc. 1362	Deed of July 1, 1903, by which the B.B.& E. R.R.Co. conveyed its entire property to the N.P.Ry. Co.
L.A.File 140	Land Assistant's file 140 "Data used in compiling return to Order No.20 - Corporate History".

EVERETT AND MONTE CRISTO RAILWAY COMPANY

Chart No. 88 & 114
Place No. 48 & 40
Map No. 68

1. Incorporation

A.S.Doc. 9960

Incorporated under the general laws of the State of Washington.

Articles are dated March 11, 1892, and were filed with the Secretary of State March 14, 1892.

Organization effected March 17, 1892.

2. Construction and Purchases

A.S.Doc. 8860

This company purchased December 15, 1892 all the property of the Snohomish, Skykomish & Spokane Railway & Transportation Company, consisting of a line of railway extending from Everett, Wash. to Snohomish, Wash., a distance of 11.41 miles. Construction was practically complete from Snohomish to Lowell, 8 miles, and considerable right of way had been acquired from Lowell to Everett.

This company did not use all of the line (8 miles) as originally constructed, but in extending the line from Lowell to Everett it commenced at a point 6.39 miles from Snohomish and constructed 5.02 miles on revised location, work being done between March 1892 and Sept. 1893.

This company also constructed a main line from Hartford to Monte Cristo, Washington, 42.12 miles between April 1892 and Sept. 1893.

3. **Operation**

L.A.File 140

This company and its receivers operated the property as follows:

	From	To	Miles	Date
Main Line	Everett	Snohomish	11.41	Oct. 1893 to Jan. 31, 1900
Main Line	Hartford	Monte Cristo	42.12	Oct. 1, 1893 to Aug. 26, 1900

This company failed and went into a receivership January 31, 1900, and the property was sold at Sheriff's Sale August 18, 1900, conveyance being by deed dated August 19, 1901, from Peter Zimmerman, Sheriff of Snohomish County, Washington to E.V. Cary. August 18, 1900 the E.& M.C. Ry. Co. also executed a deed for the property direct to E.V. Cary. On the same date Edward V. Cary executed two deeds, one to Seattle & International Railway Company conveying the line from Everett to Snohomish and one to the Monte Cristo Railway Company conveying the line from Hartford to Monte Cristo. Previous to this, on January 31, 1900, the E.& M.C. Ry. Co. had conveyed the line between Everett and Snohomish to the S. & I. Ry. Co. but the deed was not recorded until October 1, 1900.

This company had trackage rights over the Seattle Lake Shore and Eastern Ry. to connect its line between Snohomish and Hartford.

4. Present Status of Corporation

A.S.Doc. 9960

The name of this corporation was stricken from the records of the State of Washington August 31, 1909, for failure to pay annual license fees.

The records are in the custody of Mr. R. H. Relf, Assistant Secretary of the N.P.Ry.Co., St. Paul, Minn.

5. Chain of Title

	Line	From	To	Date	Form of Transfer
A.S.Doc. 8860	Everett to Snohomish	S.S.&S.Ry.&T. Co.	E.&M.C.Ry. Co.	Dec.15,1892	Deed
A.S.Doc. 247	Everett to Snohomish	E.&M.C.Ry.Co.	S.&I.Ry. Co.	Jan.31,1900	Deed
A.S.Doc. 247	All	Peter Zimmerman, Sheriff Snohomish Co.	E.V.Cary	Aug.18,1900	Cert.
A.S.Doc. 1311	Hartford to Monte Cristo	E.&M.C.Ry.Co.	E.V.Cary	Aug.18,1900	Deed
A.S.Doc. 1311	Hartford to Monte Cristo	E.V.Cary	M.C.Ry.Co.	Aug.18,1900	Deed
A.S.Doc. 247	Everett to Snohomish	E.V.Cary	S.&I.Ry. Co.	Aug.18,1900	Deed
A.S.Doc. 310	Everett to Snohomish	S.&I.Ry.Co.	N.P.Ry.Co.	Mar.21,1901	Deed
A.S.Doc. 10093	All	Peter Zimmerman, Sheriff Snohomish Co.	E.V.Cary	Aug.19,1901	Deed
A.S.Doc. 1467	Hartford to Monte Cristo	M.C.Ry.Co.	N.P.Ry.Co.	July 31,1903	Deed

SCHEDULE OF INSTRUMENTS AND RECORDS

File Ref.   **Description**

A.S.Doc. 9960   Articles of Incorporation of the Everett and Monte Cristo Railway Company.

A.S.Doc. 8860   Deed of Dec. 15, 1892, by which the Snohomish, Skykomish & Spokane Railway & Transportation Co. conveyed its entire property to Everett and Monte Cristo Railway Co.

A.S.Doc. 247   Deed of Jan. 31, 1900, by which the E. and M.C. Ry.Co. conveyed its line from Everett to Snohomish to the Seattle and International Railway Company.

A.S.Doc. 247   Deed of Aug. 18, 1900, by which E.V.Cary conveyed the Everett-Snohomish line of the E. and M.C.Ry. to the S. & I. Ry. Co.

A.S.Doc. 247   Peter Zimmerman, Sheriff of Snohomish County to E.V.Cary August 18, 1900 (Certificate of Sale) covering all E.& M.C. Ry. property.

A.S.Doc. 310   Deed of Mar. 21, 1901, by which the S.& I.Ry.Co. conveyed its entire property to N.P.Ry.Co.

A.S.Doc. 1311   Deed of August 18, 1900, by which E.V.Cary conveyed the line from Hartford to Monte Cristo to the Monte Cristo Railway Company.

A.S.Doc. 1311 — Deed from E.& M.C.Ry.Co. to E.V.Cary dated August 18, 1900 conveying Hartford to Monte Cristo line.

A.S.Doc. 1467 — Deed of July 31, 1903, by which the M.C.Ry.Co. conveyed its entire property to the N.P.Ry.Co.

A.S.Doc. 10093 — Deed of August 19, 1901 from Peter Zimmerman, Sheriff of Snohomish County, to E.V. Cary, conveying the entire property of the Everett & Monte Cristo Ry. Co.

L.A.File 140 — Land Assistant's file "Data used in compiling return under Order No.20 - Corporate History".

MONTE CRISTO RAILWAY COMPANY

Chart No. 115
Place No. 31
Map No. 68

1. Incorporation

A.S.Doc. 10010
Incorporated under the general laws of the State of Washington.

Articles are dated August 25, 1900, and were filed with the Secretary of State August 27, 1900.

M.B.522 p.24
Amended articles were filed with the Secretary of State September 26, 1900.

M.B.522 p.54
Further amended articles decreasing the amount of capital stock were filed with the Secretary of State March 19, 1901.

Organization effected August 27, 1900.

2. Construction and Purchases

A.S.Doc. 1311
This company constructed no lines but by deed dated August 18, 1900 there was conveyed to it that portion of the main line of the Everett and Monte Cristo Railway Company, extending from Hartford, Washington to Monte Cristo, Washington, 42.12 miles.

3. Operation

L.A.File 140
This company operated the property from August 27, 1900 to July 31, 1903.

4. Present Status of Corporation

A.S.Doc. 10010

The name of this corporation was stricken from the records of the State of Washington August 31, 1909, for failure to pay annual license fees.

The records are in the custody of Mr. R. H. Relf, the Assistant Secretary of the Northern Pacific Railway Co. at Saint Paul, Minnesota.

5. Chain of Title

	From	To	Date	Form of Transfer
A.S.Doc. 8860	S.S.&S.Ry.&T.Co.	E.& M.C.Ry.Co.	Dec. 15, 1892	Deed
A.S.Doc. 10093	Sheriff of Snohomish Co., Wash.	E.V.Cary	Aug. 18, 1900 " 19, 1901	Cert. Deed
A.S.Doc. 1311	E.V.Cary	M.C.Ry.Co.	Aug. 18, 1900	Deed
A.S.Doc. 1467	M.C.Ry.Co.	N.P.Ry.Co.	July 31, 1903	Deed

SCHEDULE OF INSTRUMENTS AND RECORDS

File Ref.	Description
A.S.Doc. 10010	Articles of Incorporation of Monte Cristo Railway Company.
M.B.522 p.24	Amended Articles filed Sept. 26, 1900.
M.B.522 p.54	Amended Articles filed Mar. 19, 1901, decreasing capital stock.
A.S.Doc. 8860	Deed from Snohomish, Skykomish & Spokane Ry. & Transportation Co. to the Everett & Monte Cristo Ry. Co. dated Dec. 15, 1892.
A.S.Doc. 10093	Certificate of purchase from Sheriff of Snohomish County, Wash. to E. V. Cary dated Aug. 18, 1900. (See deed below)
A.S.Doc. 1311	Deed from E.V.Cary to Monte Cristo Ry.Co. dated Aug. 18, 1900.
A.S.Doc. 1467	Deed from M.C.Ry.Co. to N.P.Ry.Co. dated July 31, 1903.
A.S.Doc. 10093	Deed from Sheriff of Snohomish County to E.V.Cary dated Aug. 19, 1901.
L.A.File 140	Land Assistant's file "data used in compiling return under Order No.20 - Corporate History".

THE WASHINGTON AND COLUMBIA RIVER RAILWAY COMPANY

Chart No. 89
Place No. 79
Map No. 69

1. **Incorporation**

A.S.Doc. 1323

Incorporated under the general laws of the State of Washington.

Articles are not dated but first acknowledgment is dated July 30, 1892. Articles were filed with the Secretary of State August 4, 1892.

Organization effected August 20, 1892.

2. **Construction and Purchases**

A.S.Doc. 8858

This company constructed no lines but made the following purchases:

	From	To	Miles	Purchased From	Date
Main Line	Pendleton, Ore.	Oreg-Wash. Line	30.42	C.B. Wright	Oct. 5 1892
Main Line	Oreg-Wash. Line	Dayton, Wash.	98.08	"	"
		Main Line Total -	128.50		
Br. Line	Smeltz (formerly Killian Jct. Oreg.)	Athena, Oreg. (formerly Centerville)	14.39	"	"
Br. Line	Eureka Jct. Wash.	Pleasant View, Wash.	19.73	"	"

		From	To	Miles	Purchased From	Date
A.S.Doc. 2578	Br. Line	Mill Creek Jct., Wash.	Tracy (formerly Dudley, Wash.)	6.13	Mill Creek R.R.Co.	Sept. 8, 1905

Branch Line Total - 40.25

L.A.File 140

This company also purchased, during the year 1900, part of the right of way for a branch line from Riverside Washington to Covello, Washington, approximately 32 miles long.

3. Operation

L.A.File 140

This company operated its lines as follows:

	From	To	Miles	Date
Main Line	Hunts Jct.	Dayton	87.40	Nov. 5, 1892 to June 30, 1907
Main Line	Hunts Jct.	Wash-Oreg. Line	10.68	Nov. 5, 1892 to June 30, 1907
Main Line	Wash.-Oreg. Line	Pendleton	30.42	Nov. 5, 1892 to June 30, 1907
Br. Line	Smeltz	Athena	14.39	Nov. 5, 1892 to June 30, 1907
Br. Line	Eureka	Pleasant	19.73	Nov. 5, 1892 to June 30, 1907
Br. Line	Mill Creek Jct.	Tracy	6.13	Sept. 8, 1905 to June 30, 1907

W. D. Tyler was appointed receiver for this company August 25, 1894 and dismissed May 24, 1895.

4. Present Status of Corporation

A.S.Doc. 1323

This corporation is still in existence.

The records are in the custody of Mr. R. H. Relf, Assistant Secretary, N.P. Ry. Co., St. Paul, Minn.

5. Chain of Title

	From	To	Date	Form of Transfer
A.S.Doc. 8859	Geo.H.Durham, Master in Chancery	C.B.Wright	Oct. 1, 1892	Deed
A.S.Doc. 8858	C.B.Wright	The W.& C.Ry. Co.	Oct. 5, 1892	Deed
A.S.Doc. 10094	M.C.F.&Mfg.Co.	The O.R.R.& N.Co.	Oct. 26, 1903	Deed
A.S.Doc. 2390	The O.R.R.& N.Co.	M.C.R.R.Co.	Nov. 23, 1903	Deed
A.S.Doc. 2678	M.C.R.R.Co.	The W.& C. R.Ry.Co.	Sept. 8, 1905	Deed
A.S.Doc. 3575	The W.& C.R. Ry.Co.	N.P.Ry.Co.	June 18, 1907	Deed

SCHEDULE OF INSTRUMENTS AND RECORDS

File Ref.	Description
A.S.Doc. 1323	Articles of Incorporation of The Washington and Columbia River Railway Company.
A.S.Doc. 8858	Deed of October 5, 1892, by which C.B. Wright conveyed what is known as the Oregon and Washington Territory System to The W.& C. R. Ry. Co.
A.S.Doc. 8859	Deed of Oct. 1, 1892, by which Geo. H. Durham, Master in Chancery conveyed property of Oregon and Wash. Territory R.R. Co. to C. B. Wright.
A.S.Doc. 2678	Deed of Sept. 2, 1905, by which the Mill Creek Railroad Company conveyed to The W.&C.R. Ry. Co. its line from Mill Creek Jct. to Tracy, 6.13 miles.
A.S.Doc. 3575	Deed of June 18, 1907, by which The W.& C.R. Ry. Co. conveyed its entire property to the N.P. Ry. Co.
L.A.File 140	Land Assistant's File "Data used in compiling return to Order No.20 - Corporate History".
A.S.Doc. 10094	Deed of Oct. 26, 1903, by which the Mill Creek Flume & Mfg. Co. conveyed its railroad to the O.R.R.& N. Co.

A.S.Doc. 2390

Deed of Nov. 23, 1903, by which the O.R.R.& N. Co. conveyed M.C.F.& M.Co. property to the Mill Creek Railroad Co.

MONTANA SOUTHERN RAILWAY COMPANY

Chart No. 91
Place No. 105
Map No. 70

1. **Incorporation**

A.S.Doc. 9935

Incorporated under the general laws of the State of Montana.

Articles are dated November 2, 1893, and were filed with the Secretary of State November 14, 1893.

Organization effected February 6, 1894.

2. **Construction**

L.A.File 140

This company secured options on right of way for a railroad between Renova, Montana and Twin Bridges, Montana, 21.90 miles, upon which the grading for 17.50 miles was completed in January 1894.

3. **Operation**

L.A.File 140

None

4. **Present Status of Corporation**

A.S.Doc. 9935

No action has been taken to dissolve this corporation but having parted with its assets it is not active.

The records are in the custody of Mr. R. H. Relf, the Assistant Secretary of the Northern Pacific Railway Co. at Saint Paul, Minnesota.

5. **Chain of Title**

	From	To	Date	Form of Transfer
A.S.Doc. 60	M.S.Ry.Co.	G.& R.V. Ry.Co.	May 29, 1897	Deed
A.S.Doc. 197	G.&R.V.Ry.Co.	N.P. Ry. Co.	Feb. 28, 1899	Deed

SCHEDULE OF INSTRUMENTS AND RECORDS

File Ref.	Description
A.S.Doc. 9935	Articles of Incorporation of Montana Southern Railway Company.
A.S.Doc. 60	Deed of May 29, 1897, by which the M.S. Ry. Co. conveyed its road-bed and grade to the Gaylord and Ruby Valley Railway Company.
A.S.Doc. 197	Deed of February 28, 1899, by which the G.& R.V. Ry. Co. conveyed its entire property to the N.P. Ry. Co.
L.A.File 140	Land Assistant's file "Data used in compiling return to Order No.20 - Corporate History".

WASHBURN, BAYFIELD AND IRON RIVER RAILWAY COMPANY

Chart No.95
Place No.133
Map No.71

1. Incorporation

A.S.Doc. 8864

Incorporated under the general laws of the State of Wisconsin.

Articles are dated August 2, 1895, and were filed with the Secretary of State August 6, 1895.

M.B.669 p.5

Organization effected August 9, 1895.

2. Construction

Construction commenced in July 1897 and was completed January 7, 1898. The line extends from Iron River, Wisconsin to Washburn, Wisconsin, 33.78 miles.

3. Operation

L.A.File 140

The line was operated by the Washburn, Bayfield & Iron River Ry. Co. from January 7, 1898 until December 17, 1901. The company failed and a decree of foreclosure was entered July 5, 1901. An amended decree of October 12, 1901 provided that the property might be sold in such parts and parcels as the Special Master might determine, and some property was sold before the decree was modified requiring that sale of property be made as an entirety.

A.S.Doc. 1130

June 14, 1902, the property was sold at public auction to the Northern Pacific Ry. Co., title passing by deed dated June 16, 1902 from Albert C. Frost, Special Master. The W.B.& I. R. Ry. Co. and Royal Trust Co. also executed deeds to the N.P. Ry. Co. June 16, 1902. The Northern Pacific Ry. Co. has since operated the road. Geo. W. Seward was appointed receiver for this company December 24, 1898, succeeded on April 6, 1899 by Edgar E. Lincoln, who in turn was followed by Albert C. Frost. The latter made final disposition of the property.

4. Present Status of Corporation

No action has been taken to dissolve this corporation, but having parted with its assets it is not active.

The records are in the custody of Mr. R. H. Relf, the Assistant Secretary of the Northern Pacific Railway Co. at Saint Paul, Minnesota.

5. Chain of Title

	From	To	Date	Form of Transfer
A.S.Doc. 1130	W.B.& I.R.Ry.Co.	N.P.Ry.Co.	June 16, 1902	Deed
A.S.Doc. 1130	Albert C. Frost, Special Master	N.P.Ry.Co.	June 16, 1902	Deed

A.S.Doc. 1130

Deeds were also executed by Albert C. Frost, Receiver, and Royal Trust Co. and Horace S. Oakley, Trustees.

SCHEDULE OF INSTRUMENTS AND RECORDS

File Ref.   Description

A.S.Doc.   Articles of Incorporation of Washburn, Bayfield
8864   and Iron River Railway Company.

A.S.Doc.   Deed of June 16, 1902, by which the N.P. Ry. Co.
1130   acquired the property of the W.B.& I. R. Ry. Co.
                This file also contains the other deeds conveying
                property to the N.P. Ry. Co.

L.A.File   Land Assistant's file "Data used in compiling re-
140   turn to Order No.20 - Corporate History".

399

SEATTLE AND INTERNATIONAL RAILWAY COMPANY

Chart No. 96
Place No. 41
Map No. 72

1. Incorporation

A.S.Doc. 9976

Incorporated under the general laws of the State of Washington.

Articles are dated June 22, 1896, and were filed with the Secretary of State June 30, 1896.

A.S.Doc. 9976

Amended Articles, increasing the membership of the managing board were filed with the Secretary of State September 26, 1896.

Organization effected June 30, 1896.

2. Construction and Purchases

L.A.File 140

This company commenced construction of the following line:

From	To	Miles	Date
Br.Line Arlington	Darrington	28.03	Aug.1900 to March 1901

The N.P. Ry. Company took over the property by deed dated Mar. 21, 1901 and completed the construction of this line.

A.S.Doc. 1336

This company acquired on July 28, 1896 the following portions of the Seattle Lake Shore and Eastern Railway Company's lines:

	From	To	Miles
Main Line	Seattle, Wash.	Sallal Prairie, Wash.	63.32
Br. Line	Woodinville, Wash.	Sumas, Wash.	102.90

A.S.Doc. 247 and A.S.Doc. 10093

    This company acquired at Sheriff's Sale August 18, 1900 the portion of the main line of the Everett and Monte Cristo Railway Company extending from Snohomish, Washington to Everett, Washington, 11.41 miles.

3. Operation

L.A.File 140

    This company operated its lines as follows:

	From	To	Miles	Date
Main Line	Seattle	Sallal	63.32	July 1, 1896 to Mar. 31, 1901
Br. Line	Woodinville	Sumas	102.90	July 1, 1896 to Mar. 31, 1901
Br. Line	Snohomish	Everett	11.41	Feb. 1, 1900 to Mar. 31, 1901

A.S.File 917-14

4. Present Status of Corporation

A.S.Doc. 9976

    The name of this company was stricken from the records of the Secretary of State of Washington August 23, 1909 for failure to pay annual license fees.

    The records are in the custody of Mr. R. H. Relf, the Assistant Secretary of the Northern Pacific Railway Co. at Saint Paul, Minnesota.

5. **Chain of Title**

	From	To	Date	Form of Transfer
A.S.Doc. 1336	Eben Smith, Spl.Master and Receivers of S.L.S.& E. Ry.Co.	Morton S.Paton, et al, Comm.of Bondholders	June 19,1896	Deed
A.S.Doc. 1336	Morton S.Paton, et al	S.& I.Ry.Co.	July 28,1896	Deed
A.S.Doc. 8860	S.S.& S.Ry. & T. Co.	E.& M.C.Ry.Co.	Dec. 15,1892	Deed
A.S.Doc. 247	E.& M.C.Ry.Co.	S.& I. Ry.Co.	Jan. 31,1900	Deed
A.S.Doc. 10093	Peter Zimmerman, Sheriff	E.V.Cary	Aug. 19,1901 # Aug. 18,1900	Deed
A.S.Doc. 247	E.V.Cary	S.& I.Ry.Co.	Aug. 18,1900	Deed
A.S.Doc. 310	S.&I.Ry.Co.	N.P.Ry.Co.	Mar. 21,1901	Deed

Certificate of Purchase exchanged for deed of Aug. 19, 1901.

SCHEDULE OF INSTRUMENTS AND RECORDS

File Ref.	Description
A.S.Doc. 9976	Articles of Incorporation of Seattle and International Railway Company.
A.S.Doc. 9976	Amended Articles dated Sept. 26, 1896.
A.S.Doc. 1336	Deeds of June 19, 1896 and July 28, 1896, by which the S. & I. Ry. Co. acquired the property of Seattle Lake Shore and Eastern Railway Company from Seattle to Sallal Prairie and Sumas.
A.S.Doc. 8860	Deed of Dec. 15, 1892, by which E.& M.C. Ry. Co. acquired the line of the S.S.& S. Ry. & T. Co. from Snohomish to Everett.
A.S.Doc. 247 and A.S.Doc. 10093	Deeds of Aug. 18, 1900 and Aug. 19, 1901 from Peter Zimmerman, Sheriff, and Everett and Monte Cristo Railway Co. respectively to S. & I. Ry. Co., covering line from Snohomish to Everett.
A.S.Doc. 310	Deed of March 21, 1901, by which S. & I. Ry. Co. conveyed its entire property to the N.P. Ry. Co.
L.A.File 140	Land Assistant's file "Data used in compiling return to Order No. 20 - Corporate History".

A.S.File   Reference to date of operation in Ass't. Secretary's
917-14
                Correspondence File.

GAYLORD AND RUBY VALLEY RAILWAY COMPANY

Chart No. 103
Place No. 96
Map No. 73

1. Incorporation

A.S. File 599-6

Incorporated under the general laws of the State of Montana.

Articles are dated March 22, 1897, and were filed with the Secretary of State March 29, 1897.

Organization effected April 20, 1897.

2. Construction and Purchases

L.A. File 140

This company acquired May 29, 1897, from the Montana Southern Railway Company all its road-bed and grade between Renova and Twin Bridges, and between November 1897 and July 1898 the N.P. Ry. Co. for account of this company completed the grading and laid the rail for a main line from Renova, Montana to Twin Bridges, Montana, 21.90 miles.

3. Operation

L.A. File 140

The line was operated by the N.P. Ry. Co. without a formal contract from August 1, 1898 to February 28, 1899.

4. Present Status of Corporation

A.S. File 599-6

The charter of this company expired by limitation

March 29, 1917 and has not been renewed.

The records are in the custody of Mr. R. H. Relf, the Assistant Secretary of the Northern Pacific Railway Co. at Saint Paul, Minnesota.

5. <u>Chain of Title</u>

	From	To	Date	Form of Transfer
A.S.Doc. 60	M.S.Ry.Co.	G.& R.V.Ry.Co.	May 29, 1897	Deed
A.S.Doc. 197	G.& R.V.Ry.Co.	N.P. Ry. Co.	Feb. 28, 1899	Deed

SCHEDULE OF INSTRUMENTS AND RECORDS

File Ref.	Description
A.S.599-6	Articles of Incorporation of Gaylord and Ruby Valley Railway Company.
A.S.Doc. 60	Deed of May 29, 1897 by which the Montana Southern Railway Company conveyed its road-bed and grade to the G. & R. V. Ry. Co.
A.S.Doc. 197	Deed of Feb. 28, 1899, by which the G. & R. V. Ry. Co. conveyed its entire property to the N. P. Ry. Co.
L.A.File 140	Land Assistant's file "Data used in compiling return to Order No.20 - Corporate History".

PORTLAND, VANCOUVER & YAKIMA RAILWAY COMPANY

Chart No.105
Place No.74
Map No.74

1. **Incorporation**

A.S.Doc.
9977

Incorporated under the general laws of the State of Washington.

Articles are dated November 22, 1897, and were filed with the Secretary of State November 30, 1897.

M.B.521
p.46

Amended articles increasing the capital stock were filed with the Secretary of State November 25, 1898.

Organization effected November 30, 1897.

2. **Construction and Purchases**

L.A.File
140

This company purchased the property of the Vancouver, Klickitat & Yakima Railroad Company November 30, 1897, consisting of a main line extending from Vancouver, Washington, northeasterly 13.50 miles to Salmon Creek, beyond Brush Prairie; the purchase being made through Messrs. R. L. Durham, Trustee, and Louis Gerlinger.

This company constructed lines as follows:

From	To	Miles	Date
Brush Prairie	Salmon Creek (New Location)	2.50	April 3 to Aug. 8, 1899
Salmon Creek	Daly's Road	.30	Approx March 1900

	From	To	Miles	Date
	Brush Prairie	Salmon Creek (Old Location)	1.40	Abandoned in 1900
	Daly's Road	Yacolt	14.10	1901 and 1902
#	Sta.247+80	Vancouver Jct.	2.60	Feb. to July 1903
	Connection with Washington & Oregon Ry.Co. in Vancouver		.40	Mar. to July 1903
		Total -	19.90	

Construction not complete

3. Operation

L.A.File 140

This company operated its lines as constructed from Dec. 1, 1897 to June 30, 1903.

4. Present Status of Corporation

A.S.Doc. 1395

By Articles dated July 3, 1903, this company was consolidated with the Washington & Oregon Railway Company, forming a new company called Washington Railway & Navigation Company.

The records are in the custody of Mr. R.H.Relf, the Assistant Secretary of the Northern Pacific Railway Co. at Saint Paul, Minnesota.

5. Chain of Title

	From	To	Date	Form of Transfer
A.S.Doc. 8863	J.Miller, Sheriff Clarke Co., Wash.	R.L.Durham, Trustee	Nov. 30, 1897	Deed
A.S.Doc. 8863	R.L.Durham, Trustee	L.Gerlinger	Nov. 30, 1897	Deed

	From	To	Date	Form of Transfer
A.S.Doc. 8863	L.Gerlinger, et ux	P.V.& Y.Ry.Co.	Nov.30,1897	Deed
A.S.Doc. 1395	P.V.& Y.Ry.Co.	W.Ry.& Nav.Co.	July 3,1903	Articles of Consolidation
A.S.Doc. 1517	# W.Ry.& Nav.Co.	N.P.Ry.Co.	Oct.19,1903	Deed

An error was discovered in this deed and a corrected deed was executed December 10, 1903.

SCHEDULE OF INSTRUMENTS AND RECORDS

File Ref.   Description

A.S.Doc.   Articles of Incorporation of Portland, Vancouver
9977   & Yakima Railway Company.

M.B.521   Amended Articles dated Nov. 25, 1898.
p.46

A.S.Doc.   Deed of Nov. 30, 1897, by which John Miller, Sheriff
8863   of Clarke County, Wash. conveyed the entire property of
                the Vancouver, Klickitat and Yakima R.R.Co. to R.L.Durham, Trustee.

A.S.Doc.   Deed of Nov. 30, 1897, by which R.L.Durham, Trustee,
8863   conveyed the above property to Louis Gerlinger.

A.S.Doc.   Articles dated July 3, 1903, by which P.V.& Y.Ry.Co.
1395   consolidated with Washington and Oregon Railway Company
                to form the Washington Railway & Navigation Company.

A.S.Doc.   Deed of Oct. 19, 1903, by which W.Ry.& N. Co. con-
1517   veyed its entire property to N.P. Ry. Co.

A.S.Doc.   Deed of Nov. 30, 1897, by which Louis Gerlinger,
8863   et ux conveyed the same property to the P.V.& Y.Ry.Co.

L.A.File   Land Assistant's file "Data used in compiling re-
140   turn to Order No.20 - Corporate History".

SEATTLE AND MONTANA RAILROAD COMPANY

Chart No.108
Place No.136
Map No.75

1. Incorporation

L.A.File 140

Incorporated under the general laws of the State of Washington.

Articles are dated March 28, 1898, and were filed with the Secretary of State March 29, 1898.

2. Construction

L.A.File 140

This company, among other things, constructed a union station and passenger terminal approximately 0.84 of a mile in length, at Seattle, Washington, between July 1903 and May 10, 1906, and also constructed an approach to said terminal by a tunnel 2.24 miles in length between May 1903 and January 1905.

3. Operation

L.A.File 140

A.S.Docs. 3192&4541

The property is operated jointly by the Great Northern Ry. Co. and the N.P. Ry. Co. Operation commenced May 10, 1906. Agreements covering operation and maintenance of the property are dated August 31, 1906 (effective May 1, 1906) and March 1, 1909 (effective July 1, 1908.)

The N. P. Ry. Co. acquired an one-half interest in the Passenger Terminal and Tunnel by two deeds dated respectively November 16, 1907 and November 25, 1907.

4. Present Status of Corporation

L.A.File 140

This corporation is still in existence.

The records are in the custody of Mr. L. E. Katzenbach, Secretary, Great Northern Railway Company, St.Paul, Minnesota.

5. Chain of Title

	Description of Property	From	To	Date	Form of Transfer
R.W.Deed 398	Undivided ½ int. in Passenger Terminal	S.&M.R.R. Co.	N.P.Ry.Co.	Nov.16,1907	Deed
R.W.Deed 400	Undivided ½ int. in Tunnel	S.&M.R.R. Co.	N.P.Ry.Co.	Nov.25,1907	Deed

SCHEDULE OF INSTRUMENTS AND RECORDS

File Ref.	Description
A.S.Doc. 3192	Temporary agreement of August 31, 1906 superseded by A.S. Doc. 4541.
A.S.Doc. 4541	Contract of March 1, 1909 covering operation and maintenance, by the N.P. Ry. Co. and the Great Northern Ry. Co. of the Seattle Passenger Terminal and Tunnel.
R.W.Deed 398	Deed of Nov. 16, 1907, by which S.& M.R.R. Co. conveys to the N.P. Ry. Co. a one-half interest in passenger terminal.
R.W.Deed 400	Deed of Nov. 25, 1907, by which S.& M. R.R. Co. conveys to the N. P. Ry. Co. a one-half interest in tunnel.
L.A.File 140	Land Assistant's file "Data used in compiling return to Order No. 20 - Corporate History".

WESTERN AMERICAN COMPANY

Chart No. 109
Place No. 16
Map No. 76

1. Incorporation

A.S.Doc. 9961

Incorporated under the general laws of the State of Washington.

Articles are dated April 12, 1898, and were filed with the Secretary of State April 18, 1898.

Date of organization is unknown.

2. Construction

L.A.File 140

This company constructed a main line from Carbonado, Washington to Fairfax, Washington, 7.10 miles, between June 1898 and February 1899.

3. Operation

L.A.File 140
and
A.S.Doc. 665

This company operated its property from February 1899 until August 3, 1901, on which date it conveyed it to the N.P.Ry.Co.

4. Present Status of Corporation

A.S.Doc. 9961

The name of this company was stricken from the records of the Secretary of State of Washington August 23, 1909 for failure to pay annual license fees.

The N.P.Ry.Co. is not in possession of this company's records and does not know who is their custodian.

5. <u>Chain of Title</u>

	From	To	Date	Form of Transfer
A.S.Doc. 665	W.A. Co.	N.P. Ry. Co.	Aug. 3, 1901	Deed

SCHEDULE OF INSTRUMENTS AND RECORDS

File Ref.   **Description**

A.S.Doc. 9961   Articles of Incorporation of the Western American Company.

A.S.Doc. 665   Deed of Aug. 3, 1901, by which Western American Company conveyed the line from Carbonado to Fairfax to N. P. Ry. Co.

L.A.File 140   Land Assistant's file "Data used in compiling return to Order No. 20 - Corporate History".

417

THE WASHINGTON CENTRAL RAILWAY COMPANY

Chart No.110
Place No.106
Map No.77

1. Incorporation

A.S.Doc. 1449

Incorporated under the general laws of the State of Washington.

Articles are dated May 28, 1898, and were filed with the Secretary of State May 31, 1898.

Organization effected May 31, 1898.

2. Construction and Purchases

L.A.File 140

This company did no actual construction but the N.P.Ry.Co. constructed for account of this company a branch line from Coulee Junction, Washington to Adrian, Washington, 21.10 miles, between November 5, 1902 and September 20, 1903.

A.S.Doc. 498

This company purchased the main line of The Central Washington Railroad Company, extending from Cheney, Washington to Coulee City, Washington, 108.66 miles, June 1, 1898.

3. Operation

A.S.Doc. 108

The lines were operated by the N.P.Ry.Co. under a lease dated June 1, 1898, as follows:

	From	To	Miles	Date
Main Line	Cheney	Coulee City	108.66	June 1,1898 to June 29,1914

	From	To	Miles	Date
Br.Line	Coulee Jct.	Adrian	21.10	Dec.1,1903 to June 29,1914

4. Present Status of Corporation

A.S.Doc. 1449

No action has been taken to dissolve this corporation but having parted with its assets it is not active.

The records are in the custody of Mr. R. H. Relf, the Assistant Secretary of the Northern Pacific Railway Co. at Saint Paul, Minnesota.

5. Chain of Title

	From	To	Date	Form of Transfer
A.S.Doc. 498	W.J.C.Wakefield, Master in Chancery	Charles T.Barney, et al	June 1, 1898	Master's Deed
	Charles T.Barney, et al	W.C.Ry.Co.	June 1, 1898	Deed
A.S.Doc. 7940	W.C.Ry.Co.	N.P.Ry.Co.	June 29, 1914	Deed

SCHEDULE OF INSTRUMENTS AND RECORDS

File Ref.	Description
A.S.Doc. 1449	Articles of Incorporation of The Washington Central Railway Company.
A.S.Doc. 498	Deed of June 1, 1898, by which The Central Washington Railroad Company's property was conveyed to The W. C. Ry. Co.
A.S.Doc. 108	Lease of June 1, 1898 from The W.C.Ry.Co. to N.P.Ry.Co. covering the entire system.
A.S.Doc. 7940	Deed of June 29, 1914, by which The W.C.Ry.Co. conveyed its entire property to the N.P.Ry.Co.
L.A.File 140	Land Assistant's file "Data used in compiling return to Order No. 20 - Corporate History".

CLEARWATER SHORT LINE RAILWAY COMPANY

Chart No.112
Place No.108
Map No.78

1. Incorporation

A.S.Doc. 1149

Incorporated under the general laws of the State of Montana.

Articles are dated November 9, 1898 and were filed with the Secretary of State of Montana on that date.

Amended articles increasing the capital stock dated November 10, 1898 were filed as follows:

With Secretary of State of Montana Nov.10,1898
" " " " " Washington Nov.28,1898
" " " " " Idaho Dec. 13, 1898.

Organization effected November 9, 1898.

2. Construction and Purchases

L.A.File 140

The N.P. Ry. Co. constructed for account of this company the following lines:

	From	To	Miles	Date
Main Line	Arrow(formerly Potlatch Jct.)Idaho	Stites,Ida.	62.91	Nov.19,1898 to Mar.24, 1900
Br. Line	Joseph(formerly Lapwai Jct.)Idaho	Culdesac,	12.00	Nov.19,1898 to Oct.30, 1899
Br. Line	Culdesac,Ida.	Grangeville, Ida.	54.78	Mar.1906 to Dec.1908

A.S.Doc.
4839

This company purchased from the Spokane, Portland and Seattle Railway Company on June 21, 1909 a branch line extending from Snake River Junction, Washington to Riparia (formerly Texas City and Lewiston Junction,) Washington, 40.97 miles.

L.A. File
140

This company purchased some right of way for but did not construct the following lines:

	From	To	Miles	Date
Br. Line	Pullman, Wash.	Penawawa, Wash.	36.00	1899 to 1901
Br. Line	Lewiston, Ida.	Riparia, Wash.	70.00	1899 to 1900
Br. Line	Lo Lo, Mont.	Summit, Mont.	18.00	1909 to 1913 Partially graded in Aug. Sept. and Oct. 1909
Br. Line	Cold Springs Creek, Ida.	Nez Perce, Ida.	10.00	1899 to 1900

R.W. Deed
92

The line Cold Springs Creek to Nez Perce was sold to Z.A. Johnson June 30, 1909.

3. **Operation**

L.A. File
140

The Company's lines were operated by the N.P.Ry.Co. without formal contract as follows:

	From	To	Miles	Date
Main Line	Arrow	Oro Fino	29.00	Nov. 15, 1899 to June 23, 1914
Main Line	Oro Fino	Stites	33.91	May 15, 1900 to June 23, 1914
Br. Line	Joseph	Culdesac	12.00	Nov. 15, 1899 to Dec. 3, 1909

	From	To	Miles	Date
Br. Line	Culdesac	Vollmer	23.00	Mar. 1, 1908 to Dec. 3, 1909
Br. Line	Vollmer	Grangeville	31.78	Dec. 22, 1908 to Dec. 3, 1909
Br. Line	Snake Riv. Jct.	Lewiston Jct. (Now Riparia)	40.97	May 3, 1909 to June 23, 1914

A.S.Doc. 5068

November 11, 1909 a contract was entered into by the Oregon Washington & Idaho Railroad Co., the N.P.Ry. Co. and the C.S.L.Ry.Co. under the provisions of which the Camas Prairie Railroad Co. was created, and operated the portion of the C.S.L.Ry. Co's line between Joseph and Grangeville, 66.78 miles. This operation commenced December 3, 1909.

4. Present Status of Corporation

A.S.Doc. 1149

No action has been taken to dissolve this corporation but having parted with its assets it is not active.

This company's charter will expire by limitation on Nov. 9, 1918.

The records are in the custody of Mr. R. H. Relf, the Assistant Secretary of the Northern Pacific Railway Co. at Saint Paul, Minnesota.

5. **Chain of Title**

	Line	From	To	Date	Form of Transfer
A.S.Doc. 4839	Snake Riv. Jctn. to Riparia formerly Lewiston Jctn.	S.P.& S. Ry.Co.	C.S.L.Ry. Co.	June 21, 1909	Deed
A.S.Doc. 7939	All	C.S.L.Ry.	N.P.Ry.Co.	June 23, 1914	Deed

SCHEDULE OF INSTRUMENTS AND RECORDS

File Ref.	Description
A.S.Doc. 1149	Articles of Incorporation of Clearwater Short Line Railway Company.
A.S.Doc. 4839	Deed of June 21, 1909, by which the Spokane, Portland and Seattle Railway Company conveyed its line from Snake River Jct. to Lewiston Jct., 40.97 miles to C.S.L.Ry.Co.
A.S.Doc. 5068	Contract of Nov. 11, 1909, by which the Camas Prairie Railroad was created and operates the line from Joseph to Grangeville.
A.S.Doc. 7939	Deed of June 23, 1914, by which the C.S.L.Ry.Co. conveyed its entire property to the N.P.Ry.Co.
L.A.File 140	Land Assistant's file "Data used in compiling return to Order No. 20 - Corporate History".
R.W.Deed 92	Deed of June 30, 1909, by which C.S.L.Ry.Co. conveyed to Z. A. Johnson the right of way for a line between Cold Springs Creek and Nez Perce.

WASHINGTON RAILWAY & NAVIGATION COMPANY

Chart No.118
Place No.67
Map No.79

1. **Incorporation**

A.S.Doc.
1395

This company was formed by consolidating the Washington & Oregon Railway Company with the Portland Vancouver & Yakima Railway Company.

It is incorporated under the general laws of the State of Washington. The articles of consolidation are dated July 3, 1903, and were filed with the Secretary of State July 13, 1903.

Organization effected July 20, 1903.

2. **Construction**

A.S.Doc.
1395

This company completed construction of the connection commenced by the P.V.& Y. Ry.Co., 2.60 miles in length, from Vancouver Jctn. to Sta. 247+80 on the Vancouver-Yacolt line in July and August 1903, and acquired July 3, 1903, by its Articles of Consolidation, the following:

	From	To	Miles
Main Line	Kalama, Wash.	Vancouver, Wash.	28.90
Br.Line	Vancouver	Yacolt, Wash.	32.00
Portion of Vancouver-Yacolt Line abandoned			1.88
		Total - -	59.02

425

After the new connection from Vancouver Jctn. was built part of the old line out of Vancouver, 1.88 miles in length, was abandoned, those portions in the City of Vancouver being thereafter operated as part of the terminal at that place. Other portions not needed for terminal purposes were abandoned in 1908 by the N.P. Ry.Co., successor in interest.

3. **Operation**

L.A.File 140

This company's lines were operated by the N.P. Ry.Co. without any formal contract, as follows:

	From	To	Miles	Date
Main Line	Kalama	Vancouver	28.90	July 1,1903 to Oct.23,1903
# Br.Line	Vancouver Jctn.	Yacolt	30.12	July 1,1903 to Oct.23,1903

\# Mileage includes tracks in Vancouver and portions of old Vancouver-Yacolt line not yet abandoned.

4. **Present Status of Corporation**

A.S.Doc. 1395

The name of this corporation was stricken from the records of the Secretary of State of Washington, July 1, 1911, for failure to pay annual license fees.

The records are in the custody of Mr. R. H. Relf, the Assistant Secretary of the Northern Pacific Railway Co. at Saint Paul, Minnesota.

5. <u>Chain of Title</u>

Kalama to Vancouver

	From	To	Date	Form of Transfer
R.W.Deed 2	Oreg.Ry.Extensions Co.	Portland &Puget Sound R.R.Co.	Aug.13,1891	Deed
R.W.Deeds 1, 2&3	P.&P.S.R.R.Co.	Wash.&Ore.Ry. Co.	Mar.19,1901 and Sept.26,1901	Cond. Decrees
A.S.Doc. 1395	W.& O.Ry.Co.	W.Ry.& N.Co.	July 3, 1901	Articles of Consolidation
A.S.Doc. 1517	# W.Ry.& N.Co.	N.P.Ry.Co.	Oct.19,1903	Deed

An error was discovered in this deed and a corrected deed was executed Dec. 10, 1903.

Vancouver to Yacolt

	From	To	Date	Form of Transfer
A.S.Doc. 8863	J.Miller, Sheriff Clarke Co., Wash.	R.L.Durham Trustee	Nov.30, 1897	Deed
A.S.Doc. 8863	R.L.Durham Trustee	Louis Gerlinger	Nov.30,1897	Deed
A.S.Doc. 8863	Louis Gerlinger et ux	P.V.& Y.Ry. Co.	Nov.30,1897	Deed
A.S.Doc. 1395	P.V.& Y.Ry. Co.	W.Ry.& N. Co.	July 3, 1903	Articles of Consolidation
A.S.Doc. 1517	W.Ry.&N.Co.	N.P.Ry.Co.	Oct. 19, 1903	Deed

SCHEDULE OF INSTRUMENTS AND RECORDS

File Ref. **Description**

A.S.Doc.
1395

Articles of Consolidation of the Washington & Oregon Railway Company with Portland Vancouver & Yakima Railway Co. to form Washington Railway and Navigation Company.

A.S.Doc.
1517

Deed of Oct. 19, 1903, by which the W.Ry. and N. Co. conveyed its entire property to the N.P.Ry. Co.

R.W.Deed
2

Condemnation Decree dated September 26, 1901, by which the W.& O.Ry.Co. acquired the bridge pier in the Columbia River at Vancouver; also refers to deed from Oregon Ry. Extensions Co. to P.& P.S.R.R. Co. conveying same pier.

R.W.Deed
1 & 3

Condemnation Decree dated Mar. 19, 1901, by which the W.& O. Ry.Co. acquired the right of way and grade of the P.& P.S.R.R.Co. between Kalama and Vancouver.

A.S.Doc.
8863

Three deeds dated Nov. 30, 1897, conveying the property of the Vancouver, Klickitat and Yakima R.R. Co. from J.Miller, Sheriff of Clarke County, Wash. to R.L.Durham, Trustee; R.L.Durham, Trustee to Louis Gerlinger; Louis Gerlinger, et ux to P.V.& Y.Ry.Co.

L.A.File 140   Land Assistant's file "Data used in compiling return to Order No.20 - Corporate History".

MILL CREEK RAILROAD COMPANY

Chart No.119
Place No.90
Map No.80

1. Incorporation

A.S.Doc. 2390

Incorporated under the general laws of the State of Washington.

L.A.File 140

Articles are dated October 12, 1903, and were filed with the Secretary of State October 19, 1903.

Organization effected October 19, 1903.

2. Construction and Purchases

A.S.Doc. 2390

November 23, 1903, this company purchased from The Oregon Railroad and Navigation Company the following narrow-gauge lines:

	From	To	Miles
Br. Line	Walla Walla, Wash.	Dixie, Wash.	10.79
Br. Line	Dudley Jct., Wash.	Tracy (formerly Dudley) Wash.	1.65

L.A.File 140

This company removed the rails from the following portions of the lines:

From	To	Miles	Date
Walla Walla	New Connection with W.&C.R. Ry.Co.	1.52	Jan.16,1905 to July 1,1905
Dudley Jctn.	Dixie	5.49	Jan.16,1905 to July 1,1905

L.A.File 140

This company carried on construction as follows:

	From	To	Miles	Date
Changing narrow-gauge line to standard	New connection with W.& C.R. Ry.Co.	Tracy	5.43	Jan.16, 1905 to July 1, 1905
New line	Connection with W.& C.R.Ry. (now called Mill Creek Jct.)		0.70	

3. Operation

M.B.530 p.27

This company's lines were operated by the Oregon Railroad and Navigation Company under a lease dated December 10, 1903, as follows:

	From	To	Miles	Date
Main Line	Walla Walla	Dixie	10.79	Nov.23,1903 to Jan.16,1905
Br. Line	Dudley Jct.	Tracy	1.65	Nov.23,1903 to Jan.16,1905

L.A.File 140

During the period between January 16, 1905 and July 1, 1905, when the lines were being reconstructed and the rails were being permanently removed from portions of them no operation was carried on.

From July 1, 1905 until September 8, 1905 the property as reconstructed, Mill Creek Jct. to Dudley (Tracy) 6.13 miles, was operated by The W.& C.R. Ry. Co. without a formal contract.

4. Present Status of Corporation

L.A.File 140

Resolution of this company praying for disincorporation granted by Court Order dated May 10, 1906.

The records are in the custody of Mr. R. H. Relf, Assistant Secretary of the Northern Pacific Railway Company, St. Paul, Minnesota.

5. Chain of Title

	From	To	Date	Form of Transfer
A.S.Doc. 10094	M.C.F.& M.Co.	The O.R.R.& N.Co.	Oct. 26, 1903	Deed
A.S.Doc. 2390	The O.R.R.& N.Co.	M.C.R.R.Co.	Nov. 23, 1903	Deed
A.S.Doc. 2678	M.C.R.R.Co.	The W.& C.R.Ry.Co.	Sept. 8, 1905	Deed
A.S.Doc. 3575	The W.& C.R.Ry.Co.	N.P. Ry. Co.	June 18, 1907	Deed

433

SCHEDULE OF INSTRUMENTS AND RECORDS

File Ref.	Description
A.S.Doc. 2390	Articles of Incorporation of Mill Creek Railroad Company.
A.S.Doc. 2390	Deed of November 23, 1903, by which The Oregon Railroad and Navigation Company conveyed to M. C. R. R. Co. its lines from Walla Walla to Dixie and Dudley Jct. to Tracy.
A.S.Doc. 2678	Deed of Sept. 8, 1905, by which the M.C.R.R.Co. conveyed to The Washington and Columbia River Railway Company its line from Mill Creek Jct. to Tracy, 6.13 miles.
A.S.Doc. 3575	Deed of June 12, 1907, by which The W. and C.R. Ry. Co. conveyed its entire property to the N.P.Ry.Co.
L.A.File 140	Land Assistant's file "Data used in compiling return to Order No.20 - Corporate History".
M.B.530 p.27	Lease of December 10, 1903, by which the property was operated by the O.R.R.& N. Co.
A.S.Doc. 10094	Deed of Oct. 26, 1903, by which the M.C.F.& Mfg.Co. deeded its lines from Walla Walla to Dixie and Dudley Jct. to Dudley to The O.R.R.& N. Co.

NORTH YAKIMA AND VALLEY RAILWAY COMPANY

Chart No.120
Place No.59
Map No.81

1. Incorporation

A.S.Doc.
3050

Incorporated under the general laws of the State of Washington.

Articles are dated July 22, 1905, and were filed with the Secretary of State July 24, 1905.

Organization effected July 24, 1905.

2. Construction and Purchases

L.A.File
140

This company constructed the following lines:

	From	To	Miles	Date
Main Line	North Yakima, Wash.	Naches, Wash.	13.07	July 1905 to July 1906
Br. Line	North Yakima	Moxee, Wash.	8.85	July 1909 to Oct. 1910
Br. Line	Granger, Wash.	Flint, Wash.	10.70	Aug. 1909 to Nov. 1910
Br. Line	Flint	Yakima Riv.	5.36	Mar. 1910 to July 1911
Br. Line	Yakima River	Parker, Wash.	1.00	July to Oct. 1911
Br. Line	Cowiche Jctn.	Spitzenberg, Wash.	2.50	Sept. 1912 to 1913
Br. Line	Spitzenberg	Weikel	2.57	Feb. 1913 to Sept. 1914

M.B.585

July 2, 1912, this company purchased the Toppenish,

Simcoe & Western Railway Company which consisted of a partly constructed main line extending rom Wesley Junction, Washington to Farron, Washington, 8.7 miles, with a right of way, partially graded, extending 7.84 miles further, to a point near White Swan, Washington.

3. **Operation**

L.A.File 140

This company operated its lines as follows:

	From	To	Miles	Date
Main Line	North Yakima	Naches	13.07	July 1906 to July 1,1914
Br. Line	North Yakima	Moxee	8.85	Oct. 1910 to July 1,1914
Br. Line	Granger	Flint	10.09	Nov. 1910 to July 1,1914
Br. Line	Flint	Yakima Riv.	6.00	July 21,1911 to July 1,1914
Br. Line	Yakima Riv.	Parker	1.00	Aug.1912 to July 1,1914
Br. Line	Cowiche Jctn.	Spitzenberg	2.50	1913 to July 1, 1914
Br. Line	Wesley Jctn.	Farron	8.57	Nov.1912 to July 1,1914

4. **Present Status of Corporation**

No action has been taken to dissolve this corporation but having parted with its assets it is not active.

The records are located as follows:

One Minute Book is in the office of the Western Land Agent, Tacoma, Wash.

The corporate records and the books of account are with the Assistant Secretary and Comptroller, respectively, of the N.P. Ry. Co., St. Paul, Minnesota.

5. Chain of Title

	From	To	Date	Form of Transfer
M.B.585 p.28 #	T.S.& W. Ry. Co.	N.Y.& V. Ry.Co.	July 2, 1912	Deed
A.S.Doc. 7942	N.Y.& V. Ry. Co.	N.P. Ry. Co.	June 24, 1914	Deed
A.S.Doc. 10234	T.S.& W. Ry. Co.	N.P. Ry. Co.	Feb. 8, 1918	Deed

The deed from the T.S.& W. Ry. Co. was lost before being recorded, and a new deed was executed Feb. 8, 1918, (A.S.Doc.10234) perfecting title in the N.P. Ry. Co.

SCHEDULE OF INSTRUMENTS AND RECORDS

File Ref.   Description

A.S.Doc.   Articles of Incorporation of North Yakima
3050   and Valley Railway Company.

M.B.585   Deed of July 2, 1912 by which Toppenish, Simcoe
p.28   & Western Railway Company conveyed its entire property to N.Y.& V. Ry. Co.

A.S.Doc.   Deed of June 24, 1914 by which N.Y.& V. Ry. Co.
7942   conveyed its entire property to the N.P. Ry. Co.

L.A.File   Land Assistant's file "Data used in compiling
140   return to Order No.20 - Corporate History".

A.S.Doc.   Deed of Feb. 8, 1918, by which T.S.& W. Ry. Co.
10234   perfected title in N.P. Ry. Co. to property conveyed in deed of July 2, 1912 to N.Y.& V. Ry. Co.

SPOKANE, PORTLAND AND SEATTLE RAILWAY COMPANY

Chart Nos. 131 & 125 & 121
Place Nos. 10 & 118 & 127
Map No. 82 & 82^1

1. Incorporation

A.S.Doc.
2650

Portland and Seattle Railway Company was incorporated under the general laws of the State of Washington.

Articles are dated August 22, 1905, and were filed with the Secretaries of the States of Washington and Oregon August 23, 1905.

Amended articles providing for the construction of some additional lines were filed with the Secretary of State of Washington October 17, 1906.

Amended articles providing for the construction of further additional lines and changing the name to Spokane, Portland and Seattle Railway Company were filed with the Secretary of State in Washington and Oregon February 1, 1908.

Amended articles increasing the capital stock were filed with the Secretary of State in Washington and Oregon April 4, 1908.

Amended articles providing for the construction of further additional lines were filed with the Secretary of the State of Washington August 22, 1910, and with the Secretary of the State of Oregon September 3, 1910.

Amended articles further increasing the capital stock were filed with the Secretary of the State of Washington February 15, 1911, and with the Secretary of the State of Oregon February 17, 1911.

Organization of Portland and Seattle Railway Company effected August 24, 1905.

2. **Construction**

L.A. File 140

This company constructed, among other lines, a branch extending from Snake River Junction, Washington to Riparia, (formerly Lewiston Junction) Washington, 40.97 miles, between June 1906 and Sept. 1908.

Also a portion of its main line extending from Vancouver, Washington to Willbridge, Oregon, 5.41 miles, between February 5, 1906 and November 17, 1908.

3. **Operation**

L.A. File 140

This company's property was operated as follows:

	From	To	Miles	Date
(1)	Snake River Jct.	Riparia	40.97	May 3, 1909 to June 21, 1909
(2)	Vancouver	Willbridge	5.41	Nov. 17, 1908 to June 30, 1917

(1) Operated by N.P.Ry.Co. without formal contract.
(2) Operated by Spokane Portland and Seattle Ry. Company.

(2) By deed of April 28, 1908 the N.P. Ry. Co. acquired 1/3 interest in this line and right to operate over it.

A.S.Doc. 5690

Under date of January 12, 1911 the Astoria & Col. Riv. R.R. Co. acquired the right to exclusive use of the line of the N. P. Ry. Co. between Willbridge and Goble, Oregon, 35.05 miles, for 999 years and this right was assigned to the S. P. & S. Ry. Co.

4. **Present Status of Corporation**

This corporation is still in existence.

The records are in the custody of Mr. W. F. Turner, Secretary and Comptroller of the Spokane, Portland and Seattle Railway Company at Portland, Oregon.

5. **Chain of Title**

	Line	From	To	Date	Form of Transfer
A.S.Doc. 2650	Entire Property	P.& S.Ry.	S.P.&S.Ry.	Feb.1,1908	Change of name
A.S.Doc. 4839	Snake River Jct. to Riparia	S.P.& S. Ry.Co.	C.S.L.Ry.	June 21,1909	Deed
A.S.Doc. 7939	Entire Property	C.S.L.Ry. Co.	N.P.Ry.Co.	June 23,1914	Deed
A.S.Doc. 4102	Undivided 1/3 interest in line Vancouver to Willbridge	S.P.& S. Ry.Co.	N.P.Ry.Co.	Apr.28, 1908	Deed

SCHEDULE OF INSTRUMENTS AND RECORDS

File Ref.   **Description**

A.S. Doc. 2650   Articles of Incorporation of Portland and Seattle Railway Company and Amendments thereto.

A.S. Doc. 4839   Deed of June 21, 1909 by which S.P.& S. Ry. Co. conveyed to Clearwater Short Line Railway Co. its line from Snake River Jct. to Lewiston Jct.

A.S. Doc. 7939   Deed of June 23, 1914, by which the C.S.L.Ry.Co. conveyed to the N.P. Ry. Co. its line from Snake River Jct. to Lewiston Jct, and all other property.

A.S. Doc. 4102   Deed of April 28, 1908, by which S.P.& S. Ry. Co. conveyed to N.P. Ry. Co. an undivided one-third interest in its line from Vancouver to Willbridge.

L.A. File 140   Land Assistant's file "Data used in compiling return to Order No.20 - Corporate History".

MISSOURI RIVER RAILWAY COMPANY

Chart No. 123
Place No. 34
Map No. 83

1. **Incorporation**

A.S.Doc. 3067

Incorporated under the general laws of the State of North Dakota.

Articles are not dated but were acknowledged June 9 and 12, 1906, and filed with the Secretary of State June 13, 1906.

Organization effected July 5, 1906.

2. **Construction**

L.A.File 140

The N.P. Ry. Co. constructed for account of this company the following lines:

		From	To	Miles	Date
(1)	Main Line	Mandan, N.D.	Stanton, N.D.	52.64	May 1909 to Oct.1912
	Main Line	Mandan, N.D.	6 miles So. of Cannonball, N.D.	42.41	May 1909 to Nov.1,1910
(2)	Main Line	6 miles So. of Cannonball, N.D.	Nosodak,	29.60	May 1909 to July 1910
	Main Line	Glendive, Mont.	Sidney, Mont.	54.81	May 4,1909 to Aug.1912

(1) A small quantity of right of way has been acquired for a possible extension of the line beyond Stanton.

(2) Grade has been constructed but no track has been laid.

3. Operation

L.A.File 140

The lines were operated by the N.P. Ry. Co. without formal contract as follows:

	From	To	Miles	Date
# Main Line	Mandan	Cannonball	36.11	Nov.1,1910 to June 20,1914
Main Line	Mandan	Stanton	52.64	Aug.1,1912 to June 20,1914
Main Line	Glendive	Sidney	54.81	Aug.1,1912 to June 20,1914

\# 6.30 miles lying south of Cannonball was not operated.

4. Present Status of Corporation

A.S.Doc. 3067

No action has been taken to dissolve this corporation but having parted with its assets it is not active.

The records are in the custody of Mr. R. H. Relf, the Assistant Secretary of the Northern Pacific Railway Co. at Saint Paul, Minnesota.

5. Chain of Title

	From	To	Date	Form of Transfer
A.S.Doc. 7935	M.R.Ry.Co.	N.P.Ry.Co.	June 20, 1914	Deed

SCHEDULE OF INSTRUMENTS AND RECORDS

File Ref.	Description
A.S.Doc. 3067	Articles of Incorporation of Missouri River Railway Company.
A.S.Doc. 7935	Deed of June 20, 1914, by which the M. R. Ry. Co. conveyed its entire property to the N.P. Ry. Co.
L.A.File 140	Land Assistant's file "Data used in compiling return to Order No. 20 - Corporate History".

WESTERN DAKOTA RAILWAY COMPANY

Chart No.122
Place No.17
Map No.84

1. Incorporation

A.S.Doc. 3068

Incorporated under the general laws of the State of North Dakota.

Articles are not dated but were acknowledged June 9 and 12, 1906, and filed with the Secretary of State June 13, 1906.

Amended articles, providing for the construction of some additional lines were filed with the Secretary of State October 1, 1908.

Organization effected July 5, 1906.

2. Construction

L.A.File 140

The N.P. Ry. Co. constructed for account of this company the following lines:

	From	To	Miles	Date
Main Line	Cannonball, N.D.	Mott, N.D.	91.35	April 26,1909 to Sept.1,1910
Br. Line	Stanton, N.D.	Golden Valley	35.00	July 1912 to Nov.1914
# Br. Line	Golden Valley	Killdeer	33.80	June 1913 to June 1914

Partly constructed only. Completed by N.P.Ry.Co.

This company acquired a considerable portion of the right of way for an extension of its line from Mott to

Marmarth, North Dakota, 79.00 miles.

3. Operation

L.A.File
140

The lines were operated by the N.P. Ry. Co. without formal contract as follows:

	From	To	Miles	Date
Main Line	Cannonball	Mott	91.35	Nov.1,1910 to June 20,1914
Br. Line	Stanton	Golden Valley	35.00	Mar. 1,1914 to June 20,1914

4. Present Status of Corporation

A.S.Doc.
3068

No action has been taken to dissolve this corporation but having parted with its assets it is not active.

The records are in the custody of Mr. R. H. Relf, the Assistant Secretary of the Northern Pacific Railway Co. at Saint Paul, Minnesota.

5. Chain of Title

From	To	Date	Form of Transfer
W.D.Ry.Co.	N.P.Ry.Co.	June 20,1914	Deed

A.S.Doc.
7936

SCHEDULE OF INSTRUMENTS AND RECORDS

File Ref.	Description
A.S.Doc. 3068	Articles of Incorporation of Western Dakota Railway Company.
A.S.Doc. 7936	Deed of June 20, 1914, by which W.D.Ry.Co. conveyed its entire property to the N.P. Ry. Co.
L.A.File 140	Land Assistant's file "Data used in compiling return to Order No. 20 - Corporate History".

BIG FORK AND INTERNATIONAL FALLS RAILWAY COMPANY

Chart No. 135 & 124
Place No. 9 & 39
Map No. 85

1. Incorporation

A.S.Doc. 3326

Incorporated under the general laws of the State of Minnesota.

Articles are not dated but were acknowledged December 28, 1906, and filed with the Secretary of State December 29, 1906.

Organization effected January 3, 1907.

2. Construction

L.A.File 140

This company constructed a main line from Grand Falls, Minn. to International Falls, Minn., 34.01 miles, between December 15, 1906 and December 2, 1907.

3. Operation

L.A.File 140

The line has been operated since December 2, 1907 by the B.F. & I. F. Ry. Co. and although the property was conveyed to the N. P. Ry. Co. June 18, 1914, the B.F.& I.F. Ry. Co. continues to operate it without formal contract.

4. Present Status of Corporation

A.S.Doc. 3326

The corporation is still in existence.

The records are in the custody of Mr. R. H. Relf,

the Assistant Secretary of the Northern Pacific Railway Co. at Saint Paul, Minnesota.

5. <u>Chain of Title</u>

	From	To	Date	Form of Transfer
A.S.Doc. 7934	B.F.& I.F.Ry.Co.	N.P.Ry.Co.	June 18, 1914	Deed

SCHEDULE OF INSTRUMENTS AND RECORDS

File Ref.	Description
A.S.Doc. 3326	Articles of Incorporation of Big Fork & International Falls Railway Company.
A.S.Doc. 7934	Deed of June 18, 1914, by which B.F. & I. F. Ry. Co. conveyed its entire property to the N.P. Ry. Co.
L.A.File 140	Land Assistant's file "Data used in compiling return to Order No. 20 - Corporate History".

THE SHIELDS RIVER VALLEY RAILWAY COMPANY

Chart No.127
Place No.7
Map No.86

1. Incorporation

A.S.Doc. 4287

Incorporated under the general laws of the State of Montana.

Articles are dated October 24, 1908 and were filed with the Secretary of State October 24, 1908.

Organization effected October 24, 1908.

2. Construction

L.A.File 140

The N.P. Ry. Co. constructed for account of this company a main line from Mission, Montana to Wilsall, Montana, 22.93 miles, between April 6, 1909 and December 1909 and partly graded 1 mile of road-bed between Wilsall and Meyersburg.

3. Operation

L.A.File 140

The line was operated by the N.P. Ry. Co. without formal contract from December 21, 1909 to June 23, 1914.

4. Present Status of Corporation

A.S.Doc. 4287

No action has been taken to dissolve this corporation but having parted with its assets it is not active.

The records are in the custody of Mr. R. H. Relf,

the Assistant Secretary of the Northern Pacific Railway Co. at Saint Paul, Minnesota.

5. <u>Chain of Title</u>

	From	To	Date	Form of Transfer
A.S.Doc. 7937	S.R.V.Ry.Co.	N.P.Ry.Co.	June 23, 1914	Deed

SCHEDULE OF INSTRUMENTS AND RECORDS

File Ref.   Description

A.S.Doc. 4287   Articles of Incorporation of The Shields River Valley Railway Company.

A.S.Doc. 7937   Deed of June 23, 1914, by which S.R.V.Ry.Co. conveyed its entire property to N.P. Ry. Co.

L.A.File 140   Land Assistant's file "Data used in compiling return to Order No. 20 - Corporate History".

TOPPENISH, SIMCOE & WESTERN RAILWAY COMPANY

Chart No.128
Place No.66
Map No.87

1. Incorporation

A.S.Doc. 4652

Incorporated under the general laws of the State of Washington.

Articles are dated May 5, 1909, and were filed with the Secretary of State on that date.

Organization effected May 10, 1909.

2. Construction

L.A.File 140

This company partly constructed a main line from Wesley Junction, Washington to Farron, Washington, 8.57 miles, between May 1909 and July 1912; and also acquired a right of way extending from Farron to a point near White Swan, Washington, 7.84 miles, which was partially graded.

3. Operation

This company operated no lines.

4. Present Status of Corporation

A.S.Doc. 4652

No action has been taken to dissolve this corporation but having parted with its assets it is not active.

The records are located as follows:

One Minute Book is in the office of the Western Land

Agent, Tacoma, Wash. (N.P.Ry.Co.)

The corporate records and the books of account are with the Assistant Secretary and Comptroller respectively, of the N.P.Ry.Co., St. Paul, Minnesota.

5. Chain of Title

	From	To	Date	Form of Transfer
M.B.585 p.28 #	T.S.& W.Ry.Co.	N.Y.& V.Ry.Co.	July 2, 1912	Deed
A.S.Doc. 7942	N.Y.& V.Ry.Co.	N.P.Ry.Co.	June 24, 1914	Deed
A.S.Doc. 10234	T.S.& W.Ry.Co.	N.P.Ry.Co.	Feb. 8, 1918	Deed

\# The deed from the T.S.& W.Ry.Co. to the N.Y.& V. Ry.Co. was lost before being recorded and a new deed was executed February 8, 1918, (A.S.Doc.10234) perfecting title in the N.P.Ry.Co.

SCHEDULE OF INSTRUMENTS AND RECORDS

File Ref.	Description
A.S.Doc. 4652	Articles of Incorporation of Toppenish Simcoe & Western Railway Company.
M.B.585 p.28	Deed of July 2, 1912 by which T.S.& W. Ry. Co. conveyed its entire property to North Yakima and Valley Railway Company. Deed lost before being recorded.
A.S.Doc. 7942	Deed of June 24, 1914 by which N.Y.& V. Ry. Co. conveyed its entire property to N.P. Ry. Co.
A.S.Doc. 10234	Deed of Feb. 8, 1918 by which T.S.& W. Ry. Co. perfected title in N.P. Ry. Co. to property conveyed in deed of July 2, 1912 to N.Y.& V. Ry. Co.
L.A.File 140	Land Assistant's file "Data used in compiling return to Order No.20 - Corporate History".

CONNELL NORTHERN RAILWAY COMPANY

Chart No.129
Place No.113
Map No.88

1. Incorporation

A.S.Doc. 5322

Incorporated under the general laws of the State of Washington.

Articles are dated May 29, 1909, and were filed with the Secretary of State June 1, 1909.

Organization effected June 2, 1909.

2. Construction and Purchases

L.A.File 140

This Company did no actual construction, but the N.P. Ry. Co. constructed for account of this company the following lines:

	From	To	Miles	Date
Main Line	Connell, Wash.	Adco, Wash.	60.95	June 5,1909 to Nov.1,1910
Br. Line	Bassett Jctn., Wash.	Schrag, Wash.	12.54	Aug.14,1909 to July 1910

This company purchased a complete right of way for a branch line from Schrag to Ritzville, Washington, 24.6 miles, which was graded Oct. 1909 to May 1910, but rail has not yet been laid.

This company also purchased some right of way for a branch line from Bassett Jctn. to Ellensburg, Wash. but the quantity of this is insignificant.

3. <u>Operation</u>

L.A.File 140

The lines were operated by the N.P.Ry.Co. without a formal contract, as follows:

	From	To	Miles	Date
Main Line	Connell	Adco	60.95	Nov.1,1910 to June 25,1914
Br. Line	Bassett Jctn.	Schrag	12.54	Nov.1,1910 to June 25,1914

4. <u>Present Status of Corporation</u>

L.A.File 140

The name of this corporation was stricken from the records of the State of Washington July 1, 1917 for failure to pay annual license fees.

The records are in the custody of Mr. M. P. Martin, Comptroller of the Northwestern Improvement Company, N.P. Ry. General Offices, Tacoma, Washington.

2. <u>Chain of Title</u>

From	To	Date	Form of Transfer
C.N.Ry.Co.	N.P.Ry.Co.	June 25, 1914	Deed

A.S.Doc. 7941

SCHEDULE OF INSTRUMENTS AND RECORDS

File Ref.	Description
A.S.Doc. 5322	Articles of Incorporation of Connell Northern Railway Company.
A.S.Doc. 7941	Deed of June 25, 1914 by which the C.N. Ry. Co. conveyed its entire property to the N.P. Ry. Co.
L.A.File 140	Land Assistant's file 140 "Data used in compiling return to Order No.20 - Corporate History".

THE CAMP CREEK RAILWAY COMPANY

Chart No.132
Place No.22
Map No.89

1. Incorporation

A.S.Doc. 6110

Incorporated under the general laws of the State of Montana.

Articles are dated May 23, 1911 and were filed with the Secretary of State June 8, 1911.

Organization effected June 10, 1911.

2. Construction

L.A.File 140

The N.P. Ry. Co. constructed for account of this company a line from Manhattan, Mont. to Anceny, Mont., 15.15 miles, between July 6, 1911 and November 18, 1911.

3. Operation

L.A.File 140

The line was operated by the N.P. Ry. Co. without formal contract from January 23, 1912 to June 22, 1914, on which date the property was conveyed to them.

4. Present Status of Corporation

A.S.Doc. 6110

No action has been taken to dissolve this corporation but having parted with its assets it is not active.

The records are in the custody of Mr. R. H. Relf, the Assistant Secretary of the Northern Pacific Railway Co. at Saint Paul, Minnesota.

5. Chain of Title

	From	To	Date	Form of Transfer
A.S.Doc. 7938	C.C.Ry.Co.	N.P.Ry.Co.	June 22, 1914	Deed

SCHEDULE OF INSTRUMENTS AND RECORDS

File Ref.   **Description**

A.S.Doc.   Articles of Incorporation of The Camp Creek Railway
6110   Company.

A.S.Doc.   Deed of June 22, 1914, by which C.C. Ry. Co. con-
7938   veyed its entire property to N. P. Ry. Co.

L.A.File   Land Assistant's file "Data used in compiling re-
140   turn to Order No. 20 - Corporate History".

CUYUNA NORTHERN RAILWAY COMPANY

Chart No.133
Place No.54
Map No.90

1. Incorporation

A.S.Doc.
6506

Incorporated under the general laws of the State of Minnesota.

Articles are dated September 20, 1911 and were filed with the Secretary of State September 25, 1911.

Amended Articles, altering the route of the lines to be constructed filed with the Secretary of State February 14, 1912.

Organization effected September 20, 1911.

2. Construction

L.A.File
140

The N.P. Ry. Co. constructed for account of this company the following lines:

From	To	Miles	Date
Deerwood,Minn.	Oreland,Minn.	3.56	Oct.23,1911 to Dec.1912
Deerwood,Minn.	Cuyuna-Mille Lac Mine	5.16	June 7,1912 to Dec.1912
# Deebee Jctn. Minn.	Duluth-Brainerd Mine	2.69	March 1,1914 to August 1914
# Loerch,Minn.	Woodrow,Minn.	1.65	June 1,1914 to April 1915

\# Completed after conveyance to N.P. Ry. Co.

3. **Operation**

L.A.File 140

The lines were operated by N.P. Ry. Co. without formal contract as follows:

From	To	Miles	Date
Deerwood	Oreland	3.56	Dec. 29, 1912 to June 18, 1914
Deerwood	Cuyuna-Mille Lac Mine	5.16	Dec. 29, 1912 to June 18, 1914

4. **Present Status of Corporation**

A.S.Doc. 6506

Corporation still in existence.

The records are in the custody of Mr. R. H. Relf, the Assistant Secretary of the Northern Pacific Railway Co. at Saint Paul, Minnesota.

5. **Chain of Title**

From	To	Date	Form of Transfer
C.N.Ry.Co.	N.P.Ry.Co.	June 18, 1914	Deed

A.S.Doc. 7933

SCHEDULE OF INSTRUMENTS AND RECORDS

File Ref.   **Description**

A.S.Doc. 6506   Articles of Incorporation of Cuyuna Northern Railway Company.

A.S.Doc. 7933   Deed of June 18, 1914, by which the C.N.Ry.Co. conveyed its entire property to N.P. Ry. Co.

L.A.File 140   Land Assistant's file "Data used in compiling return to Order No. 20 - Corporate History".

CUYUNA DOCK COMPANY

Chart No. 134
Place No. 32
Map No. 91

1. Incorporation

A.S.Doc. 6930

Incorporated under the general laws of the State of Wisconsin.

Articles are dated November 8, 1912, and were filed with the Secretary of State November 11, 1912.

Organization effected December 6, 1912.

2. Construction

L.A.File 140

This company constructed an ore dock 0.18 mile in length on the Bay Front at Superior, Wisconsin, between October 15, 1912 and October 25, 1913.

3. Operation

L.A.File 140

The dock was operated by the Cuyuna Dock Company from October 1, 1913 until August 27, 1915, on which date it was deeded to Northern Pacific Railway Company.

4. Present Status of Corporation

A.S.Doc. 6930

This company dissolved by resolution of its stockholders at a meeting held on Jan. 17, 1917, certified copy of which was accepted and filed in the office of Secretary of State Feb. 2, 1917.

Records in custody of Mr. R. H. Relf, the Ass't. Secretary N.P.Ry.Co. of St. Paul, Minn.

5. <u>Chain of Title</u>

	From	To	Date	Form of Transfer
A.S.Doc. 8553	C.D.Co.	N.P.Ry.Co.	Aug. 27, 1915	Deed

SCHEDULE OF INSTRUMENTS AND RECORDS

File Ref.	Description
A.S.Doc. 6930	Articles of Incorporation of Cuyuna Dock Company.
A.S.Doc. 8553	Deed of Aug. 27, 1915, by which C.D. Co. conveyed its entire property to N. P. Ry. Co.
L.A.File 140	Land Assistant's file "Data used in compiling return to Order No. 20 - Corporate History".

MISSOULA AND HAMILTON RAILWAY COMPANY

Chart No. 130
Place No. 131
Map No.

1. **Incorporation**

A.S.Doc. 7802

Incorporated under the general laws of the State of Montana.

Articles are dated December 31, 1910, and were filed with the Secretary of State January 5, 1911.

Organization effected February 14, 1911.

2. **Construction**

L.A.File 140

This company constructed no lines but acquired a considerable portion of the right of way for a line from Carlton, Montana to Hamilton, Montana, 30.60 miles.

3. **Operation**

L.A.File 140

None

4. **Present Status of Corporation**

A.S.Doc. 7802

This corporation is still in existence.

The records are in the custody of Mr. R. H. Relf, Assistant Secretary of the Northern Pacific Railway Company, Saint Paul, Minnesota.

5. **Chain of Title**

A.S.Doc. 9307

From	To	Date	Form of Transfer
M.& H. Ry. Co.	N.P. Ry. Co.	Nov. 1, 1916	Deed

SCHEDULE OF INSTRUMENTS AND RECORDS

File Ref.	Description
A.S.Doc. 7802	Articles of Incorporation of Missoula and Hamilton Railway Company.
A.S.Doc. 9307	Deed of Nov. 1, 1916, by which the M. & H. Ry. Co. conveyed its entire property to the N. P. Ry. Co.
L.A.File 140	Land Assistant's file "Data used in compiling return to Order No.20 - Corporate History".

INTERSTATE COMMERCE COMMISSION   COPY

Bureau of Valuation

Washington

September 30, 1921.

In reply
refer to
File Val-O-3
1787

Mr. Charles Donnelly, President,
Northern Pacific Railway Company,
St. Paul, Minnesota.

Dear Sir:

Please refer to your letter of September 17, 1921 with reference to the Corporate History of the Northern Pacific Railway Company filed in compliance with Valuation Order No. 20.

Pages 101 and 102 deal with the Utah and Northern Railway Company, the property of which is leased to, and operated by, the Northern Pacific Railway Company. Under 4 - PRESENT STATUS OF CORPORATION - the statement is made: "This corporation is still in existence."

The Corporate History of the Oregon Short Line Railroad Company states:

> "On August 1, 1886, this company (Utah and Northern Railway Company) leased to the Montana Union Railway Company for a term of 999 years all that part of its line from Garrison, Montana Territory, via Silver Bow to Butte and the mines, smelters and other industries in the vicinity thereof. On October 7, 1898, Montana Union Railway Company assigned the lease and conveyed its property of every kind to the Northern Pacific Railway Company. Northern Pacific Railway Company leased trackage rights between Silver Bow and Butte, Montana, to Oregon Short Line Railroad Company on March 1, 1898.

This Corporate History further shows the present status of

Mr. Charles Donnelly -

the corporation as follows:

"Consolidation of July 27, 1889, dissolved the Utah and Northern Railway Company and terminated its corporate existence."

The disposition of the property is shown as follows:

"The property of the Utah and Northern Railway Company was consolidated on July 27, 1889, with seven other companies to form the Oregon Short Line and Utah Northern Railroad Company, and on July 23, 1897, this property was deeded to the Oregon Short Line Railroad Company by John B. Cleland, Commissioner, and the American Loan and Trust Company."

It appears from the above that the Utah and Northern Railway Company terminated its corporate existence on July 27, 1889, and that title to the property formerly owned by that company is now held by the Oregon Short Line Railroad Company.

Will you please advise us with respect to the correctness of the above statements.

      Truly yours,

      (Sgd) C. F. Staples

        Acting Director.

October 3, 1921.

A-4

Dear Sir:

Replying to your letter of the 30th ultimo, with regard to the Corporate History filed by the Northern Pacific Railway, and especially with regard to the status of the Utah & Northern Railway Company:

So far as our records show, the Utah & Northern Railway Company was in existence as of June 30, 1917, our valuation date, and we had no information that the status of the Company had changed and that it had, in fact, been dissolved by consolidation with several other companies to form the Oregon Short Line Railroad Company in 1889. The Oregon Short Line Railroad Company is, of course, in a better position than we are to state the present status of the Utah & Northern Railway Company, and if that Company has stated that the Utah & Northern Railway Company has been dissolved and has terminated its corporate existence, we are willing to accept that statement as correct, and will be glad if you will please file a copy of your letter and a copy of this reply with our Corporate History, and I will arrange to have similar action taken as to our copies of the Corporate History.

Yours truly,

(Signed) Charles Donnelly

Mr. C. F. Staples,
Acting Director,
Bureau of Valuation,
Interstate Commerce Commission,
Washington, D. C.

From	To	Miles	Date
Silver Bow	Butte	9.20	Dec. 23, 1881 to Aug. 1, 1886
Butte	Anaconda Mine	3.40	1884 to Aug. 1, 1886
Silver Bow	Garrison	44.50	Sept. 29, 1883 to Aug. 1, 1886

4. **Present Status of Corporation**

This corporation is still in existence.

The records are in the custody of Mr. Alex Millar, Secretary of the Union Pacific System, 165 Broadway, New York City.

5. **Chain of Title**

	From	To	Date	Form of Transfer
A.S.Doc. 221	U. & N. Ry. Co.	M.U. Ry. Co.	Aug. 1, 1886	Lease for 999 years
A.S.Doc. 221	M. U. Ry. Co.	N.P. Ry. Co.	Oct. 7, 1898	Deed and Assignment of Lease

VOID
SEE REVISED
SHEET 102

Revised page 102

From	To	Miles	Date
Silver Bow	Butte	9.20	Dec. 23, 1881 to Aug. 1, 1886
Butte	Anaconda Mine	3.40	1884 to Aug. 1, 1886
Silver Bow	Garrison	44.50	Sept. 29, 1883 to Aug. 1, 1886

4. Present Status of Corporation

The property of the Utah and Northern Railway Company was consolidated on July 27, 1889, with seven other companies to form the Oregon Short Line and Utah and Northern Railroad Company, which consolidation dissolved said Utah and Northern Railway Company and terminated its corporate existence.

The records are in the custody of Mr. Alex Millar, Secretary of the Union Pacific System, 165 Broadway, New York City.

5. Chain of Title

	From	To	Date	Form of Transfer
A.S. Doc. 221	U. & N. Ry. Co.	M.U. Ry. Co.	Aug. 1, 1886	Lease for 999 years
A.S. Doc. 221	M. U. Ry. Co.	N.P. Ry. Co.	Oct. 7, 1898	Deed and Assignment of Lease

Corporate History

Northern Pacific Railway Company

June 30, 1917 - Aug. 30, 1921

470 pp., Maps - 2, correspondence.

Loaned for microfilming by Ralph W. Zimmer, P.E.
Dept. of Civil Engineering, Montana State University,
Bozeman, Montana.

FILMED BY THE
HISTORICAL SOCIETY
OF MONTANA
LIBRARY
HELENA, MONTANA

Northern Pacific Railway Company, Revised Chart — Sheet 2, As of June 30, 1917. Properties owned and Operated. Property Operated but not Owned. Properties Owned but not Operated by Respondent. Filed under Valuation Order No. 20. 478

Northern Pacific Railway Company Corporate History Map. Revised as of June 30, 1917. Each portion of the present Northern Pacific system constructed by a separate corporation formed for this purpose is made a corporate history unit. Its location is shown by number on the map, together with a summary of the chain of title from the original construction company to the present owner, the Northern Pacific Railway Company. 482

Note — These documents have been divided to fit the pages of this publication. Entire undivided versions are available in the online digital edition at https://digitalcommons.unl.edu/zeabook/127/

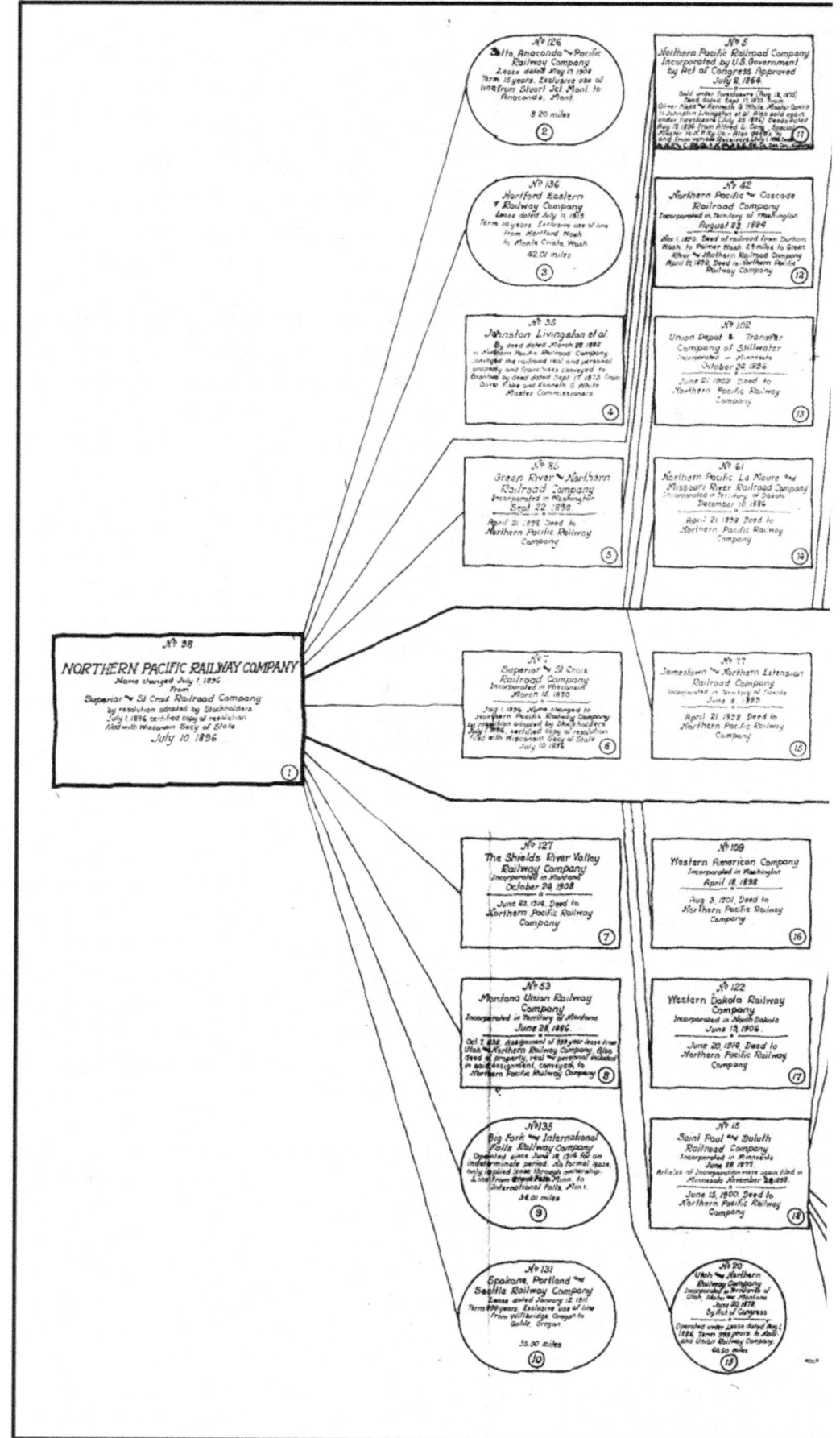

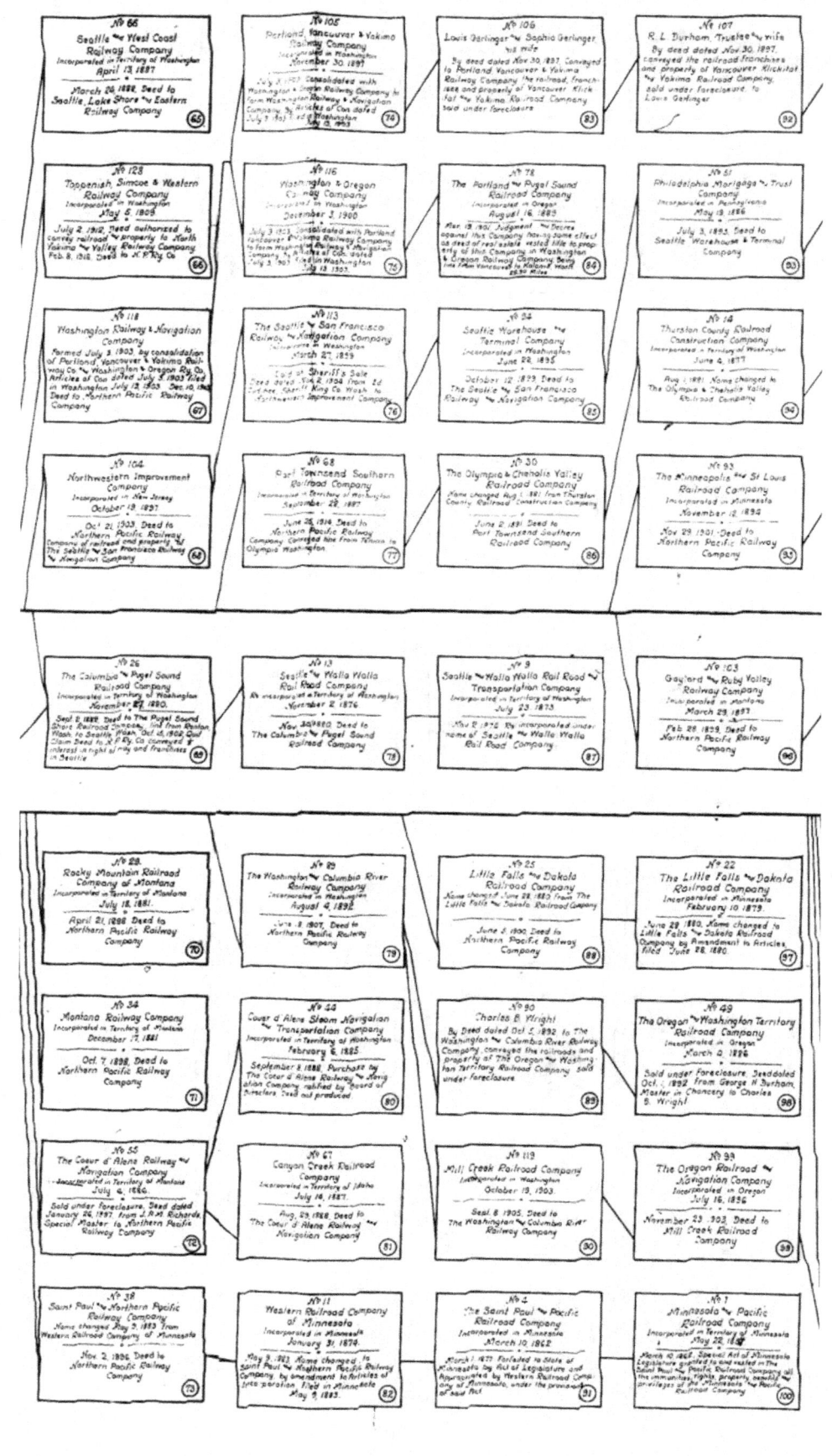

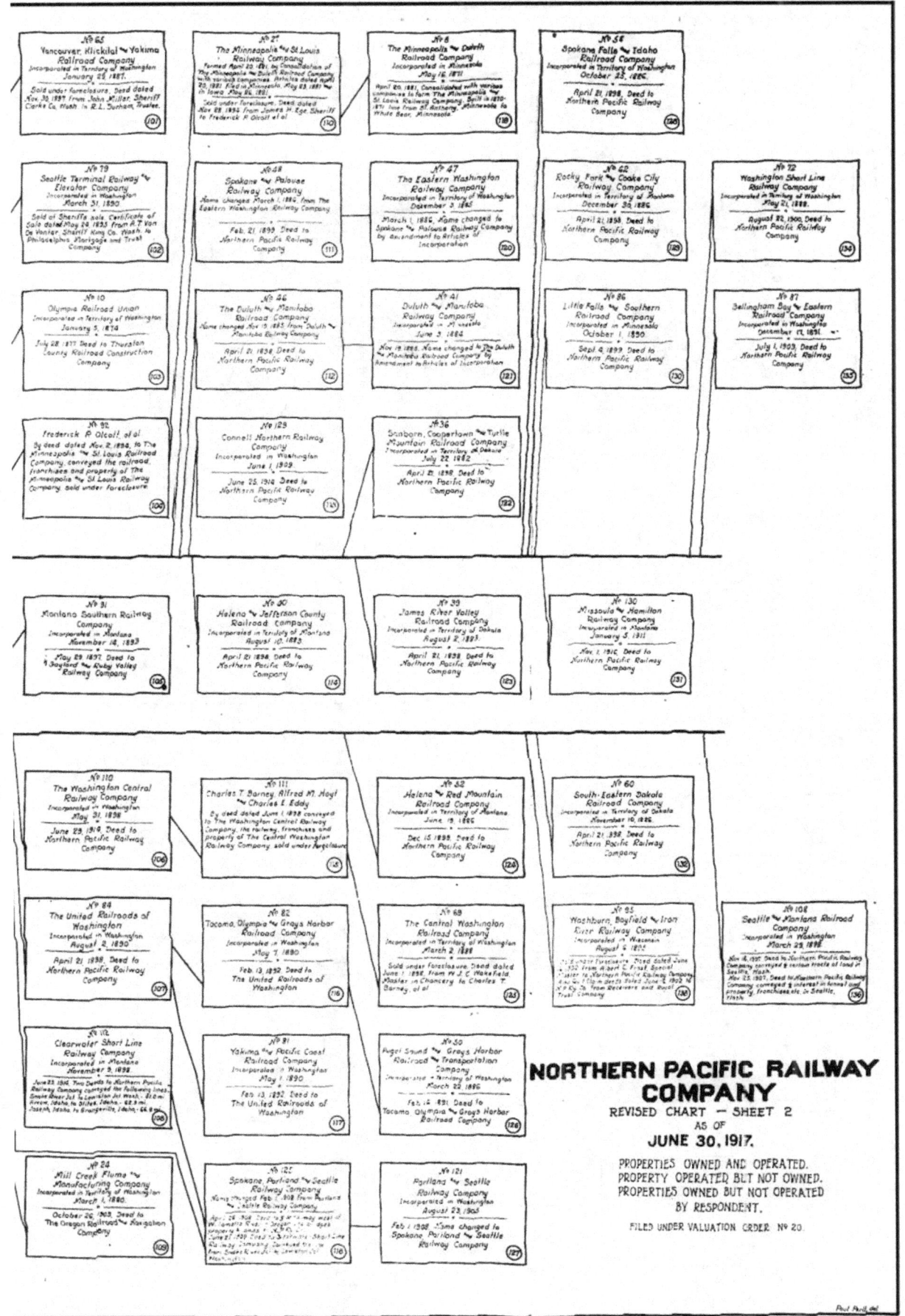

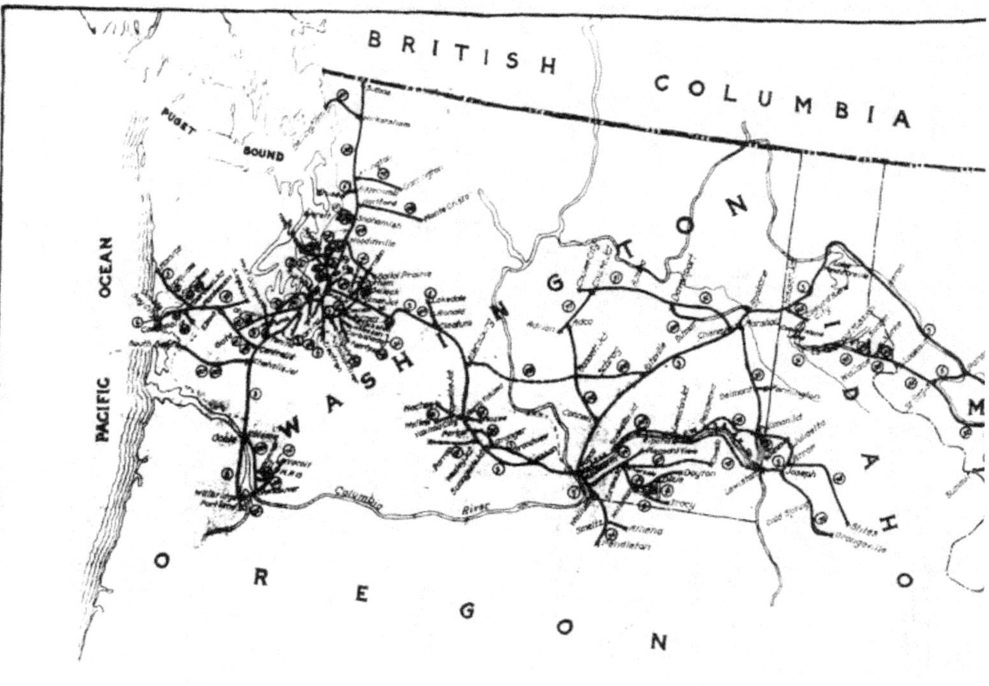

NORTHERN PACIFIC RAILWAY COMPANY
CORPORATE HISTORY MAP

REVISED AS OF JUNE 30 1917

EACH PORTION OF THE PRESENT NORTHERN PACIFIC SYSTEM CONSTRUCTED BY A SEPARATE CORPORATION FORMED FOR THIS PURPOSE IS MADE A CORPORATE HISTORY UNIT. ITS LOCATION IS SHOWN BY NUMBER ON THE MAP TOGETHER WITH A SUMMARY OF THE CHAIN OF TITLE FROM THE ORIGINAL CONSTRUCTING COMPANY TO THE PRESENT OWNER THE NORTHERN PACIFIC RAILWAY COMPANY

PREPARED UNDER VALUATION ORDER NO 20 I C C

OFFICE OF LAND ASSISTANT
ST PAUL MINN AUG 30 1921

LEGEND:—

OWNED OR CONTROLLED BY N P R R CO AT DATE OF FORECLOSURE JU...
AND ACQUIRED BY N P RY CO AT FORECLOSURE SALE ...
ADDED TO SYSTEM BY N P RY CO SINCE ACQUISITION OF N P R R CO PROPERT...
TOTAL N P RY CO SYSTEM JUNE 30 1917 ...
LINES PROJECTED - RIGHT OF WAY ACQUIRED IN WHOLE OR IN PART ...
LINES CONSTRUCTED AND OPERATED NOW ABANDONED - N P R R CO ...
N P RY CO ...

(1) 155.00 Miles
Nebraska & Lake Superior Railroad Company
Lake Superior & Mississippi Railroad Company
Saint Paul & Duluth Railroad Company
Northern Pacific Railway Company

(2) 55.00 Miles
St Paul & Pacific Railroad Company
Western Railroad Company of Minnesota
Saint Paul & Northern Pacific Railway Company
Northern Pacific Railway Company

(3) 2160.32 Miles
Northern Pacific Railroad Company
Northern Pacific Railway Company

10.70 Miles
Northern Pacific Railroad Company
Northern Pacific & Cascade Railroad Company
Northern Pacific Railway Company

6.93 Miles
Northern Pacific Railroad Company
Northern Pacific & Puget Sound Shore Rail Road Company
Northern Pacific Railway Company

(4) 12.74 Miles
The Stillwater & St Paul Railroad Company
Saint Paul & Duluth Railroad Company
Northern Pacific Railway Company

(5) 774.75 Miles
Northern Pacific Railway Company

(6) 13.62 Miles
The Minneapolis & Duluth Railroad Company
Minneapolis & St Louis Railway Company
The Minneapolis & St Louis Railroad Company
Northern Pacific Railway Company

(7) 57.10 Miles
Utah & Northern Railway Company
Montana Union Railway Company (999 year lease)
Northern Pacific Railway Company

(8) 10.10 Miles
Seattle & Walla Walla Rail Road & Transportation Company
Seattle & Walla Walla Rail Road Company
Columbia & Puget Sound Railroad Company
Puget Sound Shore Railroad Company
Northern Pacific & Puget Sound Shore Rail Road Company
Northern Pacific Railway Company

(9) 17.50 Miles
Olympia Railroad Union
The Thurston County Railroad Construction Company
Olympia & Chehalis Valley Railroad Company
Port Townsend Southern Railroad Company
Northern Pacific Railway Company

(10) 183.77 Miles
Western Railroad Company of Minnesota
Saint Paul & Northern Pacific Railway Company
Northern Pacific Railway Company

(11) 10.09 Miles
Taylors Falls & Lake Superior Railroad Company
Saint Paul & Duluth Railroad Company
Northern Pacific Railway Company

(12) 11.37 Miles
Saint Paul & Duluth Railroad Company
Northern Pacific Railway Company

40.50 Miles
Saint Paul & Duluth Railroad Company
Taylors Falls & Lake Superior Railroad Company
Saint Paul & Duluth Railroad Company
Northern Pacific Railway Company

142.36 Miles
Northern Pacific Fergus & Black Hills Railroad Company
Northern Pacific Railway Company

0.62 Mile
Stillwater Street Railway & Transfer Company
Union Depot, Street Railway & Transfer Company of Stillwater
Stillwater Union Depot & Transfer Company
Union Depot & Transfer Company of Stillwater
Northern Pacific Railway Company

11.90 Miles
St Cloud Grantsburg & Ashland Railroad Company
Saint Paul & Duluth Railroad Company
Northern Pacific Railway Company

5.14 Miles
The Grantsburgh Rush City & St Cloud Railway Company
Saint Paul & Duluth Railroad Company
Northern Pacific Railway Company

57.85 Miles
The Little Falls & Dakota Railroad Company
Northern Pacific Railway Company

13.51 Miles
Mill Creek Flume & Manufacturing Company
Oregon Railroad & Navigation Company
Mill Creek Railroad Company
The Washington & Columbia River Railway Company
Northern Pacific Railway Company

39.30 Miles
The Saint Paul Minneapolis & Manitoba Railway Company
Northern Pacific Fergus & Black Hills Railroad Company
Northern Pacific Railway Company

54.60 Miles
Rocky Mountain Railroad Company of Montana
Northern Pacific Railway Company

87.40 Miles
Fargo & Southwestern Railroad Company
Northern Pacific Railway Company

102.50 Miles
Jamestown & Northern Railroad Company
Northern Pacific Railway Company

14.83 Miles
Montana Railway Company
Northern Pacific Railway Company

36.78 Miles
Sanborn Cooperstown & Turtle Mountain Railroad Company
Northern Pacific Railway Company

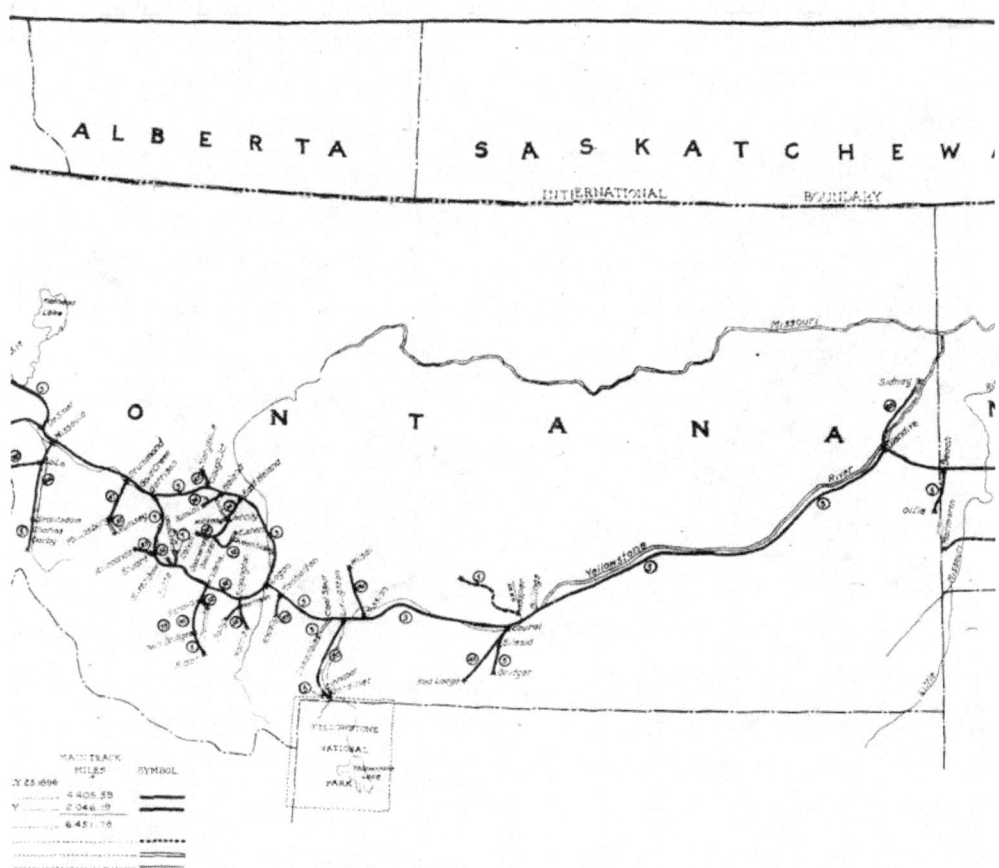

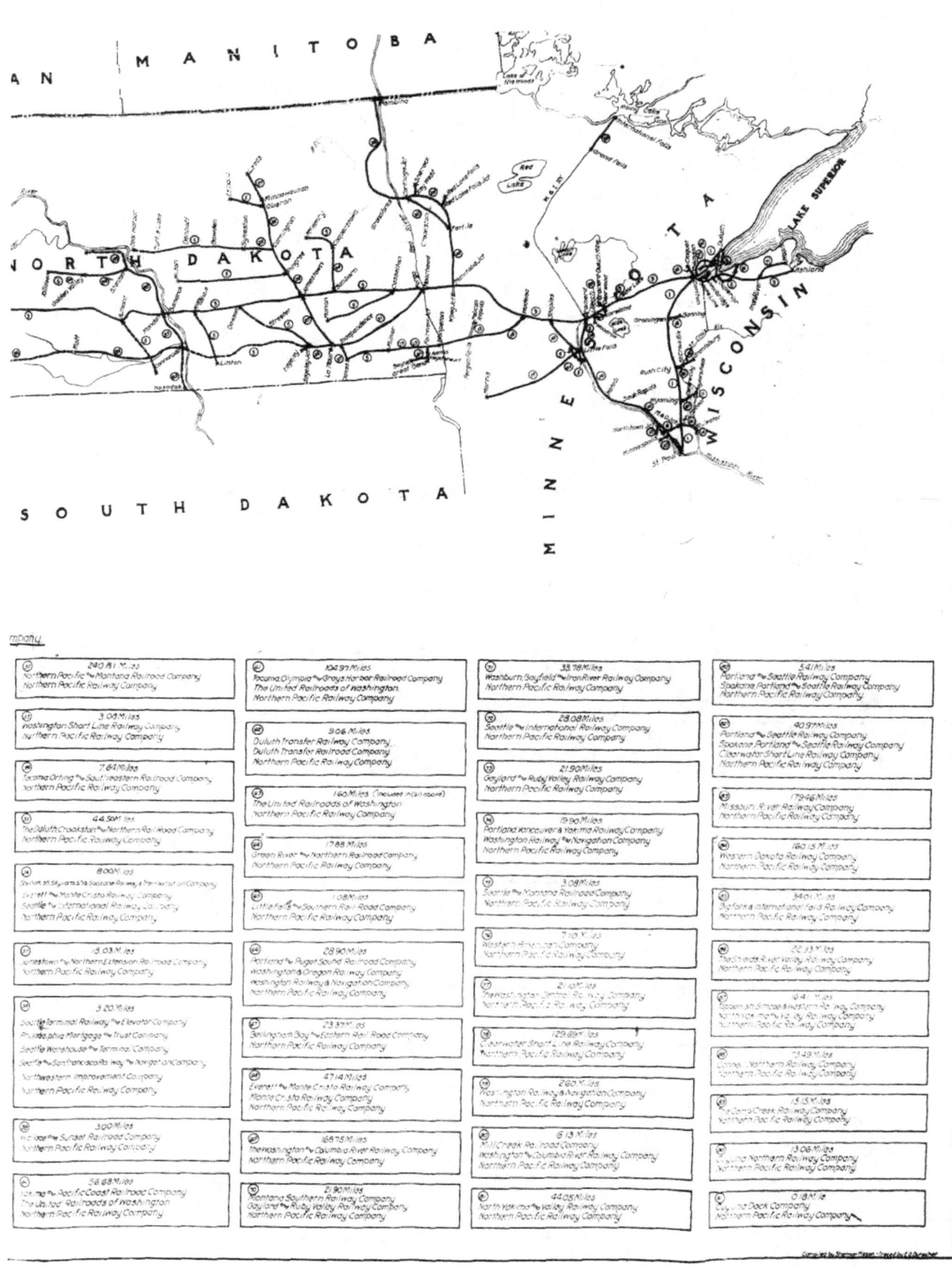

www.ingramcontent.com/pod-product-compliance
Lightning Source LLC
Chambersburg PA
CBHW080923020526
44114CB00043B/2441